A.J. CRONIN

a reference guide

A
Reference
Guide
to
Literature

Ronald Gottesman
Editor

A.J. CRONIN

a reference guide

DALE SALWAK

G.K. HALL &CO.

70 LINCOLN STREET, BOSTON, MASS.

Library of Congress Cataloging in Publication Data

Salwak, Dale.
  A. J. Cronin, a reference guide.

  (A Reference guide to literature)
  Includes index.
  1. Cronin, A. J. (Archibald Joseph), 1896—
—Bibliography. I. Title. II. Title: AJ Cronin,
a reference guide. III. Series.
Z8200.4.S27 1983   016.823'912   82-11954
[PR6005.R68]
ISBN 0-8161-8595-6

This publication is printed on permanent/durable acid-free paper
MANUFACTURED IN THE UNITED STATES OF AMERICA

for
Patti

Contents

The Author viii

Preface ix

Introduction xi

Writings by A.J. Cronin, 1931–1978 xv

Writings about A.J. Cronin, 1931–1981 1

Index 165

The Author

Dale Salwak graduated with honors from Purdue University (1969) and
received his M.A. (1970) and Ph.D. (1974) degrees in English Literature
from the University of Southern California under a National Defense
Education Act competitive fellowship program. As a faculty member of
Southern California's Citrus College since 1973, Professor Salwak spe-
cializes in contemporary English and American literature, advanced
composition, and literature of the Bible. He is also the author of
Kingsley Amis: A Reference Guide (1978), John Braine and John Wain:
A Reference Guide (1980), John Wain (1981), and Literary Voices (1982)
--a collection of interviews he conducted with Kingsley Amis, John
Braine, John Wain, and Colin Wilson. His forthcoming books include
a biographical-critical study of A.J. Cronin and the authorized biography of John Braine.

Preface

This reference guide is first and foremost an annotated listing of
the judgments passed on A.J. Cronin, the writer and the man, by his
English and American readers from 1931 until his passing in 1981.
His reputation in Europe and in other non-English-speaking countries
is, in itself, the subject for another full study. Foreign language
reviews of Cronin's books, therefore, have not been included. The
foreign language pieces that I have listed are scholarly and critical.
Also, all of the annotations are descriptive, not evaluative. In the
abstracts of interviews, bibliographies, and biographical notes, I
have emphasized scope except in the case of very brief items.

Within each year, listings are arranged alphabetically by author
and numbered consecutively. References and cross-references are to
those numbers (thus "1945.9" refers to the ninth entry for the year
1945). Names of periodicals and newspapers are given as they appear
on the title page of the issues in which the articles appeared. This
code is employed within the text to refer to reprints and replies; it
is also used in the index at the back of the guide. The index is in-
clusive, with authors, titles, and subjects interfiled.

A bibliography such as this can never be considered an individual
effort. It is a pleasure to express my gratitude to others who have
played so important a role in its compilation. To Vincent Cronin I
am indebted for helpful information. For their kind assistance in
gathering materials, my special thanks are due the members of the
staffs of the University of London Library, the University of Southern
California Doheny Memorial Library, the University of California at
Los Angeles Research Library, and the Library of Congress. For her
willing and diligent attention to my research needs, I am also grateful to Mrs. Dorothy M. Brandt of New York. For reading the introduction and offering their valued advice, I am grateful to both Mrs.
Cheryl Epler and Professor L. David Sundstrand, Citrus College.

Finally, my deepest gratitude must go to my mother, Frances H.
Salwak, who skillfully checked and corrected all three drafts of the
typescript, helped to proofread the page proofs, and performed the
tedious task of compiling the index; and to my father, Professor

Stanley F. Salwak, whose keen interest in A.J. Cronin awakened my own.

One last debt is acknowledged in the dedication.

Introduction

In the spring of 1930 a tall, sandy-haired, genial physician sold his London practice and home, moved with his family to an isolated farmhouse near Inverary, Scotland, and at the age of thirty-four wrote a novel for the first time in his life. Hatter's Castle, published the following year by Victor Gollancz, became an immediate success. It was the first work of fiction to be chosen by the English Book Society for the book-of-the-month. It was later translated into six languages, dramatized, and made into a Paramount motion picture starring James Mason and Deborah Kerr. Before long, both English and American critics hailed A.J. Cronin as a new and important author whose writing was comparable in content and style to that of Dickens, Hardy, and Balzac.

The physician-novelist is of course by no means an unfamiliar literary figure. A. Conan Doyle, W. Somerset Maugham, C.S. Forester, Oliver Goldsmith, and the Poet Laureate of England, Robert Bridges, among others, had rich medical backgrounds into which they reached for ideas for their books. However, none of these examples can quite parallel the dual career of A.J. Cronin. Medicine with him was not a stopgap or stepping-stone. He was an outstanding professional and financial success; moreover, he was ambitious, desperately tenacious, and singleminded in his pursuit of that success. It was hard-won and well-deserved. His second success, in an entirely different field, was equally substantial. Twenty novels, a play, an autobiography and one of the longest-running British television series represent a career that spans one-half of the twentieth century--1930 to 1978--and of a life that is itself as engrossing and many-sided as his fiction.

Archibald Joseph Cronin was born at Cardross, Dunbartonshire, Scotland, on 19 July 1896, the son of Patrick Cronin and Jessie Montgomerie. He had begun his medical studies at Glasgow University when the war of 1914-1918 took him into the Royal Navy Volunteer Reserve as a surgeon sub-lieutenant. Having graduated M.B., Ch.B. with honors in 1919, he was appointed physician to the outpatients in Ballahouston war pensions hospital, and later medical superintendent at Lightburn Hospital, Glasgow. From 1921 until 1924 he was in general practice in a mining area of South Wales. In the latter year he became a medical inspector of mines for Great Britain. In 1925 he took his M.D. degree with honors; a year later he prepared a report on first aid conditions in British coal mines and another report on dust inhalation in hematite mines. After his service with the Ministry of Mines was completed, Cronin moved to London and built a fashionable practice in Harley Street. Throughout these experiences and contacts with people of every kind, he kept thinking of what stories he could create.

"I have great pleasure in announcing the sudden and most surprising arrival in England of a new and most important author" (1931.21). So Hugh Walpole, himself a successful middlebrow writer, opened his review of Hatter's Castle. The general agreement among early critics in both England and America was that Cronin had indeed produced a first novel of great promise. In the Spectator, it was praised for being "brutal, violent, and full of life" (1931.19). The reviewer for the London Times Literary Supplement liked it for its "force of description, strong human sympathy and deep knowledge of the persons and scenes from which it is drawn" (1931.5). Many other reviewers saw in Hatter's Castle a return to "the solid and peculiarly English virtues of an earlier fiction" (1931.9). For good reason, Percy Hutchinson called it "the work of a novelist who is destined for the seats of the mighty" (1931.14).

But not all reviewers were as impressed with the novel as these excerpts indicate. A number of the reviews were mixed, acknowledging the novel's power while regretting its "unhealthy" subject matter, the heavy melodrama, or the author's verbosity. One critic felt that although Cronin may go far as a novelist, his "style lumbers" and his characters "seem to have escaped from old volumes of Victorian magazines" (1931.12). Helen MacAfee, writing in the Yale Review, called the book unsatisfactory because "it is so logical that it is also predictable" (1931.15). Only a few reviews were entirely negative. To Hazel Hawthorne, for instance, Hatter's Castle was "an uninspired epitome of the nineteenth-century novels." She resented that "an obviously fine talent has not directed itself into a fresher path" (1931.13).

In spite of the mixed critical reception, both publishers and retailers considered Hatter's Castle to be one of the most successful novels of 1931. The same could not be said of his next two works, Three Loves (1932) and Grand Canary (1933). Inevitably, critics hastened to compare them to Hatter's Castle, and most of them found the novels to be a disappointment. Of the former, one critic wrote: "Here is material for a fine novel. What is needed more than anything else is a judicious editorial blue pencil" (1932.6). The case against Grand Canary was put most forcibly by Graham Greene, who wrote: "[this is an] Awful Example [of the] Popular Novelist, . . . the consistency of whose inability to create a plausible human being is praiseworthy" (1933.21). In the minds of many reviewers, Cronin's reputation rested for the time, at any rate, upon his first book.

Cronin's next two novels, by contrast, did much to enhance his reputation. The Stars Look Down (1935) was commended by many readers as the best, the most readable, the most ambitious, and the most sensitive of his novels up to that time. The New York Times found him "uncannily like Dickens" and listed the work among the best novels of the year (1935.41). The New York News praised Cronin for his "surer pen" and "more penetrating eye" (1935.18). On the other hand, some reviewers found the melodrama and the length of the novel too much for their taste. Accordingly, Cronin was accused of "misusing his talents," of spoiling the tale with too many characters. The Stars Look Down was described in various reviews as "black" (1935.57), "wooden" (1935.55), "unwieldy" (1935.17), and the like.

Two years later, The Citadel appeared. To many readers, doctors particularly, the novel's main interest lay in Cronin's indictment of both the unethical practices of the medical profession and the system under which miners lived and worked. To others, the interest lay in the unmistakable similarity between the hero's personal philosophy and Cronin's own opinions. Readers found the same integrity of character, the same effort to focus attention on social forces which are responsible for many of the ills of the patients, and the same deep concern as an individual for lessening human disorder.

Other critics were more cautious in their remarks. William Carlos Williams, in the Nation, felt impelled to label the novel "a crowded story clumsily but sincerely told" before offering his more guarded opinion: "It isn't a great novel, not in the sense that Norman Douglas or Ford Madox Ford would speak of a great novel. But it's a good novel, though it is often ironical to speak of a 'good novel' today" (1937.109). The New York Times called it "pleasing reading even if it is not, as the publisher earnestly assures us, great writing" (1937.72).

The appearance of The Keys of the Kingdom in 1941 was a major turning point in Cronin's career: it expanded his audience in kind as well as number, and it changed the quality of criticism and appreciation he would receive as a writer. The book's serious subject and the respectability of the Cronin name recommended it to religious leaders who ordinarily regarded fiction as frivolous and inherently dangerous. Sectarian publications such as Churchman, Christian Century, Catholic World and Christian Index reviewed it favorably, a fact which increased phenomenally both the sales and the influence of the book. On the adverse side, The Keys of the Kingdom was called at best a good story, but misleading, melodramatic and superficial. The reviewer for Commonweal found the hero an honest character, but also "wordy and even, at times, a prig with his pointed mouthings of pious banalities" (1941.78). PM's Weekly called the novel "a classic of corn, bad taste, insufferable writing and public hoodwinking" (1941.158).

In the following years Cronin wrote thirteen more novels, all of

which met with varying critical and popular success. Reviewers of
The Green Years (1944) and its sequel, Shannon's Way (1948), felt that
both novels showed at their best those forces which formed Cronin's
writing and earned him respect as an author: his church, his dedication to medicine, his humble Scotch upbringing. Every page of Cronin's
writing, wrote Orville Prescott, "bears the stamp of an honest and
simple man, without pretense, affectation or false sophistication"
(1944.70). The Spanish Gardener (1950) also contained perhaps some
of his best work for a long time, but it is doubtful if the others--
Beyond this Place (1953), Crusader's Tomb (1956), The Northern Light
(1958), or The Judas Tree (1961), for example--did much to enhance
that reputation. Although his later novels sold well and received
generally favorable notices, they never matched the popularity of
Hatter's Castle, The Stars Look Down, The Keys of the Kingdom, or The
Green Years.

As this brief summary attempts to show, throughout Cronin's career
there has been a wide divergence of opinions about the man and his
work--ranging from praise to derision. Few readers on either side
of the Atlantic reacted to his work with indifference, which is one
reason why reading his reviews can be interesting. And yet, though
his novels sold in the millions and were handsomely adapted to the
usages of the cinema, they are a topic "strangely neglected" by aca-
demic criticism. The best essay on his work remains Francis Fytton's
"Dr. Cronin: An Essay in Victoriana," published as long ago as 1956.
There have been other essays, before and since, and there are several
perceptive pages in John T. Frederick's "A.J. Cronin" (1941.101) and
Daniel Horton Davies's book, A Mirror of the Ministry in Modern Novels
(1959.2). But further investigation needs to be made into the rapport
between Cronin and his readers; his relationship with Hollywood; the
relationship between his life and works; and his devotion to Catholi-
cism and social justice. The historical interest of his novels, their
nineteenth-century sources, influences and parallels, also are inevitable subjects for inquiry. Perhaps some of the materials in this
reference guide will provide the starting point for additional study
of this important popular novelist.

Writings by A.J. Cronin, 1931-1978

Hatter's Castle (1931)
Three Loves (1932)
Grand Canary (1933)
The Stars Look Down (1935)
Kaleidoscope in K. (1936)
The Citadel (1937)
Jupiter Laughs (1940)
The Keys of the Kingdom (1941)
Adventures of a Black Bag (1943)
The Green Years (1944)
Shannon's Way (1948)
The Spanish Gardener (1950)
Adventures in Two Worlds (1952)
Beyond this Place (1953)
A Thing of Beauty (1956; also published as Crusader's Tomb)
The Northern Light (1958)
The Judas Tree (1961)
A Song of Sixpence (1964)
A Pocketful of Rye (1969)
Desmonde (1975; also published as The Minstrel Boy)
The Lady with Carnations (1976)
Gracie Lindsay (1978)
Doctor Finlay of Tannochbrae (1978)

Writings about A.J. Cronin, 1931-1981

1 ANON. "A.J. Cronin." <u>Wilson Bulletin for Librarians</u> 6
     (November):178, 182.
         Biographical background covering Cronin's career through
     the writing of <u>Hatter's Castle</u>. "It would be difficult to
     measure Dr. Cronin's tastes and interests. The surest thing
     is that, as healer and writer, he has a deep and abiding in-
     terest in <u>people</u>--people in all walks of life."

2 ANON. "Books: Books in Brief." <u>Forum</u> 86 (September):x, xii.
         Review of <u>Hatter's Castle</u>. Finds in this novel "more
     dark misery, more cruelty, and more exquisite mental tor-
     ture than in any novel of recent years." However, because
     of Cronin's powerful writing and vivid detail, the reader
     wants to read on. Throughout the story we feel a certain
     pity for the pride-ridden father.

3 ANON. "Fiction." <u>Booklist</u> 28 (September):26.
         Brief mention of <u>Hatter's Castle</u>. This tragedy is
     reminiscent of <u>Wuthering Heights</u> (Bronte). "To some readers
     Cronin's frank details may be offensive, [but] the book is
     a unique production, filled with an amazing energy and vi-
     tality, and wholly objective in tone."

4 ANON. "New Novels." <u>Times</u> (London), 9 June, p. 10.
         Review of <u>Hatter's Castle</u>. Cronin's theme is familiar
     to those readers who are acquainted with Greek tragedy:
     "the retribution that attends an overweening man." However,
     this author has treated the theme "with a force and sympathy
     which win him great approbation." Concludes that in spite
     of its length and somberness, the novel has "real merit
     which gives great promise for the future."

5 ANON. "New Novels." <u>Times Literary Supplement</u> (London),
     11 June, p. 464.
         Review of <u>Hatter's Castle</u>. It is remarkable that a

1931

former physician should manage to write for his first novel
"a full-fledged Balzacian tragedy." Cronin realizes James
Brodie completely, "with all the granite of his nature, ugly
and yet in its way fine." Although an old-fashioned story
which has been told before, it succeeds because it is written with "force of description, strong human sympathy and
deep knowledge of the persons and scenes from which it is
drawn."

6   ANON. Review of Hatter's Castle. Pittsburgh Monthly Bulletin
        36 (October):68.
        Brief mention of Hatter's Castle with plot summary.

7   ANON. Review of Hatter's Castle. Springfield (Mass.)
        Republican, 9 August, p. 7e.
        "This is a novel of many crudities." But Cronin's story
        approaches "the verities of life," and he is successful at
        "cloaking it with powerful drama and honest tragedy."

8   CLARKE, ALAN BURTON. "Fiction." Bookman 74 (September):79-80.
        Review of Hatter's Castle. As a Victorian novel, this is
        "a long, solid, meaty book, distinguished for its objective
        writing and its rich and moving humanity." In spite of the
        occasional melodramatic scenes, "there is nothing cheap,
        nothing depressive about the novel." However, much of the
        background material is unnecessary as are many of the con-
        versations between members of the Brodie family. But the
        story is memorable because it deals with "problems and
        traits close to the center of human experience." In fact,
        this novel belongs in the same company with Of Human Bondage
        (Maugham) and The Old Wives' Tale (Bennett).

9   DANGERFIELD, GEORGE. "Decline and Fall." Saturday Review of
        Literature 7 (18 July):972.
        Review of Hatter's Castle. Finds characteristics of the
        nineteenth century novel: "a more 'literary' manner than
        we cultivate nowadays, a more obvious devotion to literary
        etiquette, which does not necessarily imply better writing;
        a slow and detailed growth with unswerving direction; and a
        respect for the privacy of its characters which did not en-
        tirely depend upon social modesty." But Cronin lacks "the
        power to round out his characters, to make them fulfil them-
        selves and their destinies." To a point the story does have
        "growth with direction: and just as certainly it afterwards
        loses direction."

10 No entry.

11 EDGETT, E.F. Review of Hatter's Castle. Boston Transcript,
       18 July, p. 8.
       A dramatic novel because Cronin chooses to tell his own
    story. "He writes with an air of detachment and aloofness
    that is as notable as it is exceptional." In spite of cer-
    tain "extravagances of characterization," every figure is
    lifelike and memorable. "It is a novel worth writing. It
    is a novel no less worth the reading."

12 HARWOOD, H.C. "New Novels." Saturday Review (London) 151
       (6 June):832.
       Review of Hatter's Castle. "What place Mr. Cronin will
    win for himself in contemporary letters it is of course too
    early to predict, but the way in which he here grips the
    reader with a violence to be appreciated only by making
    acquaintance with the book suggests that he will go very
    far indeed. But first Cronin must overcome his presbyterian
    prose and dull characterization. In one area of technique
    he has nothing to learn: "the book is perfectly propor-
    tioned."

13 HAWTHORNE, HAZEL. "Twice-Told Tale." New Republic 68
       (16 September):133.
       Review of Hatter's Castle. Finds competence rather than
    power in this novel. "The author has handled these passions
    with an able and orderly forward drive, but the book remains
    an uninspired epitome of nineteenth-century novels." Sees
    similarities with Hardy (in the characters of Mary and
    Nessie), Eliot (in the character of Dr. Renwick), and Emily
    Brontë (in the character of Brodie).

14 HUTCHINSON, PERCY. "Hatter's Castle, A Novel in the Great
       Tradition." New York Times Book Review, 19 July, p. 4.
       Although not a masterpiece, this novel is the work of a
    writer "destined for the seats of the mighty." In spite of
    glaring faults, this is the most important English novel in
    decades, for it is a restoration of the nineteenth-century
    novel.

15 MacAFEE, HELEN. "The Library of the Quarter: Outstanding
       Novels." Yale Review, n.s. 21 (Autumn):viii, x.
       Review of Hatter's Castle. Cronin's story is too logical
    and predictable. "For readers who look for their reward to
    flashes of illuminating insight or to style that has a lustre
    of its own, there is little here." It is, however, based on
    "physical fact."

16 MARSH, FRED T. "In the Great English Tradition." New York

3

1931

Herald-Tribune Books, 19 July, pp. 3-4.
Review of Hatter's Castle. Cronin's novel returns to
the tradition extending from Fielding to Hardy with "greater,
more whole-hearted abandon than any recent book." Cronin's
work is genuinely artistic. He has shaken off "contemporary,
stereotyped, journalistic formulas" by reverting to former
conventions. And yet his concerns in the novel are modern.
The novel should serve "to carry the mature reader back to
his memories of one of the great English literary traditions
--and that in itself is valuable."

17   PROTEUS [pseud.]. "New Novels." New Statesman and Nation 1
       (6 June):547.
       Review of Hatter's Castle. Comments on the presence of
an overwhelming sense of fate--a theme which controlled
Cronin.

18   ROBBINS, FRANCES LAMONT. "The New Books." Outlook and
       Independent 158 (22 July):378.
       Review of Hatter's Castle. Melodrama alone would never
make a novel. But fortunately Cronin uses it as a frame-
work for "living characterizations." Wishes there were some
humor here, for then the novel "would truly merit superlatives." Overall, however, it is "the season's most welcome
dish to lovers of solid, meaty fiction."

19   STRONG, L.A.G. "Fiction: the Rough and the Smooth." Spectator
       146 (30 May):870, 872.
       Review of Hatter's Castle. Cronin's first novel is "a
formidable one. . . . There is energy and imagination
enough in it for ten ordinary novels." His creation of
James Brodie is "magnificent." This novel is certainly "a
big achievement, tempting one to use superlatives. . . .
There can, however, be no doubt of Dr. Cronin's qualifica-
tions for his new profession."

20   Van DOREN, DOROTHY. "Death, Destruction, and Power." Nation
       133 (29 July):113-114.
       Review of Hatter's Castle. "Not since Wuthering Heights
have we had a horror story that so completely satisfies all
the requirements of the genre." But Cronin's story is different from the typical horror story because he combines
romantic terror with realism and he inspires pity for James
Brodie. Indeed, Cronin is "a novelist to be watched and
reckoned with. . . . Because of his frankness and his courage, because he is not afraid of the heights and the depths
of his characters, he achieves something of the mighty elo-
quence that must be in all novels before they are great."

21 WALPOLE, HUGH. "Books Abroad: London Letter, June." <u>New York</u>
    <u>Herald-Tribune Books</u>, 28 June, p. 9.
        Review of <u>Hatter's Castle</u>. This novel is creating a
    sensation because, above all, in the writing of it Cronin
    "has been afraid of nothing." Sees the triumph of this
    novel as a step in the return of "the objective novel to
    English fiction." Cronin's narrative gift is superb. His
    character creations are like Hardy, but he is not Hardy.
    "He writes very often badly, he does not suggest the larger
    destinies, he has none of Hardy's wonderful poetic beauty,
    but the wife of James Brodie is worthy to be set beside the
    Mayor of Casterbridge; he would not be ashamed of her com-
    pany."

22 WILLIAMS, ORLO. "Recent Fiction Chronicle." <u>Criterion</u> 11
    (October):88–89.
        Review of <u>Hatter's Castle</u>. "This was a first novel of
    undoubted merit, all the more deserving of praise in that
    its technical competence, which was up to the highest modern
    level, was not its chief virtue. . . . But to assert that
    a new star of great brilliance has suddenly risen in the
    literary sky is simply ridiculous."

1932

1   ANON. "Burns Club of London: Dr. Cronin's Tribute." <u>Times</u>
    (London), 26 January, p. 9.
        Cronin toasts the memory of Robert Burns at the 173d
    celebration of the anniversary of his birth. Said Cronin:
    "Burns was never a trifler with life, never a dilettante.
    He admitted his erratic path with a passionate self-sincerity
    that should itself disarm the Godly. He hated insincerity,
    scorned cant, spurned falsehood, and loathed tyranny. In
    his life, as in his verse, he mixed the fine and the broad,
    the ironic with the devout, the sentimental and the sublime.
    There was a tragic sweep about the life of Burns which de-
    manded not censure but compassion. In his simplicity, his
    aspirations, yes, even in his follies, Robert Burns was
    Everyman. His life, like his verse, was always in the major
    key."

2   ANON. "Book Notes: Fiction." <u>New Republic</u> 70 (14 May):335.
        Review of <u>Three Loves</u>. The characters are "less stark,
    and more complicated" than those in <u>Hatter's Castle</u>. In
    many ways, Cronin's writing has improved.

3   ANON. "Fiction." <u>Booklist</u> 28 (May):389–90.

1932

Brief mention of <u>Three Loves</u>. "This love story, less melodramatic than <u>Hatter's Castle</u>, is equally somber in its recital of personal tragedies."

4 ANON. "Lucy Moore's Three Loves." <u>New York Herald-Tribune Books</u>, 5 April, p. 5.
Review of <u>Three Loves</u>. This is "another powerful story of a remarkable woman." Like <u>Hatter's Castle</u>, it is a long novel of "power and scope."

5 ANON. "New Novels: Three Loves." <u>Times Literary Supplement</u> (London), 25 February, p. 130.
Cronin has "decidedly fulfilled the promise of <u>Hatter's Castle</u>, though it is possible that the general public will find this a less enthralling book." Cronin's greatest gift as a writer is that of "seeing his characters with entire clarity in all their goings out and their comings in." Another gift is that he brings his stories to "a finish of tragic completeness and depth." Cronin seems drawn to "the exploration of the tragedies which come from human presumption; and for the spirit that cannot yield there is no rest so long as life is in the body."

6 ANON. "Notes on Fiction." <u>Nation</u> 134 (1 June):632.
Review of <u>Three Loves</u>. Cronin's second novel "bears out much of the promise of the first and yet it is curiously disappointing." Although the story is told almost without a flaw, what is needed is some editing. "Dr. Cronin suffers from the excellent fault of too much energy, too many things to say, too much support of his central theme."

7 ANON. Review of <u>Three Loves</u>. <u>Springfield</u> (Mass.) <u>Republican</u>, 29 May, p. 7.
Cronin's technique and character delineation have grown. This novel "definitely places Mr. Cronin among the more accomplished novelists of the day who follow the older tradition of the novel."

8 BULLETT, GERALD. "New Novels." <u>New Statesman and Nation</u> 3 (5 March):300.
Review of <u>Three Loves</u>. This book commands respect because of Cronin's "imaginative energy and technical assurances." But the novel is too long. Cronin's characters are "vital enough to exist in our imaginations without all these adventitious props of circumstance." Finds that the story is tragic in the Aristotelian sense.

9 DAVENPORT, BASIL. "Chasing Balloons." <u>Saturday Review of</u>

6

Literature 8 (2 April):633.
Review of Three Loves. This is "another dour, thrawn, and memorable book." Finds a number of comparisons with Greek tragedy. Although an "unusually good book," its characterization is lacking. "It almost seems as if Mr. Cronin were more at home with abnormal psychology than with sanity. . . . Three Loves is satisfying, but abstract."

10 HARWOOD, H.C. "New Novels." Saturday Review (London) 153 (27 February):223.
Three Loves is "irritatingly depressing" because the hero's misfortunes are "largely accidental."

11 HUTCHINSON, PERCY. "Dr. Cronin's Portrait of A Stubborn Woman." New York Times Book Review, 3 April, p. 6.
Review of Three Loves. This novel is both similar to and different from Hatter's Castle. Above all, it is a "softer book," but not a romance. It is a novel "'of parts.'"

12 MARSH, FRED T. "The Pride of Possessiveness." New York Herald-Tribune Books, 3 April, p. 5.
Review of Three Loves. Although not as extraordinary a "feat of virtuosity" as Hatter's Castle, this novel is "a more genuine piece of work." Cronin's writing is "smooth and flowing, failing in emphasis, however, and lacking in original distinction." Comments on some of the strong passages involving Miss Hocking and those centered on convent life.

13 REELY, MARY KATHERINE. "New Books." Wisconsin Library Bulletin 28 (July):231.
Brief mention of Three Loves.

14 STRONG, L.A.G. "Fiction." Spectator 148 (27 February):298.
Review of Three Loves. This novel begins like a lecture and is "long-winded." The value of the book must depend upon Lucy's character, but unfortunately her portrayal is not of sufficient strength or power. "That the story has great power and distinction goes without saying, but Dr. Cronin's reputation must rest, for the present at any rate, upon his first book."

1933

1 ABELARD, PETER. "New Novels: Grand Canary." Times Literary Supplement (London), 18 May, p. 346.

1933

"This is a new experiment for Dr. Cronin, but it lacks none of the intensity of his two earlier books, displays the same powers of graphic narrative."

2   ANON. "A Doctor Discovers that He Has a Soul." <u>Salisbury</u> (N.C.) <u>Post</u>, 21 May, p. 7.
     Review of <u>Grand Canary</u>. An interesting story told with "warmth and sympathetic understanding." At the end, the hero discovers that he has a soul. Although not as fine a book as <u>Hatter's Castle</u>, somehow "it is better reading." Reprinted: 1933.3.

3   ANON. "A Doctor Finds a Way Back to Life." <u>Cincinnati Post</u>, 30 May, p. 9.
     Reprint of 1933.2

4   ANON. "Enter a He-Man." <u>Cleveland News</u>, 2 June, p. 11.
     Review of <u>Grand Canary</u>. Cronin's first novel was "fine, deep tragedy," but his new work is "popular melodrama." Unfortunately, Cronin has used "the commonplace <u>Grand Hotel</u> theme, having a religious fanatic mad over a sophisticated woman, a humorous chap for comedy relief and all the other familiar props." However, the novel does tell of the rehabilitation of a man--a stimulating subject.

5   ANON. "Fiction." <u>Booklist</u> 29 (July):341.
     Brief mention of <u>Grand Canary</u>. "It is a swift-moving story but it lacks the force and sweep of <u>Hatter's Castle</u>."

6   ANON. "<u>Grand Canary</u> Fine Regeneration Yarn." <u>Ohio State Journal</u>, 30 June, p. 3.
     Cronin has brought together "a various and amusing crowd of shipmates."

7   ANON. "New Fiction." <u>Atlanta Constitution</u>, 4 June, p. 3.
     Review of <u>Grand Canary</u>. "The reader will find exciting drama, romance, but no tragedy, and yet the book has a wider appeal than if its pages were filled with startling crime."

8   ANON. "New Novels." <u>Times</u> (London), 9 May, p. 19.
     Review of <u>Grand Canary</u>. Finds much familiar material in this novel. Although the story brings to mind Maugham, Kipling, Crosbie Garstin, London and others, "Cronin is no imitator." He has shaped "an urgent, developing story. . . . In short Dr. Cronin has given us an admirably graphic, stirring romance that deserves the popularity which will no doubt be accorded to it."

9   ANON. "Predestination?" <u>Brooklyn Daily Eagle</u>, 4 June, p. 17.
        Brief mention of <u>Grand Canary</u>. Finds here the same
    "presbyterian view of life" characteristic of <u>Hatter's
    Castle</u> and <u>Three Loves</u>.

10   ANON. Review of <u>Grand Canary</u>. <u>Boston Transcript</u>, 10 June,
     p. 8.
        No matter what Cronin writes, he will never equal "the
    tempestuous qualities and the sense of something big" that
    he put into <u>Hatter's Castle</u>, nor will he be able to create
    characters of such vitality. His second novel, <u>Three Loves</u>,
    lacked the "relentless speed" and the "vigorous fatality" of
    its predecessor, and it was more melodramatic than tragic.
    In his latest novel, the misfortunes of the characters have
    none of the inevitability found in <u>Hatter's Castle</u>. Also,
    wonders why Cronin found it necessary to spell "Plato" as
    "Playto." "How else would or could it be pronounced?"

11   ANON. Review of <u>Grand Canary</u>. <u>Columbia</u> (S.C.) <u>State</u>, 21 May,
     p. 4.
        Calls this a "dramatic romance."

12   ANON. Review of <u>Grand Canary</u>. <u>Dayton Daily News</u>, 26 May, p.
     21.
        This novel has been written with "undeniable skill."
    Recommends, however, that Cronin reread Aristotle's <u>Rhetoric</u>
    as a way of conquering some glaring errors in basic story-
    telling.

13   ANON. Review of <u>Grand Canary</u>. <u>Dayton Daily News</u>, 2 June, p.
     19.
        This is "of a more popular nature" than Cronin's previous
    novels.

14   ANON. Review of <u>Grand Canary</u>. <u>Green Bay Press-Gazette</u>,
     24 June, p. 13.
        Brief plot summary.

15   ANON. Review of <u>Grand Canary</u>. <u>Parkersburg</u> (Va.) <u>Sentinel</u>,
     2 June, p. 3.
        This has all the "fine qualities of A.J. Cronin's other
    two novels and while it is by no means a light book, it does
    lack the elements of horror and tragedy that characterized
    his earlier works."

16   ANON. Review of <u>Grand Canary</u>. <u>Springfield</u> (Mass.) <u>Republican</u>,
     18 June, p. 7.
        Many readers who respond to its "readability and romantic

1933

interest will find it all too short." Cronin's skill with character delineation has increased considerably since his first novel.

17   ANON. "Romantic and Colorful." <u>Chicago Journal of Commerce</u>, 10 June, p. 31.
        Review of <u>Grand Canary</u>. Finds a beautiful love story and a moral in this novel. "The emotions that might have been hopelessly devastating for two people are turned into the inspirations that shall henceforth guide their lives." Also present is the atmosphere of strange places, giving the novel "an added charm."

18   DAVENPORT, BASIL. "'Unhand Me, Villain.'" <u>Saturday Review of Literature</u> 9 (20 May):605.
        Review of <u>Grand Canary</u>. It is hard to believe that this novel was written by the same author of <u>Hatter's Castle</u> and <u>Three Loves</u>, for "it has nothing in common with those grim masterpieces except melodrama." Finds "a profusion of everything false and mechanical" in this latest novel.

19   DAVIS, ELRICK B. "Cronin's First Romance Promises New Audience." <u>Cleveland Press</u>, 28 June, p. 13.
        Review of <u>Grand Canary</u>. There is "little connection between manner and content of this book and the first two." This novel should win for Cronin a new audience, "though it is an old and enthusiastic and very large audience for Mr. Deeping. <u>Grand Canary</u> is another of the last of the Elsie books."

20   DOTTIN, PAUL. "La littérature anglaise en 1932." <u>Revue de France</u>, 15 September, pp. 311–332.
        Classifies Cronin's novel, <u>Three Loves</u>, as the best "psychological" study.

21   GREENE, GRAHAM. "Fiction." <u>Spectator</u> 150 (19 May):728.
        Review of <u>Grand Canary</u>. This novel is "a perfect example of the Popular Novelist. Viewed in this light his defects become positive qualities. One is inclined to praise his inability to create a plausible human being, for one real character would break the book and Dr. Cronin's importance as an Awful Example."

22   HUTCHINSON, PERCY. "Dr. Cronin's Gift for Narrative." <u>New York Times Book Review</u>, 14 May, p. 6.
        Review of <u>Grand Canary</u>. Cronin's narrative skills have advanced, but the total impact of the novel is not up to the level of <u>Hatter's Castle</u> and <u>Three Loves</u>.

23 KIRSCH, PAUL. "New Books." <u>Portsmouth</u> (Ohio) <u>Advertiser</u>,
7 July, p. 2.
Review of <u>Grand Canary</u>. Once again Cronin disregards the
usual formula of the happy ending, and yet pleases his readers. This novel of rejuvenation is possibly the best since
<u>The Man Who Came Back</u>.

24 LEMON, MARY DYER. "Note for Vacationist: Read <u>Grand Canary</u>."
<u>Indianapolis Star</u>, 16 July, p. 37.
This is a "highly imaginative and romantic" novel. The
close is "artistic . . . with none of the amenities of life"
tampered with by Lady Mary Fielding and Harvey Leith.

25 McD., M.I. "A.J. Cronin Writes of a Man's Regeneration through
New Love." <u>Milwaukee Journal</u>, 17 June, p. 11.
Review of <u>Grand Canary</u>. The story is less bleak, less
tragic than its predecessors. Because the author has "dif-
fused his power through too many characters and too much
extraneous matter," this novel is considerably less effective, however.

26 McNEILL, ALEX. "<u>Grand Canary</u>." <u>Atlanta Journal</u>, 21 May, p.
10.
<u>Grand Canary</u> will make Cronin "the undisputed champion
of the modern literary field."

27 MEADE, GILBERT W. "Theme of Novel Is Regeneration by Love's
Power." <u>Birmingham</u> (Ala.) <u>News</u>, 11 June, p. 21.
Review of <u>Grand Canary</u>. Here Cronin misses "the high
mark" he set for himself in his earlier works. Like its
predecessors, this novel focuses on one central character,
a character ruled, at least temporarily, "by an overpowering
obsession." But missing is the "all-enveloping darkness" of
<u>Hatter's Castle</u>. With each subsequent novel, his tone has
become lighter. Notable is that his power of characterization is developing and that the minor characters "shine with
individuality."

28 MURGATROYD, M. "Mr. Cronin Scores with Another Winner in <u>Grand
Canary</u>." <u>Charlotte Observer</u>, 12 June, p. 21.
Although not a profound book, this novel will "amuse any-
one who likes adventure, humor, love and tragedy." Enjoys
the clever twist of "the transmigration or reincarnation of
Harvey and Mary from another time to this."

29 N., W. "Love and Climate." <u>San Diego Union</u>, 11 June, p. 13.
Review of <u>Grand Canary</u>. In spite of faulty psychology
and awkward diction, this is bound to be a bestseller.
Cronin does well with this old-fashioned plot.

1933

30 QUENNELL, PETER. "New Novels." New Statesman and Nation 5
    (3 June):736.
        Review of Grand Canary. No doubt Cronin intended this
    novel as "poetic relief" after his grim first novel. "To
    all who make a study of popular romanticism, and the chaste
    but voluptuous exuberance of its preferred style, I recom-
    mend Dr. Cronin's latest achievement."

31 ROSS, MARY. "Cruise of the Aureola and What Followed." New
    York Herald-Tribune Books, 14 May, p. 4.
        Review of Grand Canary. Finds the same "force" and
    "vividness" that accounted for the wide reading accorded
    Cronin's earlier novels.

32 SELBY, JOHN. "Doctor Cronin Drops Tragedy." Huntington (W.Va.)
    Advertiser, 28 May, p. 11.
        Review of Grand Canary. This is not a tragedy, although
    there are tragic overtones to it. "This pleasant and not
    too involved tale Mr. Cronin tells in a curiously uneven
    prose, sometimes colorful, sometimes lush, sometimes swift
    and clean."

33 SMITH, H. ALLEN. "Physician Clicks Again." Akron (Ohio) Press,
    4 June, p. 4.
        Review of Grand Canary. This novel is "fully as impres-
    sive" as its predecessors.

34 UDEN, GRANT. "The Bookman Gallery: A.J. Cronin." Bookman 76
    (March):494.
        In Hatter's Castle and Three Loves, Cronin has given us
    characters delineated with "skill." Although they are not
    happy characters, they move with "strange compelling lights
    around them." Grand Canary, on the other hand, is a more
    romantic book. And Kaleidoscope in K. is the best thing he
    has written. In the author's hands, these characters "con-
    stitute a world as vital, as full of interplaying laughter
    and tragedy, as the greater world outside." Finds in these
    latter two books "the cutting-out of all superfluity."

35 WEEKS, EDWARD. Review of Grand Canary. Stage 13 (August):113.
        This narrative "stretches the imagination." It can be
    enjoyed "without arousing too much of one's critical ener-
    gies." But one must suspend his disbelief if he is to enjoy
    this novel. "The love story, of course, is sentimental; the
    betrayal of the missionary is old stage stuff; and the cli-
    max rings about as true as a parrot's laugh."

36 WELBACH, THOMAS. "A Change." Akron (Ohio) Press, 21 May,

p. 4.
  Brief excerpt from Grand Canary.

37 WYETH, OLA M. "Grand Canary: A Novel by A.J. Cronin."
      Savannah News, 16 July, p. 18.
        Comments on the lighter tone, the poetic quality, and
      the note of mysticism and predestination in this novel.

1934

1   ANON. Review of Grand Canary. Redwood City (Calif.) Tribune,
      19 October, p. 18.
        In this "fascinating book," Mother Hemmingway is amusing
      and Jimmy Corcoran is interesting.

2   DOTTIN, PAUL. "La littérature anglaise en 1933." Revue de
      France, 1 June, pp. 522-43.
        Studies the novels of 1933 and classifies Cronin's as
      realistic.

1935

1   A., C. "New Books." Catholic World 142 (November):242-43.
        Review of The Stars Look Down. Cronin's handling of his
      theme is fearless and able. "The book is crowded with char-
      acters, each drawn with consummate skill, and the threads of
      their lives are so artfully interwoven that the finished work
      is a satisfactory and durable fabric."

2   ANON. "Books." Time 26 (23 September):69.
        Review of The Stars Look Down. Compared with Tom Tippett's
      Horse Shoe Bottoms, Cronin's novel is "the more accomplished
      and professional." The most remarkable episode is the ac-
      count of the disaster: "a powerful piece of writing."

3   ANON. "Books: Cronin: The Stars Look Down on Life and Death
      in the Mines." Newsweek 6 (5 October):42-43.
        Review of The Stars Look Down. Cronin presents his ideas
      with "compassion and understanding, but without propaganda
      or theoretical cure-alls." The plot rushes "full gallop."

4   ANON. "Books: Dr. Cronin's New Novel." New Yorker 11 (21
      September):65-66.
        Review of The Stars Look Down. Finds enough material for
      six good novels in this "extremely rich and complex story."
      In spite of its length, occasional dullness, melodrama, and

1935

unnecessary energy and inconclusiveness, it is a fine book. "It represents a major effort to write a major novel."

5   ANON. "Dickens Characters in Tale of Miners." Chicago Journal of Commerce, 14 September, p. 22.
Review of The Stars Look Down. Unlike Robert Brifiault's Europa, Cronin's novel offers characters "whose appeal is greater because they are people of the more ordinary walks of life, to whom our sympathy goes out, and whom we learn to love." This panorama of industrial England "rings true." The story is written with conviction.

6   ANON. "Dr. Cronin's New Novel One of Life and Realism." Boston Globe, 12 December, p. 14.
Review of The Stars Look Down. A story of "rare realism, of life as it really is, with much beauty, of sordidness, of sadness and of the conflict between the good and the bad in mankind. And the whole story is admirably written."

7   ANON. "Fiction." Booklist 32 (October):42.
Brief mention of The Stars Look Down. "The book is long, diffuse, and depressing, but impressive. Some episodes will bar it from conservative libraries."

8   ANON. "New Books: The Public Library Presents." Indianapolis Times, 2 June, p. 17.
Brief mention of The Stars Look Down. This is not a pleasant book because its story is not a happy one.

9   ANON. "New Novels." Times (London), 9 April, p. 10.
Review of The Stars Look Down. This is "an average specimen" of Cronin's melodramatic writing. In spite of its powerfully dramatic scenes, his attempt to indict society as a system in which "idealism miserably fails through dishonesty, treachery, and injustice does not succeed. . . . The total impression, despite occasional vivacity and acute observation of humble interiors, is of a rather empty sound and fury."

10   ANON. "New Novels." Times Literary Supplement (London), 11 April, p. 242.
Review of The Stars Look Down. Defines this as "a good-sized chunk of the conglomerate called by Balzac la comédie humaine," but much of the novel is beyond Cronin's abilities. His portrayal of the lives of the miners' families is successful. His descriptions of a mine disaster, a riot, and an operation are realistic. In these instances "he can display his intimate knowledge of the seamy side of things; but his bent for melodrama weakens all his effects."

1935

11   ANON. Review of The Stars Look Down. Chicago News,
25 September, p. 11.
    Finds similarities between Jenny and Somerset Maugham's
Mildred (in Of Human Bondage). Not since Lawrence's Sons
and Lovers has an author given us "a destitute mining family
with such smashing realism." Although Cronin overwrites,
and although he has perhaps borrowed from other masters, he
has written, in this novel, a story which is "deeply and
disturbingly human."

12   ANON. Review of The Stars Look Down. Christian Science Monitor,
27 November, p. 10.
    "In spite of the Georgian coarseness of its diction, it
is of social and economic as well as artistic value."

13   ANON. Review of The Stars Look Down. Macon (Ga.) News,
11 October, p. 7.
    "Cronin draws no judgments. He paints no rosy pictures,
no happy endings. Life goes on for his characters, it un-
rolls unchanging for the generations. And in this, the
author shows the height of his artistic integrity."

14   ANON. Review of The Stars Look Down. Madison Journal,
29 December, p. 15.
    In his best novel yet, Cronin offers "a bitter indictment
of the system under which the miners lived and worked."

15   ANON. Review of The Stars Look Down. Philadelphia Inquirer,
26 September, p. 11.
    Finds here "evidence of authoritative knowledge, consci-
entious study and deep troubled sense of injustice." But
somehow the characters remind us of well-known types of
fiction.

16   ANON. Review of The Stars Look Down. Santa Monica Outlook,
3 December, p. 3.
    Charles G. Norris's novel Hands is a much better book.
It is truer and far less gloomy. Its characters are lifelike, not two-dimensional dolls "cut out of solid black and
white." And it is more exciting with real drama instead of
melodrama.

17   ANON. Review of The Stars Look Down. Springfield (Mass).
Republican, 13 October, p. 7.
    In spite of its massive size, this novel does not become
"unwieldy" in the author's hands.

18   ANON. "The Book of the Week." New York News, 22 September,

15

1935

p. 3.
Review of The Stars Look Down. This is an "intelligent and exciting" picture of life in a mining town from 1903 until the present day. Cronin writes with "a surer pen" and "a more penetrating eye" than he did in Hatter's Castle.

19 ANON. "The Book Shelf." Milwaukee Sentinel, 29 September, p. 10.
Review of The Stars Look Down. This novel "surges with life and power and teems with unforgettable characters and scenes."

20 ANON. "The New Books: An Outstanding Novel." Philadelphia Ledger, 20 September, p. 17.
Review of The Stars Look Down. Cronin presents "a truly stupendous canvas." This is not just another novel; this is literature.

21 ANON. "The Stars Look Down on Scene of Powerful Novel by Cronin." Charlotte News, 20 October, p. 9.
Review of The Stars Look Down. Cronin tells his story with "a soft touch, rarely rising to dramatic peaks, but always holding the reader deeply interested in the story and the characters." Praises the characterization of Jenny as perhaps "the finest drawn individual" of the novel. The mine disaster scene is described with power, too.

22 BENTLEY, FLORENCE R. Review of The Stars Look Down. Burlingame (Calif.) Advance-Star, 9 November, p. 3.
Comments on the narrative pace, the melodrama, and the themes. Concludes that Cronin "seems to have that knack of understanding characters and human nature."

23 BRICKELL, HERSCHEL. "Cronin's New Book Long, Rich Study of Real Men and Women Written Without Artificiality." New York Post, 23 September, p. 21.
Review of The Stars Look Down. Speculates that perhaps the reason Cronin's novels are not "self-consciously literary" is that the author had lived "a full and rich life before he began to express himself in words." Quotes Hugh Massingham: "'Dr. Cronin has succeeded in the real business of the novelist, which is to illuminate society by the interpretation of human lives.'" Feels that Cronin has a sense of humor, too, and an "unfailing sense of humanity."

24 BUTCHER, FANNY. "Cronin Novel Should Please His Followers." Chicago Daily Tribune, 21 September, p. 14.
Review of The Stars Look Down. This "long, detailed,

large-canvas-covered English novel" fits into the tradition
of the British novel, with obvious parallels to Dickens.
Its title is ironic. The influences of a mine disaster, a
world war, and an economic depression are as much the essence
of this novel as are the characters themselves.

25 CANTWELL, ROBERT. "A Season's Run." New Republic 85
    (11 December):152.
        Review of The Stars Look Down. Cronin's new novel "does
    not give an impression of great depth, or of offering any
    particularly original contribution, but it is written with
    a sort of narrative fluency that you find in the romances
    of a good popular magazine."

26 CATTON, BRUCE. "A Bitter Novel--But One of the Best 1935 Has
    Seen." Gastonia (N.C.) Gazette, 28 September, p. 11.
        Review of The Stars Look Down. This is a book of "vast
    power and profound human interest. It is long, but it is
    never dull; it is impassioned, but it always remains pre-
    eminently a novel, a narrative. It is very much worth read-
    ing." Reprinted: 1935.27-28.

27 _____. "Book a Day." Portsmouth (Va.) Star, 29 September,
    p. 17.
        Reprint of 1935.26.

28 _____. "Book Review." Palo Alto (Calif.) Times, 28 September,
    p. 14.
        Reprint of 1935.26.

29 DANGERFIELD, GEORGE. "A Story of Industrial England."
    Saturday Review (London) 12 (21 September):5.
        Review of The Stars Look Down. On the surface, this nov-
    el appears to contain all the ingredients necessary for a
    truly great work. And yet something is lacking. In part,
    it is the "presence of Cronin." He fails to impress his
    own self upon us. Also, the novel has no hero. None of the
    characters claims our attention more than another.

30 ELLIOTT, DOROTHY. "Dr. Cronin Proves His Pen Power." Appleton
    (Wis.) Post, 28 September, p. 14.
        Review of The Stars Look Down. Hatter's Castle was a
    classic in contemporary fiction, but Cronin's next two novels
    were "sore disappointments." Now, with his latest, Cronin
    has once again revealed his genius. "For here again we meet
    the stark realism, the tremendous power and the vital char-
    acters which the pen wielded by Cronin can create." Finds
    many Dickensian qualities in the characters of this "dramatic
    modern classic." Reprinted: 1935.31.

1935

31   ____. "New Novel by Cronin." <u>Green Bay Press-Gazette</u>,
         28 September, p. 11.
              Reprint of 1935.30.

32   FOX, SUE MAC. "<u>The Stars Look Down</u> Powerful Novel of English
         North Country." <u>Columbus</u> (Ga.) <u>Ledger</u>, 12 October, p. 11.
              Comments on the themes, characters, and plot. Cronin's
         sympathy, kindly as it is, has "no passionate depth, and so
         keeps the book from the all-time greatness it would other-
         wise take unto itself."

33   FRAME, ALEXANDER. "Interesting, Fine Novel." <u>Boston Post</u>,
         20 October, p. 3.
              Review of <u>The Stars Look Down</u>. The novel demonstrates
         that "great success is only brought with pain to others."
         In this "monumental, ever-gripping piece of work," the po-
         litical side is a secondary aspect.

34   GAY, R.M. "The Bookshelf." <u>Atlantic Monthly</u> 155 (October):20.
              Review of <u>The Stars Look Down</u>. "It would require pages
         even to suggest the skill with which the numerous strains of
         plot are interwoven with almost unfailing naturalness and
         strength. When one is through reading, one feels in spite
         of the fact that the third part is certainly weaker than
         the other two, that here is a novel of rare beauty and power
         --perhaps one that could be called great."

35   GELDER, ROBERT Van. "Books of the Times." <u>New York Times</u>,
         21 September, p. 13.
              Review of <u>The Stars Look Down</u>. This is a novel of "high
         excellence" that is likely to dominate its field for some
         time to come. The major characters "seem like figures out
         of some modern equivalent to a morality play when presented
         only in skeleton."

36   H., G. "Conflict at the Mines." <u>Nashville Tennessean</u>,
         22 September, p. 3.
              Review of <u>The Stars Look Down</u>. Cronin has extended and
         perfected his power of characterization in this novel about
         the conflict between labor and capital. His style is
         "swifter" now. The book is "a workmanlike job, worthy of
         ranking high among the sociological studies of our times,
         and handled with a clearer perspective than most."

37   HANSEN, HARRY. "The First Reader." <u>New York World Telegram</u>,
         20 September, p. 11.
              Review of <u>The Stars Look Down</u>. Calls this "capital enter-
         tainment that won't make anyone mad." Wishes Cronin had

18

known David better, as well as he did the wife in <u>Hatter's</u>
<u>Castle</u>. Reprinted: 1935.38.

38 _____. "The First Reader (the Best of the New Books)." <u>San</u>
<u>Francisco News</u>, 27 September, p. 10.
    Reprint of 1935.37.

39 HARRIS, W.E. Review of <u>The Stars Look Down</u>. <u>Boston Transcript</u>,
    21 September, p. 1.
    The earlier portions of this narrative are the best, for
    there the author maintains "pace and drive, together with
    that heightening feeling for drama which enables great fic-
    tion to illumine life." Although this is not Cronin's most
    readable novel, it is certainly his most ambitious and in
    many ways "his most sensitive attempt."

40 HOOLE, WILLIAM STANLEY. "Books and Bywords." <u>Birmingham</u> (Ala.)
    <u>News</u>, 17 November, p. 6.
    Review of <u>The Stars Look Down</u>. Calls this "the most
    powerful novel" he has read in years. Cronin's technique
    is "kaleidoscopic."

41 HUTCHINSON, PERCY. "The Clash of Capital and Labor." <u>New York</u>
    <u>Times Book Review</u>, 22 September, pp. 1, 23.
    Review of <u>The Stars Look Down</u>. Cronin's ability to keep
    "a complicated story clear at all times and also swiftly
    moving" is unmatched by most novelists. The book is "cer-
    tain to take its place among the leading novels of the year."
    Cronin is "uncannily like Dickens."

42 JACKSON, JOSEPH HENRY. "New Novel by Author of <u>Hatter's Castle</u>
    Is Work of High Quality." <u>San Francisco Chronicle</u>, 29
    September, p. 4.
    Review of <u>The Stars Look Down</u>. The author seems at home
    in the country he is describing. He follows traditional
    storytelling techniques. He works "as the old-style painters
    did--those men who did battle canvases of hundreds of gurues,
    each one painted in detail." Predicts that this novel will
    find a wide and enthusiastic audience, "both because it is
    a story and because it is a story with a meaning."

43 [MacDONALD, CLAIRE.] "Book Review." <u>Bakersfield Californian</u>,
    19 October, p. 10.
    Reprint of 1935.44.

44 _____. "The Book Parade: One of Best Novels of Year." <u>San</u>
    <u>Jose News</u>, 28 September, p. 13.
    Brief mention of <u>The Stars Look Down</u>. Cronin's best book

1935

yet. It is a novel of "vast power and profound human interest." Reprinted: 1935.43.

45 McFEE, WILLIAM. "A Vital Novel." New York Sun, 20 September,
    p. 3.
        Review of The Stars Look Down. With this novel Cronin
    has staged a comeback. He has "grown in knowledge and skill.
    He handles his material with greater ease." His characters
    are "authentic and true," and the story is "readably told."
    Finds parallels with Priestley (in English Journey) and
    Dickens. Its weakness is in its melodrama.

46 MARTIN, ROSALIND EWING. "World of Books: Author of Hatter's
    Castle Writes Another Novel of Substance and Strength."
    Chattanooga News, 23 October, p. 11.
        Brief review of The Stars Look Down. Resembles Hatter's
    Castle in that it is "long, excellently written, and not
    particularly cheerful." It keeps the reader's interest un-
    til the end.

47 MIDDLETOWN, MAY CARNEY. "Stars Look Down Is Finely, If Not
    Greatly, Written." Evanston News-Index, 14 November, p. 4.
        Cronin draws from his own experience to render clearly
    the lives of his characters. Each figure "stands out as if
    in a spotlight and their combined lives leave a vital impres-
    sion of the present day labor problems in England."

48 MORRIS, MARVIN L. "Today's Book." Macon (Ga.) Telegraph,
    25 September, p. 3.
        Review of The Stars Look Down. The novel offers "a real-
    istic picture of life, and, as in other Cronin novels, the
    chief interest lies in the characters themselves." The mine
    disaster is one of the most exciting scenes in the book.

49 NEEDHAM, WILBUR. "Great Novel of English Coal Mines Surprises."
    Los Angeles Times, 22 September, p. 16.
        Review of The Stars Look Down. The novel is "rich with
    people, with action, with vitriolic, fearless and intelligent
    piling up of evidence against the economic system, with a
    long view of the struggle that is not ended yet. These
    things are fact, not fiction." The reading races along,
    making us forget the length--forcing us to overlook some of
    the most "shockingly bad writing in history. Cronin has hur-
    ried over action, psychology, background, character, grammar,
    everything, in parts of the book not concerned with the mines
    and with social scenes and implications arising out of them."
    Excerpted: 1935.50.

50   ____ . "Survey of the Year's Best: English Coal Mine." Los
        Angeles Saturday Night 16 (14 December):4.
            Review of The Stars Look Down. In this novel Cronin
        abandons popular fiction for "proletarian literature." The
        novel is "packed with characters, action, vitriolic language,
        plot." Includes some excerpts from 1935.49.

51   PHILLIPS, ALICE SWARIGHT. "Under the Stars." Raleigh Observer,
        9 December, p. 13.
            Review of The Stars Look Down. Discusses the character
        contrasts in a book that "stirs deeply." In it, the stars
        look down on "degradation and sin and all man's frailties.
        Perhaps the doctor does not know, but they also look down
        on a very great deal of happiness and beauty."

52   PHILLIPS, MARIE TELLO. Review of The Stars Look Down. Miami
        News, 16 February, p. 14.
            Cronin's "wide experiences make him a capable interpreter
        of human life." One of the best books of the year.

53   PLOMER, WILLIAM. "Fiction." Spectator 154 (12 April):628.
            Review of The Stars Look Down. Cronin knows how to tell
        a story with little subtlety. Also obvious is that this
        chronicle "lacks that element of strangeness so inevitably
        to be found in a work of art, that it tells the ordinary
        reader little or nothing that is essentially new, and, what
        is more remarkable, . . . that it tends to describe the
        events of twenty years ago from today's point of view."

54   POPE, J.S. "The Stars Look Down." Atlanta Journal, 6 October,
        p. 11.
            This book is likely to become a literary sensation. Its
        scope is "cosmic." Its title ironically suggests "the tragic
        comedy of human striving." Comments on the "vivid character-
        ization, the stark drama of the mine disaster, the slow-swift
        movement toward the climax and the bitter recession which is
        the deep moaning flood and ebb of the tide of life." Con-
        cludes that this novel seems to be the sort of book Dreiser
        might have written "if Dreiser could write," and the "revela-
        tion of life" that Thomas Wolfe attempted without success.

55   QUENNELL, PETER. "New Novels." New Statesman and Nation 9
        (6 April):490.
            Review of The Stars Look Down. This story suits Cronin
        much better than the romantic Grand Canary. "For those who
        like their fiction argumentative, solid and thoughtful, and
        are not greatly concerned with the nuances of literary art,
        here is a book that will provide just the fare they need."

1935

Although Cronin's attempt is "slightly wooden," it is
honest.

56   RIPLEY, THOMAS. "A Doctor Understands the Soul." Atlanta
         Georgian, 27 October, p. 6.
             Review of The Stars Look Down. Notes that this novel
         appeared serially in Cosmopolitan. Calls it "a fearless and
         dramatic handling of souls minus medicine and surgery."
         There is never a dull moment in what is bound to be classed
         one of the best novels of the year.

57   ROSS, MARY. "Life Before the War." Survey Graphic 24
         (November):557-58.
             Review of The Stars Look Down. Finds bleakness in both
         the miners' lives and the frustrations that cut short "any
         gesture of idealism on the part of the miner or owner."
         Into this book has gone an enormous amount of honest feeling
         and observation. However, unlike Jules Romain's The World
         of Below, this book lacks "a capacity to look clear-eyed at
         suffering and evil and not to be submerged by it."

58   _____. "Two-Room Houses of Miners' Row: An Honest Stirring
         Novel Written from the Depths of a Compelling Despair."
         New York Herald-Tribune Books, 22 September, p. 5.
             Review of The Stars Look Down. Apparently Cronin tried
         to write a book of despair drawn from his own times. But
         the cumulative effect is "so black as to obscure its own
         meaning."

59   S., H.B. "A Novel of Class Struggle." Jacksonville (Fla.)
         Times-Union, 8 December, p. 15.
             Review of The Stars Look Down. The novel "moves swiftly"
         and is filled with every human emotion imaginable. Cronin
         gives a detailed look at the "utter destitution and helpless-
         ness" of the British laboring class. The book is "a far bet-
         ter and strengthened work" than that which appeared in serial
         form in Cosmopolitan.

60   SCRUGGS, THEODORA. "Unforgettable Realism." Nashville Banner,
         22 September, p. 4.
             Review of The Stars Look Down. "Cronin knows human nature
         so well, and has the tricks of his craft so in hand that the
         reader views the end of the story with satisfaction." Its
         message is "haunting." Of the two female characters, Jenny
         is the more convincing. Praises Cronin's realistic detail
         and method of understatement.

61   SIMMS, FENNA B. "Book Reviews." Bellflower (Calif.)

Herald-Enterprise, 7 February, p. 7.
Review of The Stars Look Down. The plot moves rapidly
in a book which "shows vividly the conflict between the
harsh in life and that which is satisfying."

62   SOSKIN, WILLIAM. "Reading and Writing: British Miners
Reaching for the Sun." America 92 (20 September):19.
Review of The Stars Look Down. Although there may be a
few "economic untruths" in this story, Cronin's treatment
is "so soundly human, so solidly built in the bedrock of
human character that his entire story seems true." It reminds us of some of Dickens's best work--"with a burning
social conscience."

63   TODD, MADONNA. "Literary Parade." San Diego Sun, 28 September,
p. 4.
Review of The Stars Look Down. The theme is labor versus
capital. But above all, the novel is about people, all "dev-
astatingly real." However, there are too many "haphazard,
unforgivably sketchy blots on the plot construction and
jolting moments of melodrama." Perhaps these weaknesses,
and the fact that the novel is so completely comprehensible,
keep it from being "a really great book."

64   Van DOREN, DOROTHY. "The Pit." Nation 141 (2 October):389.
Review of The Stars Look Down. In Hatter's Castle and
Three Loves, Cronin was "a novelist of considerable power
with ability deftly to manipulate a group of characters."
His new novel is just as strong, intelligent, with perhaps
several credible and life-size characters emerging from it.
His moral is the same as Ellen Glasgow developed in Vein of
Iron. Although his philosophy is inconclusive and although
David's integrity is a bit unsatisfying, Cronin's varied and
strong character portrayals make up for it.

65   W., A.B. "Story of Life As It Is." San Diego Union, 20 October,
p. 11.
Review of The Stars Look Down. With his fourth novel,
Cronin has earned the right to be classed with Balzac and
Hardy. In this readable book, his characters are "real
people, born of an understanding gained through years of
medical practice."

66   W., K. "A Dickensesque Touch in The Stars Look Down."
Milwaukee Journal, 22 September, p. 16.
In its absorbing detail, the novel is Dickensesque.
Moreover, Cronin has Dickens's faculty for "stating a great
social problem and not attempting a solution or preaching

1935

about it." The dominating theme is "the futility of the
British working class struggle against the greed and selfishness of the moneyed overlords." The novel will be read for
"the entertainment it affords and remembered for the strength
of its philosophy and truth of its purpose."

1936

1   ALLEN, LEROY. "Worth While Fiction of Recent Date." Social
    Science 11 (Spring):168.
        Review of The Stars Look Down. This is one of the finest
    books of the current day. "As a picture of certain phases
    of British life it is hardly to be excelled in present-day
    literature."

2   BRICKELL, HERSCHEL. "The Literary Landscape: Proletarian."
    Review of Reviews 93 (January):7.
        Review of The Stars Look Down. Calls this "a solid study
    of a Scotch mining situation with extremely well-done char-
    acterization."

1937

1   ANON. "A Challenge to Skeptics." Honolulu Advertiser,
    28 November, p. 7.
        Brief mention of The Citadel. Cronin leaves Manson "with
    the road to the ideal open but steep."

2   ANON. "A Doctor's Title for Professional Integrity." Miami
    Herald, 3 October, p. 13.
        Review of The Citadel. Finds in the plot parallels with
    Sinclair Lewis's Arrowsmith. Both novels deal with a young
    doctor who "began his career with a selfless fervor, part
    science and part zeal for service. Somewhere along the road
    this man's idealism is weakened and he follows wealth or
    fame, or both, along false paths. Nearly always a shock of
    some kind brings awareness and we leave our hero firmly re-
    established in a new start toward integrity." Comments on
    the convincing characterization, the grave charges Cronin
    makes against the medical profession, and the "sheer drama."

3   ANON. "A.J. Cronin." Green Bay Press-Gazette, 11 September,
    p. 2.
        Andrew Manson, hero of The Citadel, is "compelling, liv-
    ing and altogether real."

4   ANON. "A.J. Cronin Plans Visit in November." Huntington
        (W.Va.) Advertiser, 31 October, p. 2.
            Reports that Cronin intends to visit America in November.
        This will be his second visit. His first was made in 1935,
        several months before the publication of The Stars Look Down.
        Publisher's notice reports that The Citadel is being printed
        from two sets of plates at 10,000 copies each. As of 15
        October, a total of 105,000 copies have been printed.

5   ANON. "A Scathing Indictment." Atlanta Constitution, 3
        October, p. 7.
            Review of The Citadel. This is Cronin's "most moving and
        revealing novel." Calls it "a searing, soul-searching ac-
        count" whose heroes--Andrew and Christine--reflect Cronin's
        "greatest art."

6   ANON. "A Story of Disillusion." Knoxville Journal, 12
        September, p. 3.
            Review of The Citadel. Cronin writes with "grim feeling"
        in a novel that has "life and fire and purpose" and that
        "teaches but does not preach."

7   ANON. "A Young Doctor's Dilemma." Oakland Post-Enquirer,
        2 October, p. 9.
            Brief mention of The Citadel. Calls this "a powerful and
        absorbing story."

8   ANON. "Book Chatter." Jacksonville (Fla.) Times-Union, 26
        September, p. 3.
            Review of The Citadel. Quotes from a letter by Dr. Hugh
        Cabot of the Rochester Mayo Clinic who praises this novel as
        a great book "which may easily have a profound influence on
        the future of society."

9   ANON. "Book Notes." Boston Herald, 27 November, p. 6.
            Cronin visits Boston this week. Reports that sales of
        The Citadel have reached 148,000 copies in the U.S. and
        150,000 copies in England.

10 ANON. "Book Review." Middletown (Ohio) Press, 23 September,
        p. 2.
            Brief mention of The Citadel. Includes biographical
        background. This is "a good novel."

11 ANON. "Books." Riverside (Calif.) News, 21 October, p. 4.
            Review of The Citadel. Cronin writes with "the authority
        and experience of a practitioner." The author avoids long
        explanations, preferring to make his points through the plot

and dialogue. Predicts that doctors everywhere will find
the novel of interest.

12 ANON. "Books and Writers." <u>Southbridge</u> (Mass.) <u>News</u>, 19
November, p. 16.
Review of <u>The Citadel</u>. Cronin's first novel was "too
long, too stark and written by an unknown." His new novel,
however, is powerful, dramatic, and penetrating.

13 ANON. "Books: Doctor: England's New Dickens Reports on
Former Profession." <u>Newsweek</u> 10 (13 September):34-35.
Review of <u>The Citadel</u>. Once again Cronin is "tilting at
social evils." Comments on the reactions from the medical
profession including that of Dr. Hugh Cabot, surgeon at the
Mayo Clinic in Rochester, who congratulated Cronin for the
novel (see 1937.8).

14 ANON. "Bound to be Read." <u>Norristown</u> (Pa.) <u>Herald</u>, 17 October,
p. 2.
Brief mention of <u>The Citadel</u> with biographical details.

15 ANON. "Bound to be Read." <u>Westfield</u> (Mass.) <u>Herald</u>, 23
September, p. 5.
Review of <u>The Citadel</u> with plot summary.

16 ANON. "Cronin Not First Doctor-Author." <u>Charlotte News</u>,
14 November, p. 2.
Comments on the number of authors who began as physicians.

17 ANON. "Cronin's <u>Citadel</u> Indicts A System." <u>Hartford Times</u>,
11 September, p. 13.
Review of <u>The Citadel</u>. Calls this a propaganda novel,
"the kind of material that cannot avoid being read widely
and discussed with violence." Although as an indictment the
novel is "strong and startling," as a novel "it leaves something to be desired." Comments on the confusing medical
terminology, stereotype characters, and anticlimactic
denouement.

18 ANON. "Descent into Harley Street: Dr. Cronin's Novel."
<u>Times</u> (London), 27 July, p. 19.
Review of <u>The Citadel</u>. "What is not true is that a dis-
trict of London called 'Harley Street' is shark-infested, so
that an honest man practises there in his peril. Dr. Cronin
would deny, certainly, that he had made any such suggestion;
but it is in this sense that his indictment has been read by
many, and the excuse of misunderstanding lies within his own
pages." Nevertheless, Cronin's story is lively and dramatic.

Manson's "fall into charlatanry" is ill-prepared for, however, and the "puritanical vengeance of the later chapters
is in keeping, unhappily, with the sentimental glow of the
earlier."

19   ANON. "Dr. A.J. Cronin on Doctors." Times (London), 10
      November, p. 11.
           Cronin spoke on his motives in writing The Citadel at the
      Sun Times Book Fair. "He believed [the medical profession]
      was a profession of self-sacrifice and humanity. . . . He
      had the greatest admiration for the profession . . . but
      that did not prevent him from realizing that in the past few
      years the profession had become the victim of a paralyzing
      inertia, and of that curse of the age--commercialism." In
      the book Cronin was out to fight "the corruption of over-
      charging, and of denuding people of money which they could
      ill-afford."

20   ANON. "Dr. Cronin Pays His Respects to the Doctors."
      Philadelphia Record, 18 September, p. 16.
           Review of The Citadel. Characterization of Manson is
      "quite successful," but Christine remains "a vague and shad-
      owy figure." Although his writing is pedestrian, this is
      less objectionable than "the fact that the author makes no
      concession to popular knowledge of the technical terms of
      medicine." Doubts that the novel will benefit medicine, but
      Cronin has done his job of "telling the truth about his pro-
      fession," a profession which is "a priestly craft and there-
      fore full of curious tricks and fundamental dishonesties."

21   ANON. "Doctor's Dilemma." Times Literary Supplement (London),
      14 August, p. 591.
           Review of The Citadel. "Although Dr. Cronin has again
      written a striking novel, full of moving incident and well-
      etched characters, . . . there is more Cronin, a full measure
      of misery in these pages and an even fuller measure of de-
      testability in some of his human beings." This is his best
      novel, but lopsided propaganda. "There should have been made
      an offset to Dr. Cronin's selected types."

22   ANON. "Doctors, Nurses Inspire New Cronin Novel." Atlanta
      Georgian, 19 September, p. 3.
           Review of The Citadel. This novel will satisfy the read-
      ing audience's yearning for books about doctors and nurses.
      A lack of indepth characterization and literary merit does
      not detract from a good story.

23   ANON. "Doctor's Story about Doctor Points to Evils of

1937

Profession." New Bedford (Mass.) Standard, 19 September,
p. 3.
Brief mention of The Citadel. Comments on the plot,
strong characterization, narrative pressure and medical
terms.

24 ANON. "English Arrowsmith." Santa Monica Outlook, 16
September, p. 4.
Review of The Citadel. Praises Cronin for his storytelling ability and his "social indignation." Manson is likeable
because his zeal is of "the tough-minded kind." Feels that
Cronin's view of the British medical profession reflects a
"puritanical bias and unwillingness to give even the devil
his due." The convincing characterization and lack of melodrama makes this "a corking good story."

25 ANON. "Fiction." Booklist 34 (15 September):27.
Review of The Citadel. "Idealistic and full of human
interest, with superior characterization. A very good story,
better balanced and without the melodrama of Hatter's Castle."

26 ANON. "Gossip of the Book World." Los Angeles Times, 18 July,
p. 19.
Cronin's Manson, M.D. "promises to be one of the most
widely read books of the season."

27 ANON. "Highly Praised." Columbus Dispatch, 8 August, p. 9.
Brief mention of a favorable London press subsequent to
the publication of The Citadel, "the news of which has set
the publishers in a flurry of expectation."

28 ANON. "Important Novel about the Medical Profession." Boston
Globe, 25 September, p. 5.
Review of The Citadel. A "beautifully written" book whose
realism will carry the reader through the hero's struggles
"as if living them himself." Includes biographical background.

29 ANON. "Medical Dilemma." Van Nuys News, 7 October, p. 3.
Brief review of The Citadel. Some of these stories are
of the kind "the profession would rather keep to themselves."

30 ANON. "News." Glendale (Calif.) News-Press, 10 December, p. 3.
Reports that Cronin has sold The Citadel to MGM for
$40,000. Currently he is in Southern California for a rest.

31 ANON. "Note." Lawrence (Mass.) Tribune, 27 August, p. 2.
Reports that Cronin turned down a "very remunerative

offer" for serial rights to The Citadel so as not to inter-
fere with his publisher's efforts to make the book an even
greater success in the United States than Hatter's Castle
or The Stars Look Down.

32   ANON. "On Slum Clearance: How to Blow Up a Sewer--a Literary
       Idea." Charlotte News, 22 August, p. 7.
          Excerpt from The Citadel. Recommends the novel.

33   ANON. "Read 'Em or Not." Rutland (Vt.) Herald, 14 September,
       p. 5.
          Review of The Citadel. Calls this "a good story, with
       many telling episodes and at least two interesting charac-
       ters." Some will enjoy the medical insights here; others
       will dislike Cronin's emphasis on the "seamy side of it."
       Many will want to reread Lewis's Arrowsmith after finishing
       this.

34   ANON. Review of The Citadel. Gastonia (N.C.) Gazette, 4
       December, p. 3.
          The novel is both "a scathing indictment" of certain as-
       pects of the medical profession and a love story.

35   ANON. Review of The Citadel. Harpers 175 (November):116.
          Cronin's argument is old and rises from "the need of long
       and careful preparations for a career; in the course of this
       routine, genius is forced into the ranks with the average
       and mediocre." Cronin avoids preaching.

36   ANON. Review of The Citadel. Lawrence (Mass.) Tribune, 27
       August, p. 5.
          Reports from London that the British Medical Association
       was indignant over this novel. "Criticisms of the medical
       profession are no new thing, but never before has such a
       vehement attack been made upon it by a popular author who
       has himself had a medical training and has practised as a
       doctor." One reviewer went so far as to say that "reading
       it has made him afraid to fall ill." Because of the pub-
       licity, the advance book orders have broken every record.
       Within nine days the sales had reached 40,000 copies. Won-
       ders if sales will create similar excitement in the United
       States.

37   ANON. Review of The Citadel. Miami Herald, 12 September, p.
       11.
          Refers to Little, Brown & Company's publicity stunt to
       promote this novel. The company has been sending extracts
       to reviewers with the following comment: "a more human,

1937

less satiric version of the story Sinclair Lewis told in
Arrowsmith."

38 ANON. "St. George of the Surgery." San Francisco Call,
18 September, p. 3.
The Citadel is "honest, earnest, passionate, rich in
drama."

39 ANON. "Stirs Controversy." El Paso Herald-Post, 18 September,
p. 5.
Quotes from reviews of The Citadel appearing in a number
of British newspapers and tells of the reactions from the
British Medical Association.

40 ANON. "The Check List." Mercury 14 (November):13.
Brief mention of The Citadel. "A controversial thesis,
competently written, but not destined to add to Dr. Cronin's
stature as a novelist."

41 B., H. "Study of a Doctor's Success and Failure." Worcester
(Mass.) Telegram, 12 September, p. 3.
Review of The Citadel. This is a story "of struggle, of
triumph, and of self-sacrifice, but it is also a story of
the weakness and cheapness of men." Therefore, it is easy
to understand why some readers will like this book better
than anything Cronin has written, while others will be frustrated and disappointed.

42 B., M.H. Review of The Citadel. El Paso Times, 7 November,
p. 5.
The story itself deserves "the maximum of praise" because
it is "strong, vigorous, well able to stand on its own merit." Praises the case histories, use of medical terms,
plain-spoken language, and sincerity.

43 BANDER, NAOMI. "The Book World." Akron (Ohio) Beacon-Journal,
11 September, p. 12.
Review of The Citadel. Finds parallels between this novel and Cronin's life. Comments on the acute characterization, excellent style, absorbing story, and good motivation.
Aside from the story itself, the novel is "one of the most
powerful indictments of the medical profession" ever written.

44 BATTLE, NELL G. "At the Library." Rocky Mouth (N.C.) Telegram,
16 October, p. 4.
Review of The Citadel. This is an "absorbing, profound
and fascinating story."

45   BECKER, CHARLOTTE. "Magnificent Novel Acts As Scathing
      Indictment of Certain Aspects of British Medical Profession."
      Buffalo Sunday Times, 12 September, p. 12.
          Review of The Citadel. Notes that this novel is far less
      tragic than Hatter's Castle. Comments on the characteriza-
      tion, narration and wisdom to support calling this "a mag-
      nificent novel."

46   BERRY, LEE. "This World of Books." Milwaukee News-Sentinel,
      19 September, p. 11.
          Review of The Citadel. Like Zola, Hardy, Dickens, Tolstoy
      and a dozen other major literary figures, Cronin in this nov-
      el expresses "a sustained and passionate hatred of cruelty,
      bigotry, stupidity and injustice." In spite of a number of
      literary flaws, this is a novel of "astonishing force and
      power." Characters are flat and two-dimensional, however,
      and the author's world "tends to be a rather black and white
      affair." But praises the novel for its message, its enter-
      tainment value, and its drama.

47   BRIGHOUSE, HAROLD. "New Novels." Manchester Guardian, 20 July,
      p. 7.
          Review of The Citadel. Although Cronin continues to make
      excessive use of adjectives, this novel is "more serious in
      content than some of its predecessors, [and] is written with
      a sense of responsibility."

48   BROWN, VIOLET J. Review of The Citadel. Brooklyn Daily Eagle,
      12 September, p. 3.
          The novel is appealing because "it appeals to fundamental
      emotions without making those emotions shoddy." The central
      characters are "human and admirable." Finds a resemblance
      between Christine and the heroine of James Barrie's What
      Every Woman Knows. The minor characters are also "clear-cut
      and individual." The book will interest most readers because
      Cronin has told "the story of a whole-hearted doctor's life,
      told it honestly and told it well."

49   BUTCHER, FANNY. "Fiction." Chicago Daily Tribune, 11 September,
      p. 12.
          Review of The Citadel. "Dr. Cronin has given his hero the
      sum total of experiences which face a type, but he has writ-
      ten withal a story that keeps your eyes glued to the slowly
      turning pages." This is certain to be a best seller.

50   CHAPMAN, GLADYS D. "Bookshelf." Portland (Maine) News, 17
      September, p. 6.
          Review of The Citadel. This "new and controversial

1937

novel" is bound to generate discussion about the similarities between Cronin and Sinclair Lewis.

51 COBB, SUE. Review of The Citadel. Durham Herald, 12 September, p. 5.
    This novel should be read by every "wide-awake American."

52 COSULICH, BERNICE. "The Literary Lantern." Tucson Star, 3 October, p. 5.
    Review of The Citadel. "It is the reality of the people, the truthfulness of the situations and the justice of the exposé that makes it a really fine book."

53 DAVIES, JOE. "Of Books 'N' Things." Mahanoy City (Pa.) American, 25 September, p. 7.
    Review of The Citadel. Praises the characterization, setting, and drama in this powerful human story.

54 DEAN, MARY SCOTT. "Indictment." El Paso Herald-Post, 11 September, p. 7.
    Review of The Citadel. While the formula plot leaves little to the imagination, it is conceivable that Cronin may have added to his reputation as "a fearless reformer" because of the revelations he makes. This is a novel which one will find "readable, though scarcely absorbing."

55 DOREN, CARL Van. "Hero, in Varied Practice, Is a British Arrowsmith." Boston Herald, 11 September, p. 9.
    Review of The Citadel. Notes the parallels between Lewis's Arrowsmith and Cronin's new novel. Says that Cronin "writes like a man with his eye fixed closely on the facts before him," but he lacks the "flaring genius" of Lewis, the "electric high spirits, and the broad comedy." Nevertheless, Cronin has a genuine talent and an extremely honest mind. Finds the plot to be "stirring" and the characters "striking."

56 DuFOUR, STUART. Review of The Citadel. San Jose Mercury-Herald, 12 September, p. 11.
    This is "a gripping, fast-moving" novel that is bound to be a best seller and a revealing indictment of the medical profession.

57 EASTMAN, ELIZABETH. "The Screen: 'The Citadel' at the Empire." Daytona Beach Journal, 22 December, p. 4.
    Review of the film version of The Citadel. Robert Donat, Rosalind Russell, Ralph Richardson and Rex Harrison star in a film impressive for its "staggering force."

58   EDGETT, EDWIN FRANCIS. "A Novel by a Doctor about a Doctor."
      Boston Evening Transcript, 11 September, pp. 1-2.
          Review of The Citadel. In this novel the reader will
      learn more about the medical profession than from any other
      book. It is definitely Manson's story. Nothing in the nov-
      el is irrelevant to him. Praises the characterization,
      drama, and medical terms, but questions the advisability of
      changing the title from Manson, M.D. to The Citadel. "Not
      even by the furthest stretch of the imagination can such a
      title as The Citadel be said to have the slightest sugges-
      tion of the nature and trend of the story."

59   F., W.H. "Dr. Cronin Frowns on His Medical Brothers." New
      Orleans Times-Picayune, 26 September, p. 13.
          Review of The Citadel. "This book appears to have been
      not so much written as lived." Finds a parallel between
      Christine and Jane Austen's Elizabeth Bennett (in Pride and
      Prejudice). The clichés in the novel suggest that Cronin
      did not rewrite the first draft. "The book might be a diary,
      hastily revised. It is a good story. It is even smoothly
      written in places, and it opens a closed medical closet and
      discloses skeletons never used in class demonstrations."

60   FERGUSON, OTIS. "Men at Work." New Republic 92 (22 September):
      195.
          Review of The Citadel. Finds here, above everything else,
      "the quality of absorbing instruction, the illusion of seeing
      through a clear glass certain workings of the world, and the
      feeling that under its serene air of happen-so there is a
      detailed particular truth which both verifies and extends
      whatever of universal truth a person may know." The first
      half of the story is better.

61   G., F. "Society Doctor." Madison Journal, 17 October, p. 4.
          Review of The Citadel. This is an "absorbing and inter-
      esting story of a young doctor and his ethical struggle to
      find himself." Although Arrowsmith is a "bigger, deeper
      book, more thoughtful, powerful and passionate," Cronin's
      novel is well worth reading.

62   G., J.T. "Men Who Hold Our Lives." Cincinnati Enquirer,
      11 September, p. 3.
          Review of The Citadel. Praises the drama, Dickensian
      characters, and the eternal question which is woven into
      the narrative. "'Who are these men who hold our lives in
      their hands?'"

63   GARRARD, MAXINE. "The Citadel by A.J. Cronin Powerful Story

33

1937

of Medicine." <u>Columbus</u> (Ga.) <u>Ledger</u>, 13 September, p. 6.
Destined to be one of the year's outstanding books. Will appeal to both doctors and patients.

64 GOVAN, GILBERT E. "In a Dramatic Novel of Great Human Interest, Dr. A.J. Cronin Reveals the Illnesses of the Medical Profession." <u>Chattanooga Sunday Times</u>, 19 September, p. 21.
Review of <u>The Citadel</u>. Comments on the dramatic scenes, the romance between Andrew and Christine, and the scathing indictment of "the prejudices, ethical red tape and jealousy that clutter up the medical profession and do endless damage by retarding experimental progress." This novel is "history of the most important sort."

65 GREENE, GLADYS. "Do You Know Your Authors?" <u>Athol</u> (Mass.) <u>News</u>, 15 November, p. 3.
Review of <u>The Citadel</u>. Whether or not this is a fair picture of the medical profession will be left up to the reader. It is an entertaining novel, sincere, thoughtful, and excellent in its characterization. Includes biographical sketch.

66 H., P. "Not Only the Doctors Will Read <u>The Citadel</u>." <u>Providence Journal</u>, 11 September, p. 7.
In this splendid novel, Cronin expresses his honest fears of a profession that caters to "bogus healers" who are infesting it. Cronin avoids hysteria in this wise indictment.

67 HANSEN, HARRY. "The First Reader." <u>New York World Telegram</u>, 10 September, p. 8.
Review of <u>The Citadel</u>. Reminds us of H.G. Wells and Sinclair Lewis, both of whose novels are often tracts. Americans will read it more for its story than for its indictment of the British medical profession. Although it lacks the power of <u>Hatter's Castle</u>, the novel is a great improvement on <u>The Stars Look Down</u>. It holds the reader's interest from start to finish and emphasizes "the human side of medicine."

68 HEWES, LYDIA. "Scanning New Books." <u>Bristol Valley</u> (Conn.) <u>Herald</u>, 7 October, p. 3.
Review of <u>The Citadel</u>. Its exciting incidents, good and bad characters, and zealous crusading spirit give this book a purpose. Some events seem forced, however. Andrew's conquest of several languages occurs in too short a time. His cure of a girl's troublesome skin condition in ten days seems hard to believe. Otherwise, a credible story in which Andrew is the "most authentic" character. It invites comparison with <u>Arrowsmith</u>.

69 HOLLIS, E.E. "Young Doctor's Career." Salt Lake City Tribune,
      19 September, p. 11.
        Review of The Citadel. This is "a forceful and provoca-
      tive work, marking a new height in its author's literary
      progress."

70 K., E.C. Review of The Citadel. West Palm Beach Post, 3
      October, p. 3.
        In this novel, Cronin attempts to do for his country what
      Sinclair Lewis in Arrowsmith tried to do for his: "show up
      some of the rottenness in the medical profession." Cronin's
      approach is "more personal," however. Lewis's was impersonal,
      biting, often satiric. And yet there is far less vitality
      and life to The Citadel. This is because Andrew "lacks a
      real flesh and blood quality. He is too much a figurehead
      on which to hang the author's theories."

71 KAPLAN, CORA L. "A Doctor Looks at Doctors." Jacksonville
      (Fla.) Sunday Times-Union, 5 September, p. 12.
        Review of The Citadel. Manson is the kind of doctor one
      would like to know. Although the outcome of the plot is a
      bit too obvious, this novel is dramatic and colorful and
      holds the reader's interest from beginning to end.

72 KAZIN, ALFRED. "Dr. Cronin's Novel about the Medical
      Profession." New York Times Book Review, 12 September, p.
      6.
        Review of The Citadel. Since his first novel, Cronin's
      resemblance to Ibsen, Hardy and Charlotte Brontë has become
      "increasingly invisible." It seems that Cronin has "first-
      hand ideas and second-hand skill." This holds true for his
      latest novel, in which one is excited by "his great moral
      earnestness" but the end seems trivial. This triviality is
      due in large part to the author's conception of character.

73 KELLY, FRED C. "They're Wondering What You'll Read." Bookman
      76 (March):11.
        Brief mention of The Citadel.

74 KOLSTAD, FREDDIE. "Book News." Shreveport (La.) Times,
      12 September, p. 6.
        Review of The Citadel. An interesting story with human
      characters and convincing settings. But throughout the novel
      the extremes are emphasized. "The noble characters are a bit
      too noble to be true; the grasping, selfish ones are too much
      so." Thus the characters become mere caricatures.

75 M., W.J. Review of The Citadel. Richmond Times-Dispatch,

1937

12 September, p. 3.
Praises the "stark reality of the story, the vivid picturization of the characters," and the moral. "Apparently
without meaning to do so, Dr. Cronin has written a scathing
indictment of certain phases of the medical profession."
The theme is not new, but in the narration, the portrayal
of characters, and its simpleness, "lies the secret of Dr.
Cronin's success."

76 McFEE, WILLIAM. "A.J. Cronin, Himself a Physician, Vivisects
the Medical Profession." New York Sun, 10 September, p. 7.
Review of The Citadel. Comments on the development of
Cronin's career since Hatter's Castle and concludes that he
"has been the victim of our rage for high pressure production and large financial inducement to a popular writer to
turn out rapid rubbish." Cronin does share Dickens's weakness for melodrama, but he has none of the gift for humor or
the grotesque which sets Dickens apart from his imitators.
"But he can be definitely classed with Dickens as a novelist
whose books will be instrumental in popularizing and initiating social reforms." Hopes that one day Cronin will be responsible for a renascence in English fiction.

77 MILES, HAMISH. "Fiction." Spectator 159 (30 July):216.
Review of The Citadel. Manson is not convincing as a
living character because "one feels that his actions and reactions are so often imposed on him by Dr. Cronin." The
abundant supply of characters and episodes "makes a large,
meaty, very readable piece of dramatized pamphleteering.
Calories abound, but subtlety of flavour does not."

78 MILLER, MARY THOMAS. "Death and Rebirth of Ideals." San
Francisco Argonaut, 1 October, p. 12.
Review of The Citadel. Comments on the extremes in characterization. The good people are "too angelic" and the bad
people are painted "a bit too thick." Nevertheless, Cronin
is a fine storyteller and will keep the reader involved from
start to finish.

79 MURPHY, SPENCER. "Cronin Raps Evil Practices in Medicine."
Charlotte Observer, 31 October, p. 4.
Review of The Citadel. Cronin has become a leading storyteller. Commentators who refused to see in Hatter's Castle
another Dickens or Galsworthy or Walpole "realize by now that
they were mistaken." In his writings, it is evident that
Cronin is "a reformer at heart, a physician by experience,
and a novelist by choice." In spite of its flaws, The
Citadel is "a perfectly constructed story, logically

developed, and centered about an extremely interesting
character."

80   N., C. "A View of English Medical Practices." Augusta Labor
      Review, 1 October, p. 14.
           Review of The Citadel. "The book is medical, maybe too
      medical for some readers. But it also has plot, strong
      characterizations and a high rate of reader interest."

81   NEEDHAM, WILBUR. "Great New Novel Written by Cronin." Los
      Angeles Times, 12 September, p. 19.
           Review of The Citadel. Finds the same drama, power and
      "emotional pull" in this novel as in The Stars Look Down,
      but the material is "more controlled this time." In The
      Citadel, Cronin has tightened his command over his materials
      and characters. Finds a number of parallels between Cronin
      and Dickens.

82   NEWTON, ARTHUR LINK. "Cronin's Powerful Story of Doctor."
      Nashville Banner, 12 September, p. 3.
           Review of The Citadel. Compares this novel to Lewis's
      Arrowsmith, and finds similarities in its "ring of authen-
      ticity," its avoidance of sentimentality, its themes, and
      its central character. Only Dr. Stillman's character is un-
      believable. Otherwise, the average reader will find this
      book "absorbing, thought-inducing, . . . smooth, simple,
      powerful."

83   NOURSE, JOHN. "Book Prods Medical Profession." San Francisco
      Chronicle, 13 September, p. D3.
           Review of The Citadel. The novel is distinguished by
      "the depth to which Dr. Cronin has driven his meaning." In
      its tragic ending, Cronin shows what price must be paid for
      "competent maturity, for understanding, and intelligent
      knowledge."

84   O'N., H. Review of The Citadel. Albany Evening News, 18
      September, p. 7.
           In this "splendid book" a melodramatic but thoroughly
      confusing climax contributes to the reader's complete ab-
      sorption.

85   PATERSON, ISABEL. "Books and Things." New York Herald-Tribune,
      11 September, p. 33.
           Review of The Citadel. Calls this an "excellent and ab-
      sorbing" story conveyed by "brisk and graphic episodes in
      plausible succession--exposition by narrative." Cronin
      avoids the pitfalls inherent in most thesis novels.

1937

86   R., A.R. Review of <u>The Citadel</u>. <u>Indianapolis News</u>, 6
      November, p. 14.
         Comments on the meaning of the title and on Cronin's
      qualifications for writing this novel. "The picture Dr.
      Cronin draws is a dark one, but one which, it is to be
      feared, is window rather than distorting mirror."

87   RECTOR, BEULAH. "Dr. A.J. Cronin Has Written a Powerful and
      Revealing Novel and of the Less Pleasant Side of Medicine."
      <u>Watertown Times</u> 21 September, p. 22.
         Review of <u>The Citadel</u>. Cronin avoids "abstruse technical
      terms" and scientific explanations in a novel which allows
      us to see the worst and the best of medicine. It is a story
      told "with realism and understanding of human nature."

88   REYNOLDS, ROSSI. "Between the Covers." <u>Stockton</u> (Calif.)
      <u>Record</u> 20 November, p. 11.
         Review of <u>The Citadel</u>. Calls this a novel in "the
      Victorian manner--as solid as roast beef, as simple and
      wholesome as bread and butter." But Cronin's talents with
      characterization are not enough to meet the demands of the
      plot. "If we are prone to ask something more of a modern
      novel than life-like characters and an absorbing story, that
      is perhaps because our taste for simple things has been cor-
      rupted, a condition which it is easy enough to lament, but
      almost impossible to reform."

89   ROSS, MARY. "Doctor Pens Novel Based on His Own Profession."
      <u>Oakland Tribune</u> 19 September, p. 1.
         Reprint of 1937.90.

90   _____. Review of <u>The Citadel</u>. <u>New York Herald-Tribune Books</u>,
         12 September, p. 1.
         This novel, like his earlier ones, is a tragedy, but "the
      grasp is surer, the mastery more complete. . . . Both the
      matter of the book and the manner of the handling mark it as
      the work of a thoughtful and forceful writer who here achieves
      a new level of maturity in his second profession." Focuses
      on the theme--integrity--and on the characters of Andrew and
      Christine. Notes that Cronin is "telling a story, not preach-
      ing a sermon or writing an economic treatise." Reprinted:
      1937.89.

91   S., D.S. "Cronin Uses Vivid Characters to Flay English Medical
      Practices." <u>San Diego Sun</u>, 3 October, p. 2.
         Review of <u>The Citadel</u>. This is an "outstanding, dynamic,
      human and dramatic novel filled with unforgettable charac-
      ters" and an indictment against the medical profession.

92   S., F.M. "Doctor's Story of Doctor's Life in Fine Novel."
      Milwaukee Journal, 12 September, p. v.
           Review of The Citadel. Cronin is willing to "bare his
      soul." As a novelist he knows how "to coordinate concrete
      experiences with the psychology underneath." Sees the theme
      as being "life itself, of the effort of man to wring the
      means of existence from an unwilling world and at the same
      time to maintain his high humor." Cronin views man as "a
      magnificent being, beautifully balanced."

93   SCAIFE, ROGER L. "Beginning the Next Hundred Years: At 35."
      Saturday Review of Literature 15 (27 March):23A.
           Brief biographical background. Regarding The Citadel,
      which Cronin is at work on, he is "more than halfway through
      a new novel and 'crazy about it.'" He says, "'I simply had
      to write this book.'"

94   SELBY, JOHN. "Book Ends." Buffalo Evening News, 10 September,
      p. 2.
           Review of The Citadel. This novel is fascinating where
      his earlier ones were dull. Whether read as a tract or en-
      joyed as a piece of exciting fiction, it is a long story of
      "intelligent revolt and shocked revulsion." Suggests that
      some of the material about the surgery could be eliminated.
      Otherwise, "the writing has shrewd effectiveness throughout
      and greatness on many pages."

95   SINK, E. CARL. "Cronin Book Lives Up to His Promise."
      Winston-Salem (N.C.) Sentinel, 12 September, p. 5.
           Review of The Citadel. Comments on the book's serious-
      ness, love interest, adventure, humor (reminiscent of Mark
      Twain), and revelations. Excellent as "a book or as a pro-
      test against the status quo."

96   SMITH, NELLE EDWARDS. "Today's Book." Macon (Ga.) Telegraph,
      10 September, p. 3.
           Review of The Citadel. In all of his novels Cronin has
      proven himself to be an effective crusader because of "his
      reasonableness, his absolute honesty, and his unselfish mo-
      tives." Of all the characters in the story, Manson and his
      wife, Christine, are the most absorbing.

97   SOLOMON, GLADYS. "The Citadel Brings Another Arrowsmith."
      New Haven Register, 19 September, p. 4.
           Comments on the parallels in theme, plot and characteri-
      zation between Arrowsmith and The Citadel.

98   STAFFORD, HAZEL STRAIGHT. "Book Chats." Madison Times,

1937

10 October, p. 39.
Review of The Citadel. Comments on the "crusading power"
of this novel. Although it has the qualities that make for
popularity, it is not of high literary caliber. "It is decidedly mediocre and its plot is obvious with few surprise
angles. Christine is colorless and too goody-goody, made
by a novelist's recipe to suit his purpose but possessing
little actuality in real life. It will tax no one's intel-
ligence to read the book."

99 STEVENS, GEORGE. "Highlights of 100 Years." Saturday Review
of Literature 15 (27 March):21A.
In his review of One Hundred Years of Publishing: 1837-
1937, brief mention of Cronin's dealings with Little, Brown
& Company. Says that after Remarque came Cronin, Louis-
Ferdinand Céline, Walter D. Edmonds, James Hilton and others.

100 SWEENEY, FRANK. "Doctors' Smugness Flayed by Novelist A.J.
Cronin." Memphis Commercial Appeal, 12 September, sec. iv,
p. 5.
Review of The Citadel. A novel of "gripping episodes and
vivid personalities" that is sure to be long remembered.
Recommends it to all doctors. "It will be read in America
with a detached attitude and without applying to our own
the scathing indictment of fee-splitting, medical salesmanship and hidebound ethics."

101 THOMPSON, RALPH. "Books of the Times." New York Times,
10 September, p. 21.
Review of The Citadel. There is little that is new here.
Finds the novel disappointing after two months of publicity
surrounding its publication. "Anyone who has ever gone to a
'For Adults Only' movie and come away feeling that the sign
was less than candid should understand what I mean." As a
tract, it is too long. As a story that holds the reader's
interest, it has charm. "He does not bother to be original
or clever or profound. The style is mere workmanlike, the
development traditional, the structural devices frankly old-
fashioned. . . . It is pleasing reading even if it is not,
as the publishers earnestly assure us, great writing."

102 TOOILL, KENNETH D. "Books." Columbus (Ohio) State Journal,
22 December, p. 3.
Brief mention of The Citadel as outstanding book of the
year.

103 TORINUS, JOHN B. "A.J. Cronin Again Proves His Story Telling
Ability." Green Bay Press-Gazette, 30 October, p. 10.

Review of The Citadel. This is "a most readable, most
entertaining volume." Sees it as both an argument against
socialized medicine and an indictment against the medical
profession's "laissez faire attitude."

104   ULRICH, MABEL S., M.D. "Doctor's Dilemma." Saturday Review
      (London) 16 (11 September):5-6.
      Review of The Citadel. Notes two themes in this novel:
      the conflict between medical honesty and a competitive so-
      ciety; and married love. Like Cronin's first four novels,
      this book has "a satisfying solid and three-dimensional qual-
      ity." What Cronin has set out to do--and has done admirably
      --is to "cut through the romanticism that still surrounds
      the medical profession, and boldly expose the potentialities
      of charlatanism and dishonesty inherent in a system whereby
      a large group of men must depend for economic security on
      the real or fancied suffering of others." This situation
      applies the world over.

105   W., E.B. "Season's Best Sellers." Lewiston (Maine) Journal,
      2 October, p. 17.
      Review of The Citadel. Cronin continues to be the same
      "thoughtful, sincere and forceful writer" we saw in his
      earlier novels. He avoids preaching. His characters are
      lifelike. The dramatic episodes are convincing.

106   WAGNER, CHARLES A. "Books." New York Daily Mirror, 15
      September, p. 5.
      Review of The Citadel. This novel "excites the intel-
      ligent imagination with a constancy" not found in his earlier
      novels. Comments on the autobiographical elements.

107   WALKER, VIOLA WHITE. "Books and Authors." Lawrence (Mass.)
      Tribune, 1 October, p. 2.
      Review of The Citadel. This is a novel and not a trea-
      tise. Expresses sympathy for its hero, whose life under the
      circumstances could have followed no other course.

108   WILENSKY, HARRY. "News of New Books." Atlanta Journal,
      19 September, p. 4.
      Review of The Citadel. Predicts that the medical profes-
      sion will not like this book but the reading public will.
      Comments on its "tension," its suspense, and its development
      which has "the sweeping force of the unexpected." Finds
      parallels between Martin Arrowsmith (in Arrowsmith) and
      Andrew Manson.

109   WILLIAMS, WILLIAM CARLOS. "Books and the Arts: A Good Doctor's

1937

Story." Nation 145 (11 September):268.
Review of The Citadel. Calls this "a somewhat old-
fashioned morality using the medical profession as its
stage." Says the book ought to appeal to the self-righteous
reader, "who will thereby forget what slippery blackguards
they are themselves." This isn't a great novel, "not in
the sense that Norman Douglas or Ford Madox Ford would speak
of a great novel. But it's a good novel, though it is often
ironical to speak of a 'good novel' today." Cronin fails to
see, as Ezra Pound would say, that "it's money and its mis-
appropriation and artificial scarcity that are at the back
of our troubles, and . . . unless you see the thing through
to its source you can see nothing. Cronin of course has an
inkling of that."

1938

1   ANON. "ABA Awards Book Honors for 1937." Publishers Weekly
        133 (5 March):1106.
            The Citadel received a National Book Award for 1937.

2   ANON. "Among the Publishers." Publishers Weekly 133
        (8 January):140.
            Picture of Cronin with L.W. Harvison, Little, Brown's
        West Coast representative, autographing copies of The Citadel
        at Robinson's book department in Los Angeles.

3   ANON. "Best Sellers." Monterey Herald, 8 April, p. 4.
            The Citadel is at the top of the list of best sellers.
        One doesn't have to be a doctor to enjoy "the fine story."

4   ANON. "Between the Lines." Miami Herald, 17 April, p. 13.
            Review of Cronin's story entitled "Robinson's Lost
        Memory," which appeared in the May 1938 issue of Cosmopolitan.
        Calls it "a hastily thrown together effect."

5   ANON. "Book Review of New Books at the Eustis Memorial Library."
        Eustis (Fla.) Region, 18 March, p. 3.
            Review of The Citadel. Cronin's revelations about the
        medical profession are "infuriating." But the love story--
        the weakest part of the book--is "too sentimental and noble."
        The novel is "a courageous attempt to present to the public
        outrageous conditions which have left Dr. Cronin bitter and
        resentful." His portrait of Manson is "penetrating."

6   ANON. Review of Houseboat for Heaven. Charlotte Observer,
        9 August, p. 11.

Reports on Cronin's visit with Mr. McIntyre, during which
time he discussed the novel he is working on entitled
Houseboat for Heaven. According to the author, it involves
"an unusual presentation of a universal theme, 'the struggle
between good and evil and the human soul.'"

7   ANON. Review of The Citadel. Anderson (S.C.) Independent
    Tribune, 18 December, p. 14.
        Cronin's characters are memorable in this "fascinating
    tale." This is a thought-provoking book which should be
    read by every member of the medical profession.

8   ANON. Review of The Citadel. Boston Evening Transcript,
    14 May, p. 3.
        If there were an English equivalent to the Pulitzer
    Prize, undoubtedly The Citadel would receive it.

9   APPEL, DAVID H. "Books." Cleveland News, 24 October, p. 4.
        Review of The Citadel. This novel still holds a wide
    lead over its rivals, including Francis Brett Young's Doctor
    Bradley Remembers.

10 CHAPMAN, GLADYS D. "Bookshelf: Blue Ribbons." Portland
    (Maine) News, 21 March, p. 5.
        The Citadel was chosen by the American Booksellers
    Association as its favorite novel of 1937.

11 JACKSON, JOSEPH HENRY. "A Bookman's Notebook." San Francisco
    Chronicle, 5 March, p. 4.
        Brief mention of The Citadel as winner of the American
    Booksellers Annual Award.

12 KING, KATHLEEN. "Books." Waterloo (Miss.) Observer, 23
    September, p. 2.
        Brief plot summary of The Citadel.

13 LAMONT, WILLIAM H.F. "An Analysis of The Citadel." Education
    59 (November):157-63.
        Includes plot summary and analysis of the title, con-
    flicts, themes, characters, settings and style. Concludes
    that The Citadel is "the better type of serious popular
    novel."

14 LUENING, MURIEL LUISE. "Prize Book Review." New Orleans
    Times-Picayune, 2 October, p. 7.
        Review of The Citadel. "This portrayal of a young physi-
    cian's career through the vicissitudes of success and fail-
    ure, happiness and sorrow, is superlative in every phase,

1938

> leaving no doubt as to why it is one of the most popular of
> the new books."

15 W., T.E., Jr. "Novel of Last Year Attacks Medical System."
    Greensboro News, 9 October, p. 11.
    Review of The Citadel. Well worth reading, but be pre-
    pared for "a novel that is frank and a man who writes con-
    vincingly and says what he thinks."

16 WILSON, EMMA A. "Book Review." Chicago Record, 13 March, p.
    6.
    Review of The Citadel. Cronin's characters are too ex-
    treme. The medical terms overwhelm a bit. Romance filters
    into the novel in "a quiet insistent way." Includes brief
    biographical background.

1939

1 ANON. "Cronin Writes in Maine Cottage." Augusta Chronicle,
   28 August, p. 3.
   Cronin arrived in the United States a few days ago and
   is staying with his family until the middle of September in
   a cottage in Maine, where he is working on a new novel.

2 ANON. "News." Columbus Citizen, 13 August, p. 4.
   According to Cronin, he attempted in Jupiter Laughs to
   portray "'the failure of the individual to appreciate the
   spiritual relations between him and his creator. . . . But
   now we are on the wave of a big moral uplift. I think this
   spirit of revivalism, which may become an international experience, is a rebound from the atrocities that are being
   committed throughout the world.'"

3 ANON. Review of Vigil in the Night. Burlington (N.C.) Free
   Press, 29 April, p. 5.
   Brief mention of Cronin's new serialized novel, beginning
   this month in Good Housekeeping. Comments on Cronin's im-
   mense success as a writer and says that his home is a beautiful old manse in Sussex in the south of England.

4 KIMBALL, FREDERICK H. "Authors and Books: Doctors in
   Literature." Adams (N.Y.) Journal, 17 January, p. 6.
   Brief mention of The Citadel as "the outstanding book of
   fiction."

1940

1 ANON. "At York Harbor." <u>San Jose Mercury-Herald</u>, 28 July,
    p. 2.
        Reprint of 1940.3.

2 ANON. "Autobiographical Work." <u>Salt Lake Tribune</u>, 7 April,
    p. 3.
        Brief mention of Harold Dearden who, like Cronin, gave
    up medicine for authorship.

3 ANON. "Dr. Cronin and Family in U.S." <u>Knoxville Sentinel</u>,
    16 June, p. 3.
        After spending eight months in Hollywood, Cronin and his
    wife have arrived in New York. They will be joined later
    at York Harbor, Maine, by their youngest son, Andrew, where
    they will live for the summer. Reprinted: 1940.1.

4 ANON. Review of <u>Jupiter Laughs</u>. <u>Boston Globe</u>, 13 September,
    p. 2.
        This is "a fine piece of dramatic writing, with a con-
    cise, clear and gripping plot, a small cast of admirably
    drawn characters who spring to life and stay with the reader
    and a high quality of dramatic intensity which only a play
    can possess." Also, it is very readable.

5 ANON. Review of <u>Jupiter Laughs</u>. <u>Burlington</u> (N.C.) <u>Free Press</u>,
    17 August, p. 4.
        Brief mention that Cronin's play is to be issued in book
    form.

6 ANON. Review of <u>Jupiter Laughs</u>. <u>San Francisco Chronicle</u>,
    29 December, p. 13.
        This is "a very bad play." His attempt to do in a play
    what he has successfully done in novels results in "nothing
    but cheap and unsatisfactory melodrama." His characters are
    unattractive.

7 ANON. Review of <u>The Citadel</u>. <u>Glendale</u> (Calif.) <u>Star</u>, 3 May,
    p. 4.
        "The home, the doctor and his wife establish the comical
    but lovable family of numerable proportions, and then, of
    course, the short, surprising courtship of the doctor's
    wife-to-be" are all enjoyable examples of the many found in
    Cronin's magnificent novel.

8 BEAUFORT, JOHN. Review of <u>Jupiter Laughs</u>. <u>Christian Science
    Monitor</u>, 10 September, p. 2.

1940

Feels the play would have been "more profound and provocative" had there been less melodrama. The characters are flat and lifeless. This may make a better movie. "In a film, the story could be given more variety and pace, and, in stressing the melodrama, the film could dispense with the need of a strong character theme."

9   DUKES, ASHLEY. "The London Scene: Midwinter View." Theatre Arts 24 (November):180.
     Review of Jupiter Laughs. This play is "both escapist and history." Feels that this would make a better movie than play.

10   EATON, WALTER PRICHARD. "Plays for Stages and Students." New York Herald-Tribune Books, 8 December, p. 31.
     Review of Jupiter Laughs. A "violent and more than faintly incredible" play. Characters seem at times caricatures. "Probably in a novel these difficulties could be ironed out, but in a compact frame of a play Dr. Cronin is not skilled enough to bring it off."

11   GILDER, ROSAMOND. "Comedy Opening: Broadway in Review." Theatre Arts 24 (November):778.
     Review of Jupiter Laughs. The play "steadfastly refuses to come to life under Cronin's hand." It seems to be more a novel than a stage piece. Its movement is "laborious."

12   KRUTCH, JOSEPH WOOD. "Drama: Fun in a Hospital." Nation 151 (21 September):253-54.
     Review of Jupiter Laughs. "Here [Cronin's] theme has become merely an excuse for a melodrama in which characters and motives are simplified and exaggerated out of all verisimilitude and the criticism of organized medicine is achieved by the most elementary of devices." Also, it seems that Cronin has studied the textbooks. The play is "so theatrically sound that anyone who has ever seen a play before always knows not only what is going to happen but also just when and how it is going to be brought to pass."

13   NICHOLS, LEWIS. "Broadway in Books." New York Times Book Review, 10 November, p. 40.
     Review of Jupiter Laughs. Finds thrown together snatches of "humor, melodrama, medical terms, pathos, bathos, fine writing and dimly incredible happenings of various kinds." It is curious that the reader rather likes the characters and is "anxious to find out how it ends." But the drama critics didn't much like it.

14   P., M. Review of Jupiter Laughs. Worcester (Mass.) Telegram,
     20 October, p. 11.
        "The play is good theater against an excellently done
     background of institutional life, with its petty jealousies,
     its likes and dislikes, its monotony of interest and escapist
     love affairs."

15   VERNON, GRENVILLE. "The Stage & Screen." Commonweal 32
     (27 September):469.
        Review of Jupiter Laughs. Cronin's "strong spiritual
     sense and deep religious feeling" is present in this play.
     Obviously the real meaning of the play is "the triumph of
     the spiritual over the mundane." Hopes Cronin will attain
     a greater mastery of the dramatist's tools. Right now "he
     is still laboring under the handicap of the novelist."

16   WYATT, EUPHEMIA Van RENSSELAER. "The Drama: Jupiter Laughs."
     Catholic World 152 (October):89.
        If Cronin wished to prove that "neuroses are not the pre-
     rogative of patients," he succeeded in this play. But be-
     cause he worked to avoid sentimentality, "he has exaggerated
     the sinners." Both Ibsen and O'Neill worked with plots "just
     as crude in its colors but with more dexterous shading. Dr.
     Cronin's dialogue has no overtones." Wishes Cronin had spent
     more time with the writing of this play. There is too much
     action and too little analysis in the psychology. "But we
     know the season will not have many plays with as direct a
     purpose."

1941

1   ANON. "A Modern St. Francis As Seen by A.J. Cronin." Chicago
     News, 23 July, p. 3.
        Review of The Keys of the Kingdom. Finds in this power-
     ful novel parallels with the story in the New Testament.
     Sees Chisholm as "an imperfect and human representation of
     Christ." This is Cronin's richest, most beautifully written
     novel.

2   ANON. "A Modern St. Francis: Hero of Cronin Novel Is Catholic
     Priest Who Preaches Tolerance, Goodwill." Pasadena Star-
     News, 2 August, p. 7.
        Review of The Keys of the Kingdom. Cronin is preaching
     a sermon while telling a story. All of the characters live
     "memorably." His novel "points the way to the part the
     forces of Christianity can play in a world beset by terror-
     izing evils."

1941

3   ANON. "American Scene Dominates in Best Fiction for August."
    Dayton News, 10 August, p. 4.
        Review of The Keys of the Kingdom. Cronin has created
    in Chisholm one of his finest characters. This is a "dis-
    tinguished story."

4   ANON. "Best Best Seller." Gastonia (N.C.) Gazette, 27
    September, p. 10.
        Review of The Keys of the Kingdom. Notes that Fannie
    Hurst has written to the publishers to say that the novel is
    a "'masterpiece'" and that "'the melody lingers on' long af-
    ter she has read it."

5   ANON. "Book of the Month." Lewiston (Maine) Journal, 19 July,
    p. 2.
        The Keys of the Kingdom will be the August selection for
    the Book-of-the-Month Club.

6   ANON. "Book Review." Ruleville (Miss.) Record, 25 September,
    p. 3.
        Review of The Keys of the Kingdom. Finds this as dramatic
    as Hatter's Castle and as moving as The Citadel, but because
    of its spiritual quality, more significant than either novel.

7   ANON. "Books." Buffalo Sunday Courier-Express, 20 July, p. 5.
        The Keys of the Kingdom is a simple and sincere story
    about a good man.

8   ANON. "Books." Salt Lake City Tribune, 27 July, p. 4.
        The Keys of the Kingdom is "a volume not to be missed."

9   ANON. "Books and Book-Makers." Raleigh News and Observer,
    20 July, p. 6.
        Cronin's The Keys of the Kingdom is as moving as The
    Citadel. "There is rich drama and a little pageantry here,
    the kind of thing Dr. Cronin does so well." Father Chisholm
    will remind some readers of Francis of Assisi. Includes
    brief biographical details.

10 ANON. "Books: Goodness Made Readable." Time 38 (21 July):
    76-77.
        Review of The Keys of the Kingdom. "Cronin is a first-
    rate literary craftsman with an honest love of simple human-
    ity and a sure feel for trends." The difficulty with writ-
    ing about Christian goodness is that few believe it is pos-
    sible and few find it exciting. But Cronin succeeds "by
    simplicity, artful artlessness, complete sincerity." In-
    cludes biographical background and information about the
    writing of the novel.

11   ANON. "Books in July." <u>Watertown</u> (N.Y.) <u>Times</u>, 8 July, p. 3.
     <u>The Keys of the Kingdom</u> possesses "character portrayal,
     drama, excitement, movement." Certainly it is Cronin's
     best yet.

12   ANON. "Book Trends of the Hour." <u>Waukesha</u> (Wis.) <u>Freeman</u>,
     21 July, p. 2.
     Reprint of 1941.13.

13   ANON. "Bound to be Read." <u>Springfield</u> (Ohio) <u>News</u>, 10 August,
     p. 11.
     Review of <u>The Keys of the Kingdom</u>. "Under Cronin's sym-
     pathetic pen, Father Francis emerges a lovable, believable
     character. To this sympathetic approach, he adds the excel-
     lence of craftsmanship he has been building up over the past
     decade." Reprinted: 1941.12.

14   ANON. "Christmas Shopping List." <u>Columbia</u> (S.C.) <u>State</u>,
     21 December, p. 3.
     <u>The Keys of the Kingdom</u> is "too sentimental."

15   ANON. "Cronin." <u>Middletown</u> (Ohio) <u>Journal</u>, 17 August, p. 5.
     Review of <u>The Keys of the Kingdom</u>. In this argument for
     tolerance there is "a full quota of action, swiftly paced,
     which never lets the book become dull."

16   ANON. "Cronin Book Has Great Sales Record." <u>Asheville</u> (N.C.)
     <u>Citizen</u>, 7 December, p. 5.
     <u>The Keys of the Kingdom</u> has gone into its eighteenth
     printing, bringing the total copies in print to 527,000.
     A contract has been signed with David O. Selznik Productions,
     Inc., for the film version of the book.

17   ANON. "Cronin Forced to Rest, Becomes Great Author." <u>Charlotte</u>
     <u>Observer</u>, 3 August, p. 7.
     Brief summary of Cronin's career from <u>Hatter's Castle</u>.
     Includes review of <u>The Keys of the Kingdom</u>, which has all
     the ingredients readers of Cronin expect: characters, solid
     plot (although it seems a bit "hung together" in places).
     In spite of a few flaws, the hero "is what matters, and he
     is a splendid portrait, sincerely done, clear, and living
     long in one's memory."

18   ANON. "Fiction." <u>Los Angeles Tidings</u>, 12 September, p. 4.
     Review of <u>The Keys of the Kingdom</u>. "Some will see a sus-
     picion of indifferentism in some parts; others will dislike
     some aspects of certain characters; all in all, the book
     could probably use greater theological accuracy, but it will
     make splendid reading."

1941

19   ANON. "Fiction." <u>Washington Post</u>, 14 December, p. 9.
         Review of <u>The Keys of the Kingdom</u>. "Dr. Cronin has em-
     ployed the technical devices of the 'slick' novelist to the
     theme of sanctity, and the present tide of reaction from
     erotic romanticism and decadence has helped to carry his
     book to an almost unprecedented popularity."

20   ANON. "In Brief." <u>Nation</u> 153 (26 July):79.
         Review of <u>The Keys of the Kingdom</u>. This is another of
     Cronin's "competent, heart-warming, but hardly memorable
     stories." He has drawn on "a time-tested store of surefire
     characters."

21   ANON. "In the Library." <u>Marshfield</u> (Wis.) <u>News</u>, 25 July,
     p. 2.
         <u>The Keys of the Kingdom</u> is "a moving and significant
     novel."

22   ANON. "Jubilant Praise Greets <u>The Keys of the Kingdom</u>!"
     <u>Gastonia</u> (N.C.) <u>Gazette</u>, 2 August, p. 3.
         "Reviewers, famous authors, clergymen in all parts of
     the country are praising this novel." Excerpt from <u>The New
     York Times Book Review</u> calls the novel Cronin's "'magnificent
     story of the great adventure of individual goodness.'" Ex-
     cerpt from 1941.159.

23   ANON. "Leading Critics Pick Best Books in Annual Poll."
     <u>Nashville Banner</u>, 18 February, p. 5.
         Critics have picked <u>The Keys of the Kingdom</u> as the best
     novel of 1941.

24   ANON. "New Books at Brunswick Library." <u>Brunswick</u> (Ga.) <u>News</u>,
     23 July, p. 13.
         <u>The Keys of the Kingdom</u> is as dramatic as <u>Hatter's Castle</u>
     and as moving as <u>The Citadel</u>, but far more significant than
     either because of its theme.

25   ANON. "New Cronin Novel Great Bit of Work." <u>Lansing Journal</u>,
     3 August, p. 4.
         Review of <u>The Keys of the Kingdom</u>. "This master of sus-
     pense, of character build-up and portrayal of thought-pro-
     voking conclusions has written a book that will take its
     readers from the sacrifices of war to those of one man."
     Includes an excerpt from 1941.131.

26   ANON. "News." <u>Syracuse Sunday Herald-American</u>, 22 June, p. 11.
         Mention of <u>The Keys of the Kingdom</u>. Publication date for
     this novel is still a month away, and yet the advance

enthusiasm of the publishers is such that 230,000 copies have already been printed. One hundred fifty thousand copies will be distributed by the Book-of-the-Month Club. These figures closely parallel the recent publication history made by Hemingway's For Whom the Bell Tolls.

27 ANON. "Noble Priest's Life Struggle in Cronin Novel: Super-ficial Study Avoids Deep Conflict, Shuns Controversial." Hartford Times, 26 July, p. 9.
Review of The Keys of the Kingdom. Finds too little con-flict and too much coincidence in this novel. Wishes the conflict had been in Father Francis's soul. Also, the Chinese are "shadowy" figures and the dramatic episodes "sound like rewrites of news stories." Mother Maria-Veronica and the elder Dr. Tulloch are memorable characters.

28 ANON. "Noteworthy New Fiction." Baltimore Sun, 20 July, p. 4.
Review of The Keys of the Kingdom. Francis should rank with "the immortals of fiction as a great and humble charac-ter" in a novel which is beautiful in "its restraint, its strength of plot, and the fine flow of its language."

29 ANON. Review of Jupiter Laughs. Dayton News, 9 February, p. 2.
Brief plot summary.

30 ANON. Review of The Keys of the Kingdom. Albany (Ga.) Herald, 17 August, p. 8.
This is a brilliant novel by "a masterful writer."

31 ANON. Review of The Keys of the Kingdom. Arkansas Methodist, 19 February, p. 4.
"The story has dramatic interest and the central charac-ter a genuine nobility."

32 ANON. Review of The Keys of the Kingdom. Atlanta Constitution, 10 August, p. 13.
Favorable reviews and enthusiastic letters are pouring in, attesting to the popularity of this new novel. Notes of commendation came from Father Maurice S. Sheehy of the Catholic University of America; the Episcopal Bishop of Massachusetts; Rt. Rev. Henry Knox Sherrill, Mazo de la Roche, and other clergymen and authors. Not since the pub-lication of Remarque's All Quiet on the Western Front has there been such excitement about a book in the Little, Brown office. The publisher printed more copies prior to publica-tion than any book it has ever issued. Mentions that Cronin is currently working with the ministry of information in

1941

Washington. Soon he plans to go to Canada to study hospitalization.

33   ANON. Review of The Keys of the Kingdom. Atlanta Constitution, 7 December, p. 2.
Brief mention of Cronin's appearance on the radio program "We the People" with Eddie Dowling--in connection with the publication of his new novel.

34   ANON. Review of The Keys of the Kingdom. Baptist Messenger, 31 July, p. 11.
The most serious criticism of this book is "the teaching that God will save any man, even though he be a professed atheist, who does good." This teaching conflicts with the scriptures. "The danger of such a book as this is that it will give comfort to men and women who think that they can live selfish, worldly lives, and without repentance or faith, face a holy God and trust their good works to justify them before God."

35   ANON. Review of The Keys of the Kingdom. Boston Globe, 20 July, p. 3.
Includes brief biographical background.

36   ANON. Review of The Keys of the Kingdom. Boston Globe, 3 August, p. 4.
"It is a book that is full of the old-fashioned virtues, hence the appeal that pushes it to the head of the best seller list this week."

37   ANON. Review of The Keys of the Kingdom. Boston Herald, 4 August, p. 5.
Cronin is vacationing in Maine. Includes brief biographical background and history behind the new novel.

38   ANON. Review of The Keys of the Kingdom. Boston Post, 13 July, p. 3.
By writing this novel, Cronin is doing more for the English-speaking world "than in anything else he could do for his country of Christendom; he feeds the universal spiritual hunger of harassed people."

39   ANON. Review of The Keys of the Kingdom. Boston Post, 7 September, p. 4.
Brief mention of the popularity of Cronin's new novel.

40   ANON. Review of The Keys of the Kingdom. Charlotte Observer, 10 August, p. 11.

1941

"Advance opinions from the clergy and from famous authors, and the first reviews indicate a welcome of unparalleled enthusiasm in the experience of the publishers."

41 ANON. Review of The Keys of the Kingdom. Chicago News, 3 December, p. 21.
This is both a religious book and a novel. To date it has sold over a half million copies in America since its publication in July. "[Francis's] story, and his ability to see beyond creeds and orthodoxy, his love of decency and justice, will stir the reader."

42 ANON. Review of The Keys of the Kingdom. Columbia (S.C.) State, 10 August, p. 10.
In this novel we see what a great part religion can play in the world today. There are many interesting characters.

43 ANON. Review of The Keys of the Kingdom. Columbus (Ga.) Inquirer-Sun, 20 July, p. 4.
Brief mention of pending publication of Cronin's new novel.

44 ANON. Review of The Keys of the Kingdom. Detroit News, 29 June, p. 5.
"That this book, considering its author and its theme, will attract many readers goes without saying." Publication date was 21 July.

45 ANON. Review of The Keys of the Kingdom. Durham (N.C.) Herald, 18 August, p. 7.
"This book comes at a time when it is sorely needed because faith and religion are vital forces in a troubled world." The story is simply told, and "therein lies its greatness."

46 ANON. Review of The Keys of the Kingdom. El Paso Times, 3 August, p. 3.
Brief mention.

47 ANON. Review of The Keys of the Kingdom. Gastonia (N.C.) Gazette, 16 August, p. 11.
"The book will bring before your mind the whole great question of the part that religion can play in the world today."

48 ANON. Review of The Keys of the Kingdom. Lawrence (Mass.) Telegram, 19 September, p. 8.
Asks why the hero's way of life has not been practiced

1941

more. "That it is a practicable plan I feel certain, if all intolerance and selfishness is set aside."

49   ANON. Review of The Keys of the Kingdom. Memphis Appeal, 8 June, p. 4.
     Reports that close to $20,000 was spent on advance advertising of Cronin's new novel. Certainly this will be the most widely read novel of the season.

50   ANON. Review of The Keys of the Kingdom. New York Times, 5 May, p. 11.
     Commenting on Cronin's new novel, says that he's always readable, realistic, and that news of his new work should be exhilarating for his fans.

51   ANON. Review of The Keys of the Kingdom. Pasadena Star-News, 20 December, p. 18.
     Finds "noble idealism" in this story. Akin to its understanding of Roman Catholicism is Kate O'Brien's The Land of Spices.

52   ANON. Review of The Keys of the Kingdom. Red Bluff (Calif.) News, 12 July, p. 5.
     Calls this "a story of courage and melodrama."

53   ANON. Review of The Keys of the Kingdom. Roanoke Times, 14 September, p. 4.
     This is a "reverent piece of hagiography."

54   ANON. Review of The Keys of the Kingdom. Rockland (Maine) Courier-Gazette, 9 August, p. 4.
     This is, without a doubt, Cronin's finest novel.

55   ANON. Review of The Keys of the Kingdom. Toledo Times, 24 August, p. 6.
     Cronin's new novel is "gentle, sentimental, slow-moving."

56   ANON. Review of The Keys of the Kingdom. Tucson Star, 15 February, p. 7.
     Reports that a nationwide survey made by the Book-of-the-Month Club produced the fact that this novel is the year's best seller in the fiction field.

57   ANON. Review of The Keys of the Kingdom. Waukesha (Wis.) Freeman, 16 August, p. 8.
     Predicts that this novel will be more widely discussed than The Citadel because "it hinges on questions which deeply involve the faiths of many people."

1941

58   ANON. Review of The Keys of the Kingdom. Weaverville (Calif.)
      Trinity Journal, 21 August, p. 13.
          The book describes Chisholm's years in China: "years
      not very successful by any material standard, but richer in
      deeper spiritual values."

59   ANON. "Serious Novel: Troubled Priest Serves As Hero of
      Cronin Book." Sacramento Bee, 26 July, p. 11.
          Review of The Keys of the Kingdom. Cronin's subject is
      one which made Churchill's Inside of the Cup a compelling
      book. The subject of the discrepancy between the teachings
      of Jesus and of Christianity is dealt with clearly. Cronin
      "has achieved an unusual synthesis between the serious mes-
      sage and the tense dramatic fiction." Occasionally the
      reader is aware that the author is manipulating the charac-
      ters and narrative, however. "In spite of this weakness,
      it is a story in which a quiet and sure wisdom runs like a
      strong current beneath the exciting action."

60   ANON. "The Book Nook." West Palm Beach Post, 7 September,
      p. 10.
          Review of The Keys of the Kingdom. What Cronin did for
      the medical profession in The Citadel, he has done for the
      church in his new book. He proves his point by "indirection
      rather than direct attack." But this is "a finer, more mov-
      ing story." It is also "long and strangely interesting,
      colorful because of the sheer drama of a man's battle against
      great odds." Some of Cronin's character protrayals are
      "heavy handed"; some of the priests become types; "but his
      principal character never lacks true structure and genuine-
      ness." The general idea behind the book is somewhat similar
      to John Rathbone Oliver's Victim and Victor.

61   ANON. "The Citadel by A.J. Cronin." Waycross (Ga.) Journal-
      Herald, 28 May, p. 14.
          This "soul-searching" account will be of interest to
      those who are fascinated by both medicine and good litera-
      ture. In this book there is both pathos and humor.

62   ANON. "The Keys of the Kingdom: In His Third Best Seller
      Scotland's Writing Doctor Takes Faith for His Theme." Life
      11 (24 October):62, 64.
          Biographical background. In his latest novel, Cronin
      "reveals the same driving narrative power, the same concern
      with medical matters and care of the poor, the same melo-
      dramatic plot, and the same searching, if sentimentalized,
      humanity of feeling." Includes plot summary. For the cre-
      ation of Father Chisholm, the author drew on his memories

1941

of his uncle. Includes a description of the conception and writing of the novel.

63 ANON. "The Ways of Fame." Chelsea (Mass.) Record, 26 July, p. 2.
    Reports that over 250,000 copies of The Keys of the Kingdom were sold by advance orders.

64 ALLRED, PEARL Q. "Book of the Week." Ogden (Utah) Examiner, 3 August, p. 2.
    Review of The Keys of the Kingdom. Although this is "a good and sincere" novel, it is questionable whether it will advance Cronin's literary stature. In it there is a restoration of the nineteenth century English novel.

65 APPEL, [DAVID]. "Radio/Books: Cronin's First Novel in Four Years Paints Unforgettable Picture of a Priest's Soul." Cleveland News, 21 July, p. 14.
    Review of The Keys of the Kingdom. Finds this a better novel than The Citadel, because of its more direct appeal, its greater intensity, an adult grasp of the techniques of writing, and a more profound theme. Chisholm is Cronin's "masterpiece."

66 APPLEBY, JOHN T. "Books: Dr. Cronin's Study in Sanctity." Washington Post, 20 July, p. 13.
    Review of The Keys of the Kingdom. Comments on the bad priest, the worldly priest, and the good priest in this novel. Finds that Cronin's writing "lacks the harsh realism" of his earlier novels. Because Chisholm is described almost wholly from the outside, there is "a slightly unreal air about it." Wishes the author had left the hero in Scotland. Then the story would have been "a more compelling and more convincing study of a priest's life."

67 B., H. "Cronin's New Book Greatest." Akron Journal, 10 August, p. 11.
    Review of The Keys of the Kingdom. Not a dogmatic book, this is one of "'harrowing simplicity'" about the fact that "'individualism is rather a dangerous quality in a theologian.'"

68 B., L.B. "Religion Presented Logically: A.J. Cronin Triumphs with Novel of a 'Mr. Chips' of the Church." Richmond Times-Dispatch, 20 July, p. 14.
    Review of The Keys of the Kingdom. Both churchmen and nonchurchmen will learn a good deal from this story. The most obvious truth is that the man who is different will

face disappointment and failure in the eyes of the world. This truth is developed through the comparison of Francis Chisholm and his friend, Anselm Mealey. As usual, Cronin's "forceful and easy style" makes his novel a joy to read.

69   B., M.   "Cronin Writes Worthy Defense of Catholic Priest in New Volume." Dallas Times-Herald, 27 July, p. 9.
     Review of The Keys of the Kingdom. Like Stevenson's Father Damien, Cronin has written through his hero a magnificent defense of a Catholic priest. Finds parallels between the experiences of Chisholm and those of David Copperfield, too. Calls this Cronin's "finest achievement."

70   B., M. duQ.   "Author of the Week: Cronin Polishes Up Religion in His Best Novel." Columbia (S.C.) State, 27 July, p. 11.
     Review of The Keys of the Kingdom. In spite of its conventional plot, this novel is packed with "vigor and drama." It is his best book to date. "Tolerance, humility and courage are the three virtues" of his chief character.

71   B., M.H.   Review of The Keys of the Kingdom. El Paso Times, 20 July, p. 16.
     Cronin's chief character is the portrait of a man with a soul. The excellent characterization and the exciting drama compensate for the lack of romance in this novel.

72   BARISH, MILDRED.   "Vicar Dedicates Life to Mankind." Los Angeles Times, 20 July, p. 27.
     Review of The Keys of the Kingdom. Not unexpectedly, Cronin in these perilous times looks back to a period less imperiled when men could "concentrate on tolerance, humility and spiritual brotherhood." His perception of Chisholm is "quiet and keen." There is in this book "an almost Dickensian richness, color and breadth of background detail."

73   BEALS, HELEN.   "Scotch Priest in Fight for Right." Worcester (Mass.) Telegram, 20 July, p. 5.
     Review of The Keys of the Kingdom. This book is needed by "a broken but not contrite world. It can do more good than any novel we know today."

74   BELL, HERBERT C.F.   "The Atlantic Bookshelf." Atlantic Monthly 177 (August):x.
     Review of The Keys of the Kingdom. "This is a stirring book, a virile book, and yet a wistful and tender book. It is dramatic in narrative, but soothing in its style and its philosophy."

1941

75   BENNETT, ALICE KIZER. "Heroic Priest Is Protagonist in New
      Novel by A.J. Cronin." Dallas Times, 20 July, p. 14.
          Review of The Keys of the Kingdom. The deep spiritual
      significance of this novel will surprise readers of Cronin's
      previous novels.

76   BERRY, LEE. "This World of Books." Toledo Blade, 26 July,
      p. 2.
          Review of The Keys of the Kingdom. Although not a great
      novel, it is "a fine job of storytelling, and its pointblank
      insistence on the spiritual values of life is particularly
      suited to the mood [of 1941]." It is certainly "the most
      memorable and persuasive novel" about the life of the theo-
      logian to appear in many years.

77   BIHN, HAZEL E. "Books." Palos Verdes (Calif.) Estates
      Bulletin, 14 August, p. 2.
          Review of The Keys of the Kingdom. Not an attack on the
      Church, Cronin's novel is "an attack on those two unlovely
      sins, intolerance and complacency." This is by far the best
      of his novels.

78   BINSSE, H.L. "Fiction." Commonweal 34 (1 August):354-55.
          Review of The Keys of the Kingdom. Cronin's serious sub-
      ject may deceive people into thinking that this is a serious
      book. "In its way the book represents a small tragedy. Such
      subjects need to be treated and have been treated by Mauriac,
      Bernanos, Graham Greene and Kate O'Brien. Undoubtedly Dr.
      Cronin's intention was good. It is painful to have to re-
      port that he has dealt with a great theme on too melodramatic
      a level. The result is indeed a 'good story,' but it is mis-
      leading." See 1941.90.

79   BOND, ALICE DIXON. "A.J. Cronin's Moving Novel Tells Story
      of Scotch Priest." Boston Herald, 23 July, p. 4.
          Review of The Keys of the Kingdom. This story is "time-
      less, . . . exciting and provoking." The China incident is
      filled with adventure and entertainment. "With perceptive
      sympathy and genuine understanding Dr. Cronin has used the
      keys of tolerance and humility to open the doors of his
      Kingdom."

80   BOUWHUIS, Rev. ANDREW L., S.J. "Canisius Reader." Buffalo
      Union and Echo, 25 July, p. 2.
          Review of The Keys of the Kingdom. Although the theme
      is different, Cronin continues to draw on his storytelling
      abilities in this latest novel. Unfortunately, he has made
      the mistake of presenting his own opinions through Chisholm.

Some of the opinions are inconsistent with the character of the good Father. However, this is not to imply that Cronin is anti-religious.

81 BRADSHAW, MICHAEL. "Cronin's Latest Novel Immensely Readable." Dayton Journal-Herald, 27 July, p. 6.
    Review of The Keys of the Kingdom. This novel deserves the popularity it will receive. "Its plot is significant without being profound. Its treatment is melodramatic without being shallow. Its characters are convincing without being particularly real."

82 BRITTON, BEVERLEY. "Balancing the Books." Richmond Times-Dispatch, 22 June, p. 8.
    Brief mention of The Keys of the Kingdom.

83 BURCHER, DOROTHY GRAY. "From My Book Shelf." Chowchilla (Calif.) News, 4 September, p. 33.
    Review of The Keys of the Kingdom. This novel should be read by people of all creeds. "It is highly dramatic and full of pathos, and overwhelms the reader with the importance of religious and racial tolerance."

84 BURGARD, AUGUSTA C. "A.J. Cronin's Latest Novel Is Outstanding Book of Month." Columbus (Ga.) Sunday Ledger-Enquirer, 3 August, p. 6.
    Review of The Keys of the Kingdom. Cronin's characters seem to be lifted from the pages of Dickens. His China is borrowed from Pearl Buck. His problems and their solutions come from the pages of a detective novel or western adventure story. His atmosphere abounds in "theatrical unrealness." But the novel is exciting, readable and bound to be widely discussed.

85 C., J.A. "Dr. Cronin's New Book Is About Missionary." Durham Herald, 20 July, p. 8.
    Review of The Keys of the Kingdom. This great novel is about the fundamental things of life. Comments on the many "lovable" characters and the dramatic scenes of conflict on both the physical and spiritual levels.

86 CARPENTER, H.A. "Literature: English and American." Library Journal 66 (July):614.
    Brief review of The Keys of the Kingdom. Cronin's character delineation is excellent. The book is highly recommended.

87 CASWELL, WILBUR LARREMORE. Review of The Keys of the Kingdom.

1941

Churchman 155 (1 September):21.
Hopes that the savage attack on this book by the literary
critic in the newspaper P.M. "will not prejudice anyone
against this great novel." Every clergyman should read it.
See 1941.158.

88 CHENEY, ROBERT J. Review of The Keys of the Kingdom. Portland
(Maine) Express, 26 July, p. 17.
Cronin now turns "his immaculate prose and fine sense of
construction to a religious theme." In spite of this, all
readers should enjoy reading it.

89 COOLIDGE, CHRISTINE. "Books and Their Writers: Cronin Makes
You Angry." San Francisco Chronicle, 20 July, p. 18.
Review of The Keys of the Kingdom. Readers will love
Chisholm and detest Monsignor Sleeth. The reader must be
the sort of person "for whom the characters in a book are
as real as his next door neighbor." Cronin employs Dickens's
"trick of descriptive nomenclature," but his humor is not as
"broad and boisterous."

90 CORT, JOHN C. "Communications." Commonweal 34 (29 August):447.
Review of The Keys of the Kingdom. In a letter to the
editors, he defends Cronin's novel and protests the
Commonweal's tough review (see 1941.78). Granted Cronin
has not written a great book, but he has written "a very
fine book." It is a good story with "realism, humor, warmth
and vitality." And Father Chisholm is "a thoroughly human,
likable and interesting person." But above all, Cronin has
written a popular book and has made "Christianity, Catholi-
cism and even sanctity seem desirable things."

91 DAVENPORT, BASIL. "The Universals of A.J. Cronin." Saturday
Review (London) 24 (19 July):7.
Review of The Keys of the Kingdom. Because of its religious theme, Chinese setting, and melodramatic incidents,
this book is bound to sell well. Unfortunately, many readers will take this as an important moral treatise--which it
is not.

92 DeCASSERES, BENJAMIN. "The March of Events." American
Editorial, 4 August, p. 3.
Review of The Keys of the Kingdom. In his hero Cronin
has portrayed a "super-humanist, a man that towers, in his
gentleness, humility and fearlessness, over the age he lives
in."

93 DUNTON, EDITH K. "Read 'Em or Not." Rutland (Vt.) Herald,

29 July, p. 5.
The Keys of the Kingdom is "an enthralling story built
around the finest qualities of humanity."

94   F., B.W. "Turning the Pages." Cincinnati Times-Star, 25 July,
      p. 2.
        Review of The Keys of the Kingdom. The novel reads like
      poetry. It is far removed from the problems of today's war.
      "In a literal interpretation the book relates how one man
      found the keys; in its deeper implication it portrays the
      present trend back to religion."

95   F., R.B. "Melodrama Fills New Cronin Novel." New York Journal,
      10 August, p. 11.
        Review of The Keys of the Kingdom. "Few novelists today
      can equal A.J. Cronin in patterning a plot, utilizing every
      possible wisp of melodrama in its futherance, making virtu-
      ally all his contrasts explosive, and in hanging so adroitly
      on to the long arm of coincidence. His craftsmanship is
      well-nigh flawless and his novels sell like hotcakes."

96   FADIMAN, CLIFTON. "Books: Inside a Nazi--Dr. Cronin's Saint."
      New Yorker 17 (26 July):46, 49.
        Review of The Keys of the Kingdom. Except for a few ex-
      citing scenes, this novel is "an elaborate, carefully writ-
      ten, and deeply moral piece of tedium." It is unclear why
      the book is not moving. Perhaps it is because Cronin takes
      so many pages and yet fails "to move the reader to a deep
      awareness of spiritual beauty." Maybe Cronin is too skill-
      ful a novelist. He knows the tricks of the trade, yet this
      is not "the way the lives of saints are played out in this
      world."

97   FELD, ROSE. "Books and Things." New York Herald-Tribune Books,
      21 July, p. 21.
        Review of The Keys of the Kingdom. Cronin's priest is of
      such stature as to stand beside the doctor-hero in The
      Citadel. The China incident makes the bulk of this "full-
      bodied novel." Cronin's details are well-chosen and his
      knowledge of background is excellent. "Cronin writes with
      deep compassion, but his compassion is flooded with bitter-
      ness at the stupidity of mankind."

98   FERGUSON, Mrs. WALTER. "Escape." San Francisco News, 22 July,
      p. 11.
        Recommends The Keys of the Kingdom to all "who are weary
      of evildoing."

1941

99 FITT, FRANK. "The Saint As a Best Seller." <u>Christian Century</u>
58 (3 September):1081-82.
Review of <u>The Keys of the Kingdom</u>. Cronin's hero is a
refreshingly "flesh-and-blood" character. "There is so much
of him that is in all of us and so much more that we would
like to obtain that for every reader there is certain to be
a blessing." Also, the novel carries for all of us a rebuke,
for "the horror of so much of our social order today is seen
in the environment of Francis Chisholm as a youth." But
there is a positive side as well, for Cronin deals with
"eternal and redemptive values for our tragic world."

100 FLINT, DORIS. "The Book Shelf: Late Book Reviews and Literary
Criticism." <u>Ionia</u> (Mich.) <u>News</u>, 18 September, p. 3.
Review of <u>The Keys of the Kingdom</u>. Enjoyable reading
but at times a bit boring. "There is a great deal of good
to be derived from the story if one is inclined to look for
it."

101 FREDERICK, JOHN T. "A.J. Cronin." <u>College English</u> 3
(November):121-29.
Considers whether or not Cronin may be considered a great
novelist in light of his flaws as a writer. Discusses
<u>Hatter's Castle</u>, <u>Grand Canary</u>, <u>The Citadel</u>, <u>The Stars Look
Down</u> and <u>The Keys of the Kingdom</u>, and concludes: "It is
not important that Mr. Cronin has written some bad books.
Most great writers have done that. It is important that he
has not yet written a wholly good book." On the negative
side, finds in Cronin's novels a lack of humor, an absence
of stylistic grace, an obvious construction, and some feeble
characters. On the positive side, he finds a "deliberate
choice of fictional material of the highest value and importance, unquestionable earnestness of purpose and--most important of all--positive evidence of capacity for self-
criticism and for growth."

102 GARDINER, H.C. Review of <u>The Keys of the Kingdom</u>. <u>America</u>
99 (26 July):442.
Finds two points to criticize. In trying to "be all
things to all men," Chisholm often seems indifferent, "that
he would just as soon quote a saying of Confucius as one of
Christ." Also, Mother Maria-Veronica's attitude is expressed
in an insolent language unseemly for a nun to speak. "These
points remarked, the book is thrilling and, in places, inspiring reading."

103 GOVAN, GILBERT E. "In New Novel, A.J. Cronin Tells Colorful
and Inspiring Life of a Scottish Missionary." <u>Chattanooga</u>

1941

Times, 3 August, p. 13.
Review of The Keys of the Kingdom. Notices that Cronin's
themes became matters of public importance beginning with
The Stars Look Down. Here he doesn't attack religion.
Rather, he attacks human weakness encountered in all institutions. Unfortunately, some readers may lose sight of the
message while focusing on disagreeable details such as occasional faults in style.

104 GRAUER, OTTO C. "Back of Books." Buffalo Courier-Express,
     1 June, p. 10.
     Discusses the publisher's promotional activities behind
     The Keys of the Kingdom.

105 H., C.P. Review of The Keys of the Kingdom. Social Progress
     36 (November):31-32.
     "To read this volume is to feel oneself as a congregation
     of one." The theme is "'What makes a clergyman successful?'"
     The answer is developed with "literary skill, with spiritual
     sensitiveness, . . . and with tolerance toward some of the
     complexities in the total situation." Humility is seen as
     the Christian virtue.

106 HANSEN, HARRY. "How Author Feels When He Sees Film Version of
     His Book." Chicago Sunday Tribune, 31 December, p. 2.
     Reports on Cronin's reactions after seeing for the first
     time the film version of The Keys of the Kingdom. The au-
     thor praised Gregory Peck's portrayal of Father Chisholm.
     He felt the settings were not quite faithful to Tynecastle
     and the southern border. "'One of the things that interests
     me,' he said, 'is the way a brief episode in a story becomes
     an important dramatic episode in a film.'" He also felt that
     the death of Francis's parents and the revolutionary sequence
     in China were "disproportionately emphasized." According to
     Cronin, "the integrity of the individual" has always been
     uppermost in his mind when planning a book.

107 _____. "The First Reader: Dr. Cronin Pits Kindness and
     Generosity Against Violence and Hate in His New Book, The
     Keys of the Kingdom." New York World Telegram, 21 July,
     p. 11.
     Readers will find the novel "healthy, invigorating, opti-
     mistic; they will welcome its elevation of decency, kindness
     and goodwill in human relations." Like The Citadel, the nov-
     el presents "the eternal battle of good intentions against
     selfish interests." Has reservations about the characteri-
     zation of Mother Maria-Veronica.

1941

108   HART, EVELYN. "Books of the Week: Cronin's Novel Points Value
       of Ordinary Human Kindness." Dayton Daily News, 27 July,
       p. 10.
              Review of The Keys of the Kingdom. Reminiscent of the
       childhood of David Copperfield. Though tragic early in the
       story, it ends on a note of triumph. "It is a thorough job
       of writing, with excellent character development underlying
       the progress of events." Sees this as an indictment of the
       modern world.

109   HART, PHILOMENA. "Fisherman, Scots Priest: Cronin's Story of
       an Old Man's Wisdom." Providence Journal, 20 July, p. 7.
              Review of The Keys of the Kingdom. Cronin is never
       preachy in this new novel. Rather, he informs the reader
       through his central character. The novel is superbly con-
       structed. Most important of all is its recognition of spir-
       ituality in today's world that is "eminently convincing."

110   HATCHER, HARLAN. "Book of the Summer--and Autumn." Columbus
       (Ohio) Citizen, 27 July, p. 9.
              Review of The Keys of the Kingdom. This is a good story
       about an unusual character. "Like the great Victorians from
       whose rich tradition he springs, his people are either good
       or bad. . . . The evil are punished, the good are rewarded."

111   HAYES, SIBYL C. "Dr. Cronin's New Novel." San Jose Mercury
       Herald, 10 August, p. 33.
              Review of The Keys of the Kingdom. "Dr. Cronin's ideas
       about men in the church apply to the world in general."
       This novel will make the reader think.

112   HOLLIS, EVA E. "Cronin's Newest Novel Strikes Vital Note,
       Creates Strong Figure." Salt Lake City Tribune, 24 August,
       p. 6.
              Review of The Keys of the Kingdom. This novel "exalts
       tolerance, humility and love of mankind in a day when the
       world suffers through the lack of these virtues." Even
       those who are reluctant to read books with religious themes
       will enjoy this one. That is because of Cronin's narrative
       facility, melodrama, and sincere approach.

113   JESSUP, LEE CHENEY. "'Deeply Significant Today.'" Nashville
       Banner, 27 August, p. 5.
              Review of The Keys of the Kingdom. Once again we see
       that Cronin is "a superb story-teller who does not hesitate
       to employ pure melodrama to produce the desired dramatic em-
       phasis." Like Hatter's Castle and The Citadel, Cronin uses
       strong character contrasts to delight his readers. Cronin

is obviously a man with "a sincere love for humanity and a
finger on the pulse of time."

114   KENDRICK, ALEXANDER. "Book of the Week: A.J. Cronin's Fine
      Novel of a Priestly Career." Philadelphia Inquirer, 23 July,
      p. 14.
         Review of The Keys of the Kingdom. Finds this novel both
      "more understanding and more universal" than The Citadel.
      Cronin's characters, conflicts and humanity are more pro-
      found. Most vivid of all is his portrait of Father Chisholm.

115   KIESSLING, E.C. "Fine Novel of Piety by A.J. Cronin."
      Milwaukee Journal, 20 July, p. 13.
         Review of The Keys of the Kingdom. Like Willa Cather's
      Death Comes for the Archbishop, Cronin demonstrates that "a
      great religious leader's life might provide excellent mater-
      ial for a fascinating story." What The Citadel did for the
      medical profession this novel does for the Church. "It is
      part entrancing story, part satire, part also expression of
      personal faith." The author succeeds in all three purposes.

116   KINGSBURY, WILLIAM. "Noble and Exciting: A.J. Cronin's Novel
      Something to Delight the Fastidious Reader." Nashville
      Tennessean, 20 July, p. 8.
         Review of The Keys of the Kingdom. Cronin surpasses the
      drama of Hatter's Castle and the power of The Citadel in
      this novel with a "noble theme, dramatic, well-written and
      not vapidly sentimental" story. Cronin avoids sentimentality
      through a couple of ironic twists in the dream sequence.

117   L., A.F. "Keys of the Kingdom by Dr. A.J. Cronin." Lewiston
      (Maine) Journal, 12 July, p. 22.
         This novel leaves the reader pondering "what is real re-
      ligion." Obviously Cronin has written "with profound con-
      viction, and in the spirit of the Man of Nazareth."

118   LAPPIN, HENRY A. "Dr. Cronin Invades the Church." Buffalo
      Evening News, 26 July, p. 10.
         Review of The Keys of the Kingdom. Although he is a
      Catholic, it is obvious that Cronin has much to learn about
      priests and nuns. "Parts of the book ring with a rich ab-
      surdity; and some of the author's employments of the deus
      ex machina are unforgivable in a novel we are expected to
      take seriously."

119   LAYCOCK, EDWARD A. "Notes and Comment." Boston Globe,
      10 August, p. 8.
         Brief mention of The Keys of the Kingdom as being on the
      best seller list.

1941

120   LEE, CHARLES. "Books of the Week: Cronin's New Hero a Priest."
      Philadelphia Record, 20 July, p. 9.
            Review of The Keys of the Kingdom. This novel is "packed
      with solid portraiture, convincingly realistic backgrounds
      and dramatic incident." There is also humor here, as well
      as satire, constructive criticism, and a challenge to orga-
      nized religion--a "plea for universal sanity and tolerance."

121   LEWIS, R.J., Jr. "Speaking of Books." Albany (N.Y.) Times-
      Union, 20 July, p. 11.
            Review of The Keys of the Kingdom. This is a "rich, warm
      story--gentle and humorous," and probably Cronin's best nov-
      el yet. "It is the story of a good man that every reader,
      regardless of creed, will love and admire."

122   McCABE, WARD. "Today and For Ever." Alexandria (Va.) Gazette,
      25 November, p. 3.
            Review of The Keys of the Kingdom. A moving novel which
      concerns the problems of the priest and the Church.

123   McCLEARY, DOROTHY. "Good Reading." New Republic 105 (28 July):
      125.
            Review of The Keys of the Kingdom. Cronin's latest novel
      is "painstakingly documented, and written with narrative
      frenzy and craftsmanship." But because the story is told
      through the eyes of a single character--Father Francis--the
      book lacks "emotional unity." As a novel based on a spiri-
      tual theme, this is "oddly superficial." But it is "'clean
      and sound'" as an adventure story and travel story "packed
      with melodramatic action."

124   McFEE, WILLIAM. "Dr. Cronin Writes Story about Church and
      Life." Youngstown (Ohio) Vindicator, 27 July, p. 4.
            Reprint of 1941.125.

125   _____. "The Book of the Day." New York Sun, 21 July, p. 5.
            Review of The Keys of the Kingdom. Ever since Hatter's
      Castle, Cronin has lost the "freshness and power" which
      distinguished him as a writer. This recession in his career
      continues with his latest novel. "It is not a creation but
      a manufactured article." It is a Marie Corelli romance
      brought up to date. Reprinted: 1941.124.

126   McINTYRE, ALFRED. "A.J. Cronin." Book-of-the-Month Club News
      (July), pp. 3-4.
            Brief biographical background. Cronin "does not believe
      in the Novel with a Purpose." Out of his experience came
      The Citadel. Three years passed before he found a theme

66

that satisfied him for his next novel. When he had completed
the first draft of The Keys of the Kingdom, he wrote, "'While
simple and very moving, I think it is by far the most important thing I have ever done, and deeply significant today.'"

127   McSORLEY, JOSEPH. "New Books." Catholic World 153 (August):
      631-32.
          Review of The Keys of the Kingdom. "The characters are
      pawns, wooden images, caricatures crudely fashioned, or
      crudely distorted. . . . If Dr. Cronin regards himself as
      a liberal-minded man he has much to learn about the qualities
      which make for balanced judgment and fair representation."

128   MARCHAND, LAFAYETTE. "Week's Books: Unforgettable Portrait
      of Priest Given in The Keys of the Kingdom." Boston Globe,
      20 July, p. 9.
          Cronin now has the courage to ponder "a more intense
      theme." The story of Father Chisholm is "deeply moving"
      and tragic, building to a powerful climax in the last chap-
      ter. As a writer Cronin has come to full maturity.

129   MILLER, MARGARET. "Novel Revolves Around Life of Priest in
      China, Scotland." San Diego Union, 27 July, p. 10.
          The Keys of the Kingdom is "a dramatic story, not all
      dealing with religion."

130   MILLER, MARY THOMAS. "Dr. Cronin's Sixth Success." Argonaut
      (15 August):4.
          Review of The Keys of the Kingdom. This is a deeper,
      more smoothly written novel than anything Cronin has yet
      written. "We see, through Dr. Cronin's eyes, the develop-
      ment of a man and his soul, and his finding of the keys."

131   MORLEY, CHRISTOPHER. "The Keys of the Kingdom." Book-of-the-
      Month Club News (July), pp. 2-3.
          The hero does not fit easily into ecclesiastical disci-
      pline. At many points Cronin's story touches upon "matters
      of doctrine and devotion which involve painful paradox."
      This is a novel which, "though it has no bearing upon our
      present horrors, is none the less full of invigorating cour-
      age." Excerpted: 1941.25.

132   NAYLOR, PAULINE. "A.J. Cronin Turns to the Field of the
      Spirit." Fort Worth Telegram, 20 July, p. 4.
          Review of The Keys of the Kingdom. Father Chisholm's
      story may give readers an answer for what the world can turn
      to for the survival of spiritual qualities. This is Cronin's
      most dramatic story yet.

1941

133   OWENS, OLGA. "Bookstall Gossip." <u>Boston Post</u>, 20 July, p. 5.
       Brief biographical mention. "Dr. Cronin's personal vigor
       is reflected in all his novels."

134   PEKAR, JOE. "A Pre-Issue Best Seller." <u>Omaha World-Herald</u>,
       20 July, p. 6.
       Review of <u>The Keys of the Kingdom</u>. What Cronin does is
       write about something that will apply to the world at large.
       Religion is a perilous topic, to be sure, but Cronin "gets
       away with it nicely."

135   RADIN, DOROTHEA P. "A.J. Cronin's Latest Novel." <u>Oakland
       Tribune</u>, 3 August, p. 2.
       Review of <u>The Keys of the Kingdom</u>. "The book is a glori-
       fication of the virtues of tolerance and humility, virtues
       now so little popular as to make their defense both desperate
       and timely." As usual, Cronin's ability to hold the reader's
       attention accounts in part for the book's success. Its only
       faults are occasional "well-worn" episodes, melodrama, and a
       romantic discovery near the end which seems "far-fetched."

136   REELY, MARY KATHERINE. "New Books: Fiction." <u>Wisconsin
       Library Bulletin</u> 37 (October):155.
       Brief mention of <u>The Keys of the Kingdom</u>. Compares it
       to <u>The Citadel</u>.

137   ROBERTS, MARY-CARTER. "Priest Is Main Character in New Cronin
       Novel." <u>Washington</u> (D.C.) <u>Star</u>, 27 July, p. 11.
       Review of <u>The Keys of the Kingdom</u>. Follows to some degree
       the pattern in <u>The Citadel</u>. But instead of the medical pro-
       fession, the priesthood is held up to examination. If we
       put together the two novels, "we may conclude in more general
       terms that Dr. Cronin holds that idealism, anywhere and of
       any kind, is unrewarding in the worldly sense, and that hu-
       manity in general prefers a comfortable sham to a demanding
       and difficult reality." The story seems a bit manipulated
       by the author, however.

138   ROBINSON, TED. "Catholic Missionary Is Hero of A.J. Cronin's
       Latest Novel." <u>Cleveland Plain-Dealer</u>, 20 July, p. 9.
       Review of <u>The Keys of the Kingdom</u>. In dramatic effect
       this novel goes beyond anything Cronin has yet written. Al-
       though many writers say it is more difficult to make virtue
       as interesting as vice, Cronin accomplishes that. At the
       same time, he makes his hero "human and understandable and
       likable."

139   ROSS, MARY. "A Most Appealing and Memorable Book: Cronin's

New Novel Will Be the Subject of Wide Discussion." New York
Herald-Tribune Books, 20 July, p. 1.
    Review of The Keys of the Kingdom. "As readers of Dr.
Cronin's earlier novels will anticipate, his present story
has vigor and drama. It also has beauty, gentleness and
humor." Because it involves questions of faith, this novel
will most likely appeal to a wider readership than did The
Citadel. Includes extensive plot summary.

140   SELBY, JOHN. "Books." Columbus (Ohio) State-Journal, 28 July,
       p. 3.
           Reprint of 1941.142.

141   [SELBY, JOHN.] "Dr. A.J. Cronin Writes Story of Catholic
       Church." New Haven Register, 20 July, p. 5.
           Review of The Keys of the Kingdom. Cronin uses the
       Catholic Church to picture the world, and what he says
       through Francis applies not only to the Church but also to
       the entire world. Suggests that the novel might have been
       just as affecting if it were a bit less sentimental and if
       Cronin had not exploited the obvious quite so often. Re-
       printed: 1941.140, 142-48.

142   SELBY, JOHN. "Dr. Cronin's New Novel Is Story of a Catholic
       Priest." Charlotte Observer, 27 July, p. 5.
           Reprint of 1941.41.

143   [SELBY, JOHN.] "Reviews in Brief of Recent Worthwhile Books."
       Savannah News, 10 August, p. 3.
           Reprint of 1941.41.

144   ____. "Shopping List." Gastonia (N.C.) Gazette, 20 December,
       p. 7.
           Reprint of 1941.41.

145   ____. "The Literary Guidepost." Wausau (Wis.) Record-Herald,
       21 July, p. 10.
           Reprint of 1941.41.

146   ____. "What's Best Between Bookends: Cronin Masters A
       Difficult Theme." Rochester Democrat and American, 27 July,
       p. 4.
           Reprint of 1941.41.

147   ____. "What's Best Between Bookends: Your Christmas Book
       List." Rochester Democrat and American, 21 December, p. 2.
           Reprint of 1941.41.

1941

148 _____. "Writes New Novel." <u>Green Bay Press-Gazette</u>, 26 July,
p. 5.
Reprint of 1941.41.

149 SHANNON, T.V. "Msgr. T.V. Shannon Calls <u>The Keys of the</u>
<u>Kingdom</u> Catholic Book of the Year." <u>Chicago News</u>,
3 December, p. 10.
"Deep tragedy with its moods of pity and terror redeem
the novel of minor faults."

150 STAFFORD, RUSSELL HENRY. "The Author of <u>The Citadel</u> Writes
His Greatest Novel." <u>Boston Post</u>, 20 July, p. 7.
Review of <u>The Keys of the Kingdom</u>. Cronin's best book.
In it he has told an interesting story about a good man.
"It is refreshing to come upon a novel so close to experience
as this, so revealing and so memorable, yet with not a single
bitter or dirty line in it. Nor is there any shadow of big-
otry or mere moralizing."

151 STEVENS, MARION. "Dr. Cronin Dramatizes Virtue in His New
Best-Selling Novel." <u>Miami Herald</u>, 3 August, p. 6.
Review of <u>The Keys of the Kingdom</u>. Spiritual goodness
is made "readable and intensely absorbing" by Cronin's expert storytelling abilities. The scope is larger than <u>The</u>
<u>Citadel</u>. Cronin "comes closer to humanity itself." Perhaps
because of this and an enhanced dramatic style, we find the
novel "more vital, more readable and infinitely more stirring."

152 TEMPLETON, LUCY CURTIS. "Books Old and New." <u>Knoxville</u>
<u>Sentinel</u>, 27 July, p. 4.
Review of <u>The Keys of the Kingdom</u>. In <u>The Citadel</u>, Cronin
revealed the hypocrisy in the medical world. In his new novel, his targets are "religious arrogance and hypocrisy."
Cronin could have been equally convincing about the short-
comings of Presbyterians or "the Establishment South of the
Border."

153 THOMPSON, RALPH. "Books of the Times." <u>New York Times</u>,
21 July, p. 13.
Review of <u>The Keys of the Kingdom</u>. Cronin is a novelist
whose reputation as a "great" writer is perhaps exaggerated.
He himself may have helped to foster this notion by writing
about "broad and unquestionably major-novelist themes."
However, in both <u>The Citadel</u> and his new novel, his doctrine
is trite. The story is "pure contrivance" in many places.
"Practically everything else in his book is sheer story in
the familiar Cronin manner."

154   THOMSON, WILLIAM S. Review of <u>The Keys of the Kingdom</u>.
      <u>Atlanta Journal</u>, 10 August, p. 7.
            This is Cronin's most significant work to date. It will
      demand attention beyond that given to <u>The Citadel</u>.

155   TOBIAS, ROWENA W. "Dr. Cronin Scores Again." <u>Charleston News</u>,
      20 July, p. 11.
            Finds appealing the melodrama and the highly suspenseful
      scenes in <u>The Keys of the Kingdom</u>.

156   WAGNER, CHARLES A. "Books." <u>Chicago Daily Mirror</u>, 23 July,
      p. 26.
            Review of <u>The Keys of the Kingdom</u>. Finds this to be a
      disappointing novel because it does not come from Cronin's
      heart. Like <u>Grand Canary</u>, the story means little to the
      reader. His problem continues to be a problem of having
      little to say.

157   WALKER, CHRISTIN. "Close to Heaven and Earth." <u>Columbus</u> (Ohio)
      <u>Dispatch</u>, 20 July, p. 5.
            Review of <u>The Keys of the Kingdom</u>. Father Chisholm comes
      as near to being Christ-like as any fictional character, but
      Cronin avoids becoming preachy in his story about the priest.
      Finds parallels between this novel and <u>The Citadel</u>.

158   WEIDMAN, JEROME. "Books: Dr. Cronin's New Novel Full of
      'Incredible Hokum.'" <u>PM's Weekly</u>, 20 July, p. 44.
            Review of <u>The Keys of the Kingdom</u>. "Obviously the good
      doctor didn't have a moment, during the first three and a
      half decades of his life, to waste on writing. It is plain
      that he was too busy, up to the age of 34, reading and memo-
      rizing all the other lines of fiction that had ever been
      written." Says that this novel is "a classic of corn, bad
      taste, insufferable writing and public hoodwinking." See
      1941.87.

159   WOODS, KATHERINE. "A Modern Saint Is the Hero of A.J. Cronin's
      Novel." <u>New York Times Book Review</u>, 20 July, p. 5.
            Review of <u>The Keys of the Kingdom</u>. "No one who has read
      Dr. Cronin's earlier work needs to be told with what compact
      dramatic skill event has followed event and idea has been
      held safely back from the edge of symbolism." But this novel
      is better than <u>The Citadel</u> because it has "greater warmth and
      vitality." Unfortunately, some readers may see this novel
      as an attack on the Church, for "the breadth of his attack
      is against the ancient deadly evil of intolerance and greed
      and arrogant complacency." In spite of some flaws--such as
      redundancy and overemphasis--"one is struck by the subtlety

1941

of thought which slowly gathers its thrust." In all, the
novel is "a magnificent story of the great adventure of individual goodness." Excerpted: 1941.22.

160   Z., A.J. "Cronin's Latest Is Dramatic Story." Springfield
(Mass.) News, 1 August, p. 2.
    Review of The Keys of the Kingdom. In spite of the emo-
tion in this novel, "the reader cannot help but notice the
quiet dignity that pervades all."

1942

1   ANON. "Cronin, A(rchibald) J(oseph)." Current Biography 1942.
Edited by Maxine Block. New York: The H.H. Wilson Co.,
pp. 167-70.
    Biographical background and stories behind the writing
and publication of Hatter's Castle, Three Loves, Grand
Canary, The Stars Look Down, The Citadel, Jupiter Laughs and
The Keys of the Kingdom. Includes brief bibliography of
secondary sources.

2   ANON. "Fiction." Fort Wayne Protestant Voice, 30 January,
p. 5.
    The Keys of the Kingdom is "a tender and lovable story"
and one of Cronin's most readable.

3   ANON. "1941's Best Books." Atlanta Journal, 1 March, p. 10.
    The Keys of the Kingdom has been designated "leader of
the ten outstanding novels of 1941."

4   CRAIG. "A.J. Cronin Scores Triumph in The Keys of the Kingdom."
Stanford University Daily, 29 January, p. 5.
    "Dr. Cronin's facility for color and moving drama in his
descriptions and scenes makes this book even more absorbing
than his previous ones. Beneath it is a deep conviction
that tenacious faith cannot fail to carry the world over
even the most tragic and heartbreaking vicissitudes. The
chief character serves as a fine example of the part that
religion has the chance to play in our world today."

5   DITTEMORE, ELDON. Review of The Keys of the Kingdom. Christian
Index (19 February), p. 7.
    "The main ideas of this book seem to me to be: Christ
and the Church teach that no one acting in good faith can
ever be lost. . . . This is because of the mercy of God."

6   KNAPP, VALERIE. Review of The Keys of the Kingdom. Gloucester

72

(Mass.) Times, 24 January, p. 3.
The novel is particularly significant to those readers
seeking spiritual stability. "There is a depth of human
understanding, of logical spiritual intercourse, and so
much of truth here that one cannot fail to be touched or
moved or at least aroused."

7   V., M.J. "Social Fiction." Sociology and Social Research 26
    (January-February):298.
    Review of The Keys of the Kingdom. Because of Cronin's
    storytelling abilities, the reader must read on. "To read
    the novel is not only a delightful experience but an en-
    lightening one."

8   W., G. "Speaking of Books." Murray (Utah) Eagle, 23 July,
    p. 4.
    Readers familiar with Cronin's works will find in The
    Keys of the Kingdom many interesting hours of reading pleas-
    ure.

1944

1   ANON. "A.J..Cronin Writes One of Season's Better Books in The
    Green Years." San Jose Mercury Herald, 19 November, p. 5.
    "Each character is drawn in Cronin's best manner, until
    the family is a living and breathing entity. It is a power-
    ful story, splendidly executed."

2   ANON. "Another Cronin Book to Provoke Discussion." Cleveland
    Catholic Universe Bulletin, 8 December, p. 18.
    Review of The Green Years. As with his earlier books,
    this novel will provoke discussion because the author has
    "a provocative way of introducing the Church into his writ-
    ings." Canon Roche's arguments are pitifully weak. The
    First Communion scene is beautifully rendered, but "its
    aftermath rather profanes what should be a lovely day."
    Concludes that the author seems to take "perverse delight
    in upsetting the apple-cart just so far in every narrative
    that portrays Catholic customs. If he could remedy this
    fault he would be a much better writer."

3   ANON. "Book Review." Beloit (Wis.) News, 13 November, p. 5.
    Calls The Citadel "first-rate reading."

4   ANON. "Books: Adolescence à la Cronin." Newsweek (11
    November), pp. 92, 95-96.
    Review of The Green Years. Biographical background.

1944

"All Cronin's novels, like his latest, are slow, quiet, intense accounts of credible human beings placed in credible situations." The Green Years is typical of Cronin. It is "sentimental and understanding, and peopled with dour, small-town characters who have about them the ring of reality."

5   ANON. "Boy Against the World." Atlantic Monthly 174 (December):127, 129.
     Review of The Green Years. In The Citadel, Cronin was at his best in depicting the "humbler Scottish folk." Similarly, in his latest novel, "it is in a small and provincial community that Cronin the novelist finds the human nature and the warmth with which to kindle the best of his novels." The hero's experiences evoke echoes of the reader's own past. "The strength of the story lies in its Scotch honesty and aspiration; the weakness . . . is its lack of force and subtlety, especially in times of crisis."

6   ANON. "Boy's Courage Theme of Tale." Memphis Commercial Appeal, 26 November, sec. iv, p. 10.
     Review of The Green Years. This novel of adolescence is written with "sympathetic insight" and wins the reader's attention from the start. Cronin focuses on "school, religion, a romantic ideal, an overwhelming ambition to become a doctor." Recommends the book for both adults and young readers.

7   ANON. "Briefly Noted: Fiction." New Yorker 20 (18 November): 90.
     Review of The Green Years. Cronin portrays the grandparents' family with "skill and warmth, and the author has an admirable way of telling a story, but unfortunately there is not much of a story to tell."

8   ANON. "Calvinism and Scant Fare." Dayton Journal-Herald, 4 December, p. 6.
     Review of The Green Years. Says that Howard Spring could have handled this story of an adolescent growing up with "great verisimilitude."

9   ANON. "Cronin's Genius Creates Beautiful Tale of Youth." St. Louis Globe-Democrat, 14 November, p. 11.
     Review of The Green Years. In this "intensely autobiographical" novel Cronin blends "power and authority," charity and sympathy.

10   ANON. "Cronin's Latest Doesn't Ring the Bell." Detroit Free Press, 17 December, p. 10.

Review of The Green Years. "In all the essentials of thought, writing and atmospheric quality," this novel is sound. But the story is too slight for it to compare with The Stars Look Down or The Keys of the Kingdom. Comments on Cronin's continuing interest in science and the Catholic Church.

11   ANON. "Dr. Cronin Popular." Pasadena Star-News, 2 December, p. 8.
      Review of The Green Years. Reports that advance orders from bookstores for Cronin's new novel totaled 185,000 copies on 13 November--the day of publication. The sixth printing before publication has just been ordered, bringing the total number of copies to 220,000. In advance orders and printings, this breaks all records at Little, Brown.

12   ANON. "Dusting the Library Shelves." Ft. Atkinson (Wis.) Union, 1 December, p. 8.
      The Green Years is a "deeply moving" novel which has all of the qualities that made his earlier works so popular.

13   ANON. "Editor's Choice: What of the Dry?" Commonweal 41 (17 November):130-31.
      Review of The Green Years. Finds here a combination of Cronin's narrative skill and "an almost inevitable tendency to stack the cards against his hero--object: pity."

14   ANON. "Fiction." Booklist 41 (15 November):89.
      Review of The Green Years. "Sympathetic understanding in characterization and humor in the telling, but the book may not have the wide appeal of some of the author's earlier books." This was serialized in Redbook.

15   ANON. "Green Years Goes into Sixth Printing." Memphis Commercial Appeal, 17 December, p. 4.
      All records have been broken at Little, Brown for advance sales.

16   ANON. "Highlights from New Books." Riverside (Calif.) Enterprise, 20 November, p. 3.
      Plot summary of The Green Years.

17   ANON. "His 'Mortal Sin.'" Middletown (Ohio) Journal, 12 November, p. 6.
      Comments on the "rich" humor, the "genuine" pathos, and the surprising climax in The Green Years.

18   ANON. "New Books." Beloit (Wis.) News, 14 December, p. 9.

1944

>   Review of The Green Years. Although the book may not
> have the wide appeal of his earlier novels, the story is
> told with "understanding and humor."

19   ANON. "New Books Arrive at City Library." Norway (Mich.)
>   Current, 14 December, p. 7.
>   Review of The Green Years. Calls this a "deeply moving
>   novel, one which will keep the reader's emotions constantly
>   in play." Its humor, excitement, and inspiration give the
>   novel "its most poignant episodes a warm, comforting glow."

20   ANON. "New Cronin Novel." San Jose News, 12 December, p. 5.
>   Brief mention of The Green Years.

21   ANON. Review of The Green Years. Boston Globe, 29 November,
>   p. 30.
>   Comments on Cronin's "tender eye." Grandpa will become
>   "one of the memorable and heroic rascals of fiction."

22   ANON. Review of The Green Years. Chelsea (Mass.) Record,
>   23 December, p. 11.
>   "You can always depend on A.J. Cronin to tell a good
>   story, and he doesn't disappoint us in his latest novel."
>   Notes that The Keys of the Kingdom will soon be released as
>   a major film by Twentieth Century-Fox.

23   ANON. Review of The Green Years. Chicago News, 13 December,
>   p. 8.
>   The novel is "rich to overflowing with character por-
>   traits," but Grandpa steals the show. "Technically, this
>   is Dr. Cronin's top performance, a master work by a master
>   storyteller."

24   ANON. Review of The Green Years. Chippewa Falls (Wis.) Herald
>   Telegram, 18 December, p. 10.
>   This "sensitive story" is "rich in incident and back-
>   ground."

25   ANON. Review of The Green Years. Cleveland News, 14 December,
>   p. 2.
>   Rates this as Cronin's best novel.

26   ANON. Review of The Green Years. Cleveland Press, 14 November,
>   p. 3.
>   Calls this a "splendid novel" that will not disappoint
>   Cronin fans.

27   ANON. Review of The Green Years. Green Bay Press Gazette,

1944

25 November, p. 6.
Recommends that Roddy McDowell play the hero in the film
version of the novel. Says this is "a dour story of poverty,
work and heartbreak." There is little humor except for
Grandpa.

28 ANON. Review of The Green Years. Marshfield (Wis.) News-
Herald, 24 November, p. 10.
Comments on Shannon's development into manhood from "a
sensitive, trusting boy beset from every side with crushing
difficulties."

29 ANON. Review of The Green Years. Miami Herald, 31 December,
p. 8.
Cronin's most "charming" book, because Cronin "abandons
drama for fine and sensitive observation of life." Says
this surpasses any American novel because, typical of British
fiction, it has "a quality of writing, of steady point of
view, of complete integration of matter and manner which
touched literary heights which few modern nervous, staccato,
vivid, even dashing, even powerful American novels can."

30 ANON. Review of The Green Years. Pacific Grove Tribune,
8 December, p. 3.
Feels that Cronin has "a sympathetic understanding of
human frailties and emotions and portrays them with intense
sincerity."

31 ANON. Review of The Green Years. Religious Book Club
(December), p. 3.
This is "a heart-warming story, with a heavy accent on
youthful hardships, undefeatable ambition, and religious
faith."

32 ANON. Review of The Green Years. Richmond Times-Dispatch,
26 November, p. 7.
This is a "lovable and charming" book in which the author's concern with the "crises, loves, ambitions, loneli-
ness, and ecstasy of a boy's life from childhood to manhood"
is universal.

33 ANON. Review of The Green Years. San Francisco News, 1
December, p. 8.
Brief mention of Cronin's storytelling abilities.

34 ANON. Review of The Green Years. Washington Post, 19 November,
p. 4.
Cronin is becoming "increasingly dull, careless or perhaps

1944

weary in fabricating his stories." Notes that Cronin has
also become "intensely Roman" in his point of view and is
bitter toward his Protestant characters and the typical Scot.
Not nearly as well executed as Hatter's Castle, The Stars
Look Down or The Keys of the Kingdom. Says this is a "rather sad, rather tired manufacture with a slightly unbelievable
happy ending."

35 ANON. Review of The Green Years. Washington (D.C.) Star,
    12 November, p. 4.
        Whereas the earlier novels had a social theme, this book
    is wholly about people. It is a simple novel, lacking the
    social implication and the complicated structure of his
    earlier works. Comments on the autobiographical elements,
    too.

36 ANON. "The Green Years Is Affecting Tale of a Scotch Family."
    San Jose Mercury Herald, 18 November, p. 13.
        Calls this "a finely drawn picture in prose" of a family
    in Scotland. The characters are lifelike and the narrative
    flows smoothly.

37 ANON. "Weekly Book Review." Lawrence (Mass.) Tribune,
    10 November, p. 6.
        The Green Years is "heart-warming stuff" which once again
    demonstrates Cronin's skill as a storyteller.

38 ANON. "Writers at Work." New York Times, 30 April, pt. II,
    p. 3.
        Quotes Cronin as saying that his chief purpose in life
    --to "'improve'" as a writer--is a desire "'clearly handi-
    capped by success.'" He goes on to say: "'No one is more
    vulnerable than an author who sells well.'" Moreover, he
    finds writing is "'a great sweat, often an agony.'" He
    can't type, he won't dictate, and his new book, The Green
    Years, was written at only one-fifth the speed of his first
    novel--1,000 words a day. Cronin confirms that the novel
    has its autobiographical side, too. Alexander Gow was mod-
    elled after his great-grandfather, "who really had a Bergerac
    nose and who was extremely kind to his great-grandson when
    sober and 'even kinder when he was not.'"

39 APPEL, DAVID. "Turning a New Leaf." Chicago News, 15 November,
    p. 39.
        Review of The Green Years. In Cronin's novels one finds
    "the crusader's fire and the preacher's zeal." Finds over-
    tones of Dickens, Maugham, and Barrie, but always "there is
    the unmistakable stamp of the born storyteller." In his

latest novel, Cronin's talents come "to full bloom." Discusses the drama and humor in this "subtle unveiling of a boy's soul."

40   B., E.M. Review of The Green Years. Springfield (Mass.)
     Republican, 12 November, p. 4.
         Cronin's fans will find this a "pleasant successor" to
     The Citadel, in spite of the subtle drama and slight problem. New readers of Cronin's will find in this book "a
     heartwarming evening or two of enjoyment."

41   BOND, ALICE DIXON. "The Case for Books." Boston Herald,
     15 November, p. 14.
         Review of The Green Years. Points out that this is
     Cronin's shortest book and, in artistry and quality, it
     seems the best. Finds the story both realistic and moving
     because of the author's perception, tenderness, and humor.
     Comments on the spiritual overtones--a distinctive feature
     of The Keys of the Kingdom--and on Shannon's character. "In
     one small and lucid segment Dr. Cronin has given us the life
     of a boy beset by terror and hardship and often aching disappointments, yet alive to beauty and love and ambition."

42   BULLOCK, FLORENCE HAXTON. "Cronin's Enchanting Novel of a
     Boy's Life." New York Herald-Tribune Books, 12 November,
     p. 3.
         Review of The Green Years. In this novel Cronin "understands life and has the gift of sharing that understanding
     with us in a wholly enchanting fashion." As in his earlier
     novels, Cronin leaves us with the sense that life is not
     "static."

43   CRONIN, J.F. "Growth of Character." Cincinnati Enquirer,
     18 November, p. 6.
         Review of The Green Years. While all of the characters
     are drawn vividly, all are important only as they relate to
     the hero. Most interesting of these characters are Grandpa
     Gow, Papa Leckie, and Mrs. Leckie. Finds parallels between
     this novel and one by Warwick Deeping. "Its interest is
     wholly dependent on the development of its characters, its
     setting is in a small town in the British Isles, the viewpoints of its characters are small-town people." Compared
     with Cronin's earlier novels, The Green Years will be a disappointment. Read alone, it will be enjoyable though "light"
     reading.

44   DANCOKE, CHARLES, S.J. "Cronin's Green Years Merits Few
     Laurels." Milwaukee Herald Citizen, 2 December, p. 4.

1944

Review of The Green Years. Finds Shannon's development follows conventional lines. His reversal might have been more convincing "if the reader were convinced beforehand that Robert's religious feeling were deep and strong." The most serious artistic defect is that Robert's character does not develop and seems incapable of growing in wisdom as the result of experience. "The impression is inevitable that Robert will go on the rest of his days the victim of moods and circumstances, forever incapable of becoming complete master of himself." This is a "minor" novel in which only one phase is handled well: the friendship of Robert and Gavin.

45   DuBOIS, WILLIAM. "Scenes from a Frustrated Boyhood." New York Times Book Review, 12 November, p. 3.
Review of The Green Years. Comments on the combination of "quiet charm and the special brand of heartache" that Cronin is so adept at fashioning. Complains about the plotting, which is familiar and too carefully planned by the author. Drama is stifled at times by "drabness." The catalogue of poverty at times seems merely a catalogue. The death of Gavin "seems merely a gratuitous blow of fate." And the final solution of Shannon's despair is "redeemed from pure corn only by the author's quick curtain." Nevertheless, the novel is "stirring" and even "eloquent."

46   DUNCAN, ROBERT. "The Book Corner." Columbus (Ga.) Ledger, 12 November, p. 12.
Review of The Green Years. Comments on the humor, the pathos, and the climax. Cronin is indeed a skillful storyteller.

47   ERSKINE, JOHN. "Fine and Warmly Human Story of an Old Man and a Lad." Chicago Sun Book Week, 12 November, p. 25.
Review of The Green Years. Says that this "splendidly written story will delight Dr. Cronin's admirers. It will open their eyes as all his books have done, to pleasant as well as to unpleasant possibilities of life, with a strong accent on courage and cheerfulness." In spite of its title, the book is actually about old people. Shannon is the only youthful character on whom Cronin spends any time, and his character is "transparent." Calls it a "magnificent" story, but complains that the ending comes too soon.

48   GOULD, RAY. "Enchanting, Unforgettable New Novel Already Among Best-Seller Lists." Montgomery Advertiser, 26 September, p. 11.
Review of The Green Years. Cronin proves once again that

80

"a novel can reach heights without resorting to off-color writing." Comments on the lifelike characters and the warm, sympathetic tone.

49   HANSEN, HARRY. "The First Reader." New York World Telegram, 13 November, p. 23.
      Review of The Green Years. Finds possible parallels between this novel and Richard Llewellyn's How Green Is My Valley. Obviously Cronin understands Shannon's sensitivity. He "writes beyond his behavior to what stirs in his heart and writes the best novel of Scottish boyhood since Kidnapped." Cadger Gow will become one of the "immortals" of the British novel.

50   HILL, VICTOR. "Book of Youth." Providence Journal, 19 November, p. 9.
      Review of The Green Years. Finds reasons to suggest that this novel is autobiographical: "his profound sympathy with people whose worthiness often has less than an even chance against their struggles, his association with the Roman Catholic Church and his sense of the religious, and his agonizing, cragged sense of conflict."

51   HILLYER, DOROTHY. Review of The Green Years. Boston Globe, 15 November, p. 16.
      "Dr. Cronin has the ability to dramatize a very real perception of the inner processes of life. As an author he writes the way all people hope their doctor sees and feels. No wonder he is successful!"

52   HUDSON, THOMAS FRANKLYN. Review of The Green Years. Social Progress (December), p. 16.
      Comments on the drama, the religious bigotry, the insight into human frailties and emotions, and the deep understanding of people's passions in this exceptional tale by an exceptional novelist.

53   JULKA, LUCILE. "Cronin's Novel, Tale of Youth and Idealism." Milwaukee Journal, 12 November, p. 6.
      Review of The Green Years. Praises Cronin's "philosophy of hope without bitterness." Deeper than the story of an adolescent, this novel "is the tale of a youth's search for the things of the soul and how he managed to find them."

54   KNIGHT, ELIZABETH B. "Some Very Nice Middle-of-Road Scotch-Irish." Dallas Times-Herald, 3 December, p. 5.
      Review of The Green Years. Comments on the themes of science and religion that run throughout Cronin's works.

1944

Concludes that the author's philosophy--conservative and
optimistic--will please many readers. "While he may not
hit the heights, nor the depths, his style is easy and
gracious," and the characters are lifelike.

55   LAPPIN, HENRY A. "Cronin's Latest Falls Below Earlier Works."
     <u>Buffalo Evening News</u>, 11 November, p. 7.
        Review of <u>The Green Years</u>. The pages in which Cadger Gow
     appears are "the most diverting in a not notably diverting
     book." Speculates that this novel may have been written
     early in Cronin's career. "It certainly exhibits no advance
     in his art."

56   LEE, CHARLES. "Book of the Week." <u>Philadelphia Record</u>,
     12 November, p. 6.
        Review of <u>The Green Years</u>. Calls this novel "long, warm-
     hearted, somewhat familiar, unadrenalized, occasionally
     humorous but for the most part somber, over-detailed, some-
     times exciting, frequently dull and sluggish." But the book
     is bound to be a success, and its success is bound to be
     temporary.

57   LOWREY, JACOB H. "<u>The Green Years</u> Described as Best A.J.
     Cronin Novel." <u>Columbia</u> (S.C.) <u>State</u>, 3 December, p. 4.
        In spite of its less than sensational story, this novel
     comes closer to what is known as literature. The author
     infuses commonplace events with "his own acute sense of
     drama." The characters are lifelike. The author creates
     the illusion of covering more ground than he actually does.
     Concludes that the novel accomplishes a difficult task:
     "searching exploration of the mind of youth."

58   McFEE, WILLIAM. "A.J. Cronin Mixes Religion with Science in
     New Novel." <u>Youngstown Vindicator</u>, 3 December, p. 7.
        Review of <u>The Green Years</u>. Says that the author is more
     convincing about science than religion. Attributes his suc-
     cess to two elements: He is a born storyteller, and he has
     the exact intellectual range of his readers.

59   McVICKER, DAPHNE ALLOWAY. "The Book Mark." <u>Columbus</u> (Ohio)
     <u>Citizen</u>, 12 November, p. 3.
        Review of <u>The Green Years</u>. Cronin achieves much in this
     novel because he once again successfully sets "character
     against an almost personal background" and because he cre-
     ates characters that are genuine.

60   MARTIN, GERTRUDE A. "With the New Books." <u>Jackson Leader</u>,
     11 December, p. 4.

1944

Review of The Green Years. "We leave the book with the feeling that these are real people; that this is a real town with life going on in all gradations of experience: humor, pathos, the heights of spiritual exaltation and the depths of despair. They are all there--for that is what makes an A.J. Cronin novel."

61 MEALAND, RICHARD. "Books into Films." Publishers Weekly 146 (14 October):1585.
    Discusses the purchase of The Green Years and other novels by film studios. Almost everything that Cronin has written has sold for films. "Like Arnold Bennett, Cronin has always watched every penny he has earned." He is probably "the canniest and shrewdest trader in the writing game with or without the help of agents."

62 MERLIN, MILTON. "Decisive Decade of Man's Life Depicted by Cronin." Los Angeles Times, 19 November, pp. 3-4.
    Review of The Green Years. Calls this an "ingratiating novel" filled with incident and several memorable characters.

63 MORLEY, CHRISTOPHER. Review of The Green Years. Book-of-the-Month Club (December), pp. 9-10.
    Comments on the lack of melodrama, the excellent settings, the "character and shrewd local color that make this story so appealing." It is an honest narrative, engaging, and irresistibly readable.

64 NICHOLS, ELIZABETH P. "New Books Appraised: Fiction." Library Journal 69 (1 November):936.
    Review of The Green Years. "Usual expert character delineation and subtle humor of Cronin are here with a tenderness and warmth equalled only in The Keys of the Kingdom."

65 NORTH, STERLING. "Today's New Book: Calvinism and Scant Fare." New York Post, 17 November, p. 17.
    Review of The Green Years. The reading is dull and the writing is careless. This is "a rather sad, rather tired manufacture with a slightly unbelievable happy ending."

66 OREBAUGH, VERNON. Review of The Green Years. Toledo Blade, 10 November, p. 8.
    Although short on plot, the characterization is excellent and the detail satisfying.

67 OWENS, OLGA. "The Reading Glass: Current Reviews." Boston Sunday Post, 12 November, p. 18.
    Review of The Green Years. A satisfying novel which is

1944

bound to be another best seller for Cronin. The "spiritual overtones" are far more impressive than the preaching found in Maugham's The Razor's Edge.

68   P., M. "Irish Youth in Family of Scotch Miser." Worcester (Mass.) Telegram, 19 November, p. 16.
     Review of The Green Years. Reading this novel is like "taking a vacation--a vacation from the war. . . . If one can lose oneself in any book and forget for a bit the present cataclysm, here is the chance." Hopes there will be a sequel.

69   PETERSEN, SCARBOROUGH. "Green Years Given Praise by Reviewer." Beverly Hills Citizen, 1 December, p. 1.
     Says this is as "gripping, but much more pleasant" than Hatter's Castle. It is also entertaining and thought-provoking.

70   PRESCOTT, ORVILLE. "Books of the Times." New York Times, 13 November, p. 17.
     Review of The Green Years. Tries to find in this latest novel the secret to Cronin's success. Notes the obvious plot, the sentimentality, the stilted and stiff prose, but finds that it "still stands serene and forthright, a book that arouses interest and commands respect." Its ability to do this stems from the author's own character, his view of life and of the world. "Every page Dr. Cronin writes bears the stamp of an honest and simple man, without pretense, affectation or false sophistication." There is universal quality to the man and his vision that gives life to his characters and "understanding to his books."

71   REELY, MARY KATHERINE. "New Books: Fiction." Wisconsin Library Bulletin 40 (December):160.
     The Green Years is a "simpler and less ambitious novel."

72   ROBINSON, TED. "Author of The Citadel Has New Tale." Cleveland Plain Dealer, 2 November, p. 8.
     Review of The Green Years. Calls the novel "original, human, humorous, obviously genuine."

73   ROTHMAN, NATHAN L. "A.J. Cronin Creates Robert Shannon." Saturday Review (London) 27 (18 November):22.
     Review of The Green Years. This novel is "rather a weak and tentative effort, lacking both the assurance and the dramatic outline which are generally characteristic of his work." Attributes this weakness to the hero's character, which has "none of the spirit of youth, none of the spine of maturity. He seems in fact to have been created expressly

to appeal to our least critical sentiments, a cautious, affecting little man of sugar and water, sweet and harmless,
no visible character." None of the characters is successful
or full of life.

74 S., M.B. "Boy's Story." New Orleans Picayune, 17 December,
    p. 5.
        Review of The Green Years. In this "comfortable" novel,
    Cronin is at his best in "the life of the spirit, in the
    psychology of the growing boy." Cronin shows understanding
    and insight in his depiction of an adolescent growing up.
    The characters surrounding the hero highlight his problems.

75 SELBY, JOHN. "Calls Cronin Book 'Most Rewarding' of All His
    Novels." Charlotte Observer, 19 November, p. 7.
        Reprint of 1944.76.

76 ____. "The Green Years by Dr. A.J. Cronin." Asheville (N.C.)
    Citizen, 19 November, p. 9.
        This is "a solid and justly proportioned novel." Shannon
    is a genuine character. Great-grandfather is endurable.
    Reprinted: 1944.75.

77 SIMS, MARIAN. "Myself When Young." Atlanta Journal, 19
    November, p. 3.
        Review of The Green Years. This would have been a better
    book if written in the third person point of view. Cronin
    has told a familiar story "without adding enough to make the
    book very interesting or very important."

78 SULLIVAN, ROBERT. "Well Worn Material Is Made Vital." Chicago
    Tribune, 12 November, p. 22.
        Review of The Green Years. Cronin uses familiar situa-
    tions in a way that are "new and fresh and satisfying." But
    in spite of this, "the writing is often blurry and weak,"
    filled with generalities. Sees possibilities for a sequel,
    however.

79 TAYLOR, HOWARD. "A Fine New Novel by A.J. Cronin." Philadelphia
    Inquirer, 5 November, p. 4.
        Review of The Green Years. Because Cronin is not crusad-
    ing for anything in this novel, finds it "the most convincing
    and the most worthwhile of all Dr. Cronin's novels."

80 TOWNEND, MARION. "New Cronin Novel Delightful Story of Orphan
    Youth." Charlotte Observer, 3 December, p. 15.
        Review of The Green Years. "A richly satisfying, sincere"
    story written as a combination of two points of view. "It is

1944

a record of young Robert Shannon but viewed nostalgically, half-objectively by the author-narrator."

81 VOILES, JANE. "A Purpose of Pity and Tenderness." San Francisco Chronicle, 26 November, p. 17.
Review of The Green Years. Hardly an objective study, this novel is "thinner in substance" than The Keys of the Kingdom. Cronin tells the story with that peculiar "tenderness that, at its worst verges on the sentimental and, at its best, reveals the universal qualities of suffering and hope."

82 WARE, HARLAN. "Cronin's Latest Novel Gleams with Integrity." Pasadena Star-News, 11 November, p. 6.
Review of The Green Years. Says that Cronin has produced "a work of the imagination which has in it the breath of life." Praises the author's integrity.

83 WERNER, HAZEN G. "Ideals of Adolescence Stormed by Adults." Dayton Journal-Herald, 31 December, p. 5.
Review of The Green Years. Says the book is an excellent account of the "ideals of adolescence stormed upon by an adult world that neither saw nor felt the inner hurts of a growing soul." Notes a similarity between Cronin's great-grandfather and Dickens's Macawber.

84 Z., R. "An Irish Child in Scotland." Hartford Courier, 19 November, p. 10.
Review of The Green Years. Cronin poignantly depicts childhood in "all its richness, joy and pain."

1945

1 ANON. "Between Book-Ends." Ontario (Calif.) Herald, 11 January, p. 4.
Cronin doesn't disappoint readers expecting a good story in The Green Years.

2 ANON. "Book-of-the-Month Club Dividend." Chelsea (Mass.) Record, 20 August, p. 4.
Cartoon depicting Cronin's early years and his experience writing The Green Years.

3 ANON. Review of The Green Years. Attleboro (Mass.) Sun, 6 February, p. 2.
Cronin tells Shannon's story with "insight and sincerity."

4 ANON. Review of The Green Years. Columbia (S.C.) State,

21 January, p. 6.
"It is a moving novel, but it also has humor and excitement."

5   ANON. Review of The Green Years. Detroit News, 25 February,
p. 15.
This is not Cronin's "best effort."

6   ANON. "The Innkeeper's Wife." St. Louis Globe, 28 December,
p. 3.
Review of Cronin's story which appeared recently in The
American Weekly. As expected the story is "warm and inspiring, and beautifully told." It imagines what might have
happened to the innkeeper and his wife, both of whom owned
the stable in which Christ was born.

7   B., M.H. Review of The Green Years. El Paso Times, 25 March,
p. 15.
"With something of the warm, sensitive penetration of
Richard Llewellyn's How Green Was My Valley, Mr. Cronin, in
delicate literary style that contradicts the vigor of the
life he portrays, tells the poignant story of Robert Shannon."
Cronin never lets his readers down in his depiction of "real
life, most richly portrayed."

8   BRÉGY, KATHERINE. "New Books." Catholic World 160 (January):
375.
Review of The Green Years. "It is a story for the mature
and sophisticated reader, told with artistry, verisimilitude
and the irony of the backward perspective."

9   F., M. Review of The Green Years. Charleston News, 11 February,
p. 5.
"The strength of Dr. Cronin's handling of his work (and
here he differs from many other authors) is that his men re-
main intact after the plunge. They are still the same indi-
viduals, though subject, like other live organisms, to
change, to degeneration or to triumphant growth."

10 FLETCHER, MARIE. "Book Review." Eugene Register Award,
31 August, p. 10.
Review of The Green Years. Sees similarities between
this novel and David Copperfield, Oliver Twist, Rob Roy and
Guy Mannering. The novel "plumbs the heights and depths of
human experience," just as does Beethoven's Fifth Symphony.

11 FREER, Rev. HAROLD WILEY. "Book Reviews by Westlake Pastor."
Lakewood (Ohio) Suburban News and Herald, 29 June, p. 11.

1945

Review of <u>The Green Years</u>. A weaker novel this time, Robert's days in school suggest similar scenes in <u>How Green Was My Valley</u>. The most serious weakness occurs when Robert turns against his religion. "Cronin here is writing as a Protestant outside of the Church whose imagination has gone beyond his reach. Nevertheless, this is yet another color-ful story by Cronin."

12 HOLLIS, EVA E. "Alien in Scotland . . . A New Cronin." <u>Salt Lake City Tribune</u>, 8 January, p. 2.
Review of <u>The Green Years</u>. Cronin reveals his characters with "fine artistry and the sharpness and sympathy with which boyhood's thoughts and problems are set forth might suggest something autobiographical in Robie's story." As in his other novels, we find here Cronin's "warm humanity, the pene-trative insight and sincerity of purpose."

13 McFEE, WILLIAM. "The Book of the Day: A.J. Cronin's New Novel Will Please His Audiences." <u>New York Sun</u>, 14 November, p. 9.
Review of <u>The Green Years</u>. Reading this, one wonders whether Cronin ever really gave up medicine. His religious theme is barely convincing. He is more convincing about science. <u>Hatter's Castle</u> announced the arrival of a major new novelist, but with his formula, Cronin "is seen as some-thing less than great."

14 PAIGE, MARY. "Mary Paige Reports." <u>Wickenburg Sun</u>, 18 January, p. 4.
Review of <u>The Green Years</u>. This is "a magnetic and com-pletely human story." The author's understanding of human frailties is sympathetic.

15 PRESCOTT, ORVILLE. "Outstanding Novels." <u>Yale Review</u> 34 (Winter):382-83.
Review of <u>The Green Years</u>. "Cronin writes clumsily, with-out originality or distinction of any kind." But there are qualities to his writing that redeem many of his shortcom-ings. These "have their source in Dr. Cronin's own character, his intimate knowledge of the troubles of life, his warm sympathy, his identity with almost universal human experience. . . . Dr. Cronin writes of life the way the average intel-ligent reader feels it to be."

16 RINKER, MAXINE. "Books." <u>Hermosa Beach</u> (Calif.) <u>Review</u>, March, p. 2.
Review of <u>The Green Years</u>. "Here Cronin is at his best in depicting the spiritual conflict that precedes maturity, and Robert's story is an appealing one."

17 VASSALO, CAROL. "Books of the Week." Arcadia (Calif.) Tribune,
    22 February, p. 3.
        Review of The Green Years. "In spite of the unhappy in-
    cidents that are a part of Robert's growing up, the book is
    not a sad one, owing to the flashes of real humor which run
    through the story."

                            1946

1   ANON. "Book Notes." Hayward (Calif.) Review, 17 August, p. 6.
    Brief mention of The Green Years.

2   ANON. "Cronin Arrives." New York Times, 1 December, p. 26.
    Cronin arrives to make his home in Connecticut.

3   ANON. "Senior High Group." Catholic Messenger, 5 December,
    p. 3.
        Review of The Green Years. An "interesting, enrapturing
    and heart warming" story. In this novel Cronin equals all
    of his other books. "He is forthright in portraying his
    characters, bringing to light both good and bad qualities.
    He shows his deep understanding of human nature by not mere-
    ly judging from Robie's exterior behavior, but looking into
    his heart to find the motives that actuate his conduct.
    Definitely one of the best boyhood novels ever written."

4   ANON. "This Week's Reprints." New York Post, 2 May, p. 6.
        Reprint announcement of The Green Years. The novel is
    "obvious in plot, but honest, unaffected and full of charm
    and warmth."

                            1947

1   ANON. "A.J. Cronin." Philadelphia Bulletin, 23 February, p.
    2.
        Cronin often works from 9 A.M. until midnight, like
    Sinclair Lewis.

2   O., P. "Archibald Joseph Cronin." Catholic Authors:
    Contemporary Biographical Sketches 1930-1947. Edited by
    Matt Hoehn. Newark: St. Mary's Abbey, pp. 175-76.
        Biographical background through The Keys of the Kingdom.

3   WILLIAMINA, Sister M., S.S.J. "When Fiction Invades the
    Convent." San Francisco Monitor, 1 February, p. 9.
        Studies the history of the treatment of nuns in fiction,

1947

including a mention of their "unfortunate treatment" in The
Keys of the Kingdom. Cronin has made Mother Maria Veronica
"almost into an agent of deviltry." It is clear that this
treatment violates "the canons of art and truth."

1948

1   ADKINS, SAM. "Cronin's Orphan Grows Up." Louisville Courier-
     Journal, 1 August, p. 3.
          Review of Shannon's Way. The novel is far too similar
     to Arrowsmith, but "without the power of Sinclair Lewis'
     writing." Notes that this is supposed to be a sequel to
     The Green Years, and that "it lives up to the old saw that
     no really great story has had an adequate sequel."

2   AHEARNE, DANIEL E. "English Arrowsmith." Hartford Courant,
     18 July, p. 5.
          Review of Shannon's Way. Calls this another "pleasantly
     light and readable tale," but one which will add nothing to
     Cronin's stature as a writer.

3   ALBRIGHT, LETTY. "Another Novel." Little Rock Gazette,
     10 October, p. 7.
          Review of Shannon's Way. That this book is a best seller
     indicates that "the reading taste of the general public is
     on the decline." Says that Cronin has "sold his birthright
     for a mess of pottage."

4   ANDERSON, BETT. "A.J. Cronin's Somber Portrait of Knight in
     White." Philadelphia Inquirer, 18 July, p. 11.
          Review of Shannon's Way. Cronin's anger, first to sur-
     face in The Citadel, appears once again. "Stupidity, pro-
     fessional jealousy, intolerance, red tape in life-and-death
     matters--these are the human frailties alleged and deplored
     again by a man of words who happens also to be a man of medi-
     cine." Questions the reason for choosing such "dreary" stock
     characters, but admits that this problem is offset by the
     author's ability to build drama and intensity. Given its
     subject, however, it would be hard to find "a more depressing
     portrait of the human race."

5   ANON. "A.J. Cronin's Latest Novel is Shannon's Way." Vallejo
     (Calif.) Times-Herald, 25 July, p. 4.
          Although Cronin once again writes well of the problems
     and life of his doctor-hero, the thin plot and unrealistic
     characters result in "a mere pot-boiler tossed off by a
     writer who has done many superior jobs."

1948

6   ANON. "A Summer Mixture: Saarinen May Be Caviar, but Cronin
     and Paul Are Plain Fare." Boston Globe, 21 July, p. 5.
          Review of Shannon's Way. This novel has all the earmarks
     of a best seller: it is about a doctor, it is a love story,
     it has a happy ending, it is "a self-contained sequel" to
     The Green Years, and "it requires no effort on the part of
     the reader."

7   ANON. "Books: Briefly Noted: Fiction." New Yorker 24
     (31 July):61.
          Review of Shannon's Way. "Dr. Cronin's mediocre attempt
     to exploit a truth he laid bare, possibly inadvertently,
     some ten years ago, with the publication of The Citadel--
     that the doctor as fictional hero has a great way with the
     reading public."

8   ANON. "Books: Public Library: Fiction." Berlin (N.H.)
     Reporter, 29 July, p. 4.
          Review of Shannon's Way. Comments on Cronin's abilities
     as a storyteller and his "sympathetic understanding of human
     frailties and emotions."

9   ANON. "Browsings from Parlin Library." Everett (Mass.) News-
     Gazette, 29 July, p. 11.
          Review of Shannon's Way. Notes the contrast between this
     novel and The Citadel, in which the hero is tempted by mate-
     rial success. Says that Cronin is "an excellent storyteller.
     His characters are well drawn and he shows a deep understand-
     ing of human nature and human emotions."

10   ANON. "Cronin Almost Missed Becoming Famous Author." Charlotte
     Observer, 4 July, p. 2.
          Reviews how Cronin became an author and mentions the
     forthcoming publication of Shannon's Way. Reprinted:
     1948.27.

11   ANON. "Cronin on His Methods." Little Rock Gazette, 8 August,
     p. 5.
          Excerpt from 1948.38.

12   ANON. "Cronin's New Doctor Story." Newark Evening News,
     20 July, p. 6.
          Review of Shannon's Way. Cronin's power as a storyteller
     is obvious from the beginning in a novel that is less compli-
     cated in plot, character and theme than earlier works. In
     one respect Cronin has added "a fresh element that lends the
     story he tells genuine interest"--the hero is a research
     assistant.

1948

13   ANON. "Engrossing and Fine Story." <u>Boston Herald</u>, 21 July,
       p. 5.
           Brief plot summary of <u>Shannon's Way</u>. Comments on the
       abundance of difficulties facing the hero.

14   ANON. "Fiction." <u>Booklist</u> 44 (17 July):373, 384.
           Brief mention of <u>Shannon's Way</u>. Finds "less agonizing"
       here than in <u>The Green Years</u>.

15   ANON. "Fiction." <u>Kirkus Reviews</u> 16 (15 May):239.
           Review of <u>Shannon's Way</u>. "Dr. Shannon is an oddly prick-
       ly individual; he tells his own story, and neither in his
       own telling nor in the reactions of others in his story does
       one feel any warmth of affection, scarcely even liking for
       him." This is one of Cronin's "lesser efforts."

16   ANON. "Fiction." <u>Oakland Tribune</u>, 18 June, p. 6.
           Review of <u>Shannon's Way</u>. Comments on "the course of sci-
       ence as well as the course of true love" in this new novel.

17   ANON. "Good Enough but Too Late." <u>Sacramento Union</u>, 7 November,
       p. 2.
           Review of <u>Shannon's Way</u>. The story suffers from having
       been told all too often. "Cronin can write, but it is too
       bad that the man who produced <u>The Keys of the Kingdom</u> and
       <u>The Citadel</u> didn't write this story 17 years ago"--when he
       was a doctor in the West End of London but vacationing in
       Scotland.

18   ANON. "<u>Green Years</u> Again." <u>Charlotte Observer</u>, 8 August,
       p. 3.
           Review of <u>Shannon's Way</u>. Lacks the "rich, Scotch-broth
       atmosphere which endeared <u>The Green Years</u> to so many readers."
       Because Cronin's world is "a good world," the reader knows
       from the beginning that the hero will attain a successful
       career and marry the heroine.

19   ANON. "Guild Chooses Cronin." <u>Pittsburgh Press</u>, 2 May, p. 2.
           <u>Shannon's Way</u> has been chosen by the Literary Guild for
       its August selection.

20   ANON. "Illness Proved Boon." <u>St. Petersburg Times</u>, 1 August,
       p. 4.
           Biographical background. Printing order for <u>Shannon's
       Way</u> has reached 800,000 copies.

21   ANON. "Medicine and Morals." <u>Times Literary Supplement</u>
       (London), 23 October, p. 593.

Review of <u>Shannon's Way</u>. "Dr. Cronin's competent new novel is reminiscent of nothing so much as the act of a once-promising variety artist whose performance has staled with repetition."

22 ANON. "Medic's Career in Coming Novel." <u>Chicago News</u>, 2 June, p. 5.
    Observes that Cronin's early medical career helped him to write <u>Shannon's Way</u>. Excerpt from 1948.38.

23 ANON. "Mostly Trade." <u>New York Herald-Tribune</u>, 18 April, p. 11.
    Brief mention that <u>Shannon's Way</u> will be the August selection of the Literary Guild.

24 ANON. "New Books for Fall Reading." <u>Sacramento Bee</u>, 4 September, p. 10.
    Review of <u>Shannon's Way</u>. Although this novel lacks the "depth and penetration" of his earlier works, "it is an absorbing story." Feels that this is a "tender and genuine love story" as well.

25 ANON. "New Cronin Book Relates Doctor's Bitter Struggles." <u>Oakland Tribune</u>, 25 July, p. 6.
    Review of <u>Shannon's Way</u>. Notes similarities and differences between this novel and Sinclair Lewis's <u>Arrowsmith</u>. "But it is simply impossible to worry over much. Although you feel for young Shannon in his trials and tribulations you never doubt in his darkest hours that a happy ending is just around the corner."

26 ANON. "Novels for Summer Reading." <u>Quincy</u> (Mass.) <u>Patriot Ledger</u>, 26 July, p. 9.
    Review of <u>Shannon's Way</u>. Like the earlier novels, this is "an inspiring reading experience." Unlike the hero of <u>The Citadel</u>, Robert Shannon is not tempted by material success.

27 ANON. "Of Books and Men." <u>Brooklyn Daily Eagle</u>, 11 July, p. 2.
    Reprint of 1948.10.

28 ANON. "Research for Life." <u>Atlantic Monthly</u> 182 (August):100, 102.
    In both <u>The Citadel</u> and <u>Shannon's Way</u>, Cronin blends the knowledge of "a practitioner and the skill of a dramatist." Rates the latter as the best book yet because "in it those forces which have formed his writing--his church, his

1948

dedication to medicine, and his humble Scotch upbringing--
combine to give deep feeling and authenticity to his story
of a struggling young biologist." Concludes that the author
"writes with the sure touch of sympathy. Injustice and intolerance, man-made and enforced by profession or church--
these are the themes which find such human expression in
his story."

29   ANON. "Research Lab." Atlanta Journal, 25 July, p. 3.
Review of Shannon's Way. From his material Cronin has
written "a highly effective and expert novel. He tells his
story with admirable facility and feeling."

30   ANON. "Reviewers on Library." Attleboro (Mass.) Sun, 5 August,
p. 4.
Review of Shannon's Way. This novel goes back to the
"mood and tempo" of his earlier novels. Finds an "old-
fashioned sort of aura" which many readers may enjoy.

31   ANON. Review of Shannon's Way. Chicago Rotarian (November),
p. 2.
Comments on Cronin's sincerity, genuine feeling for his
characters, and authority. Shannon seems "excessively stupid" at times, and the resolution is "somewhat artificial."

32   ANON. Review of Shannon's Way. Christian Century 65
(3 November):1177.
"Cronin is one of the very few contemporary novelists
whose stories this reviewer regularly takes time to read
for pleasure and profit, not as an onerous professional
duty." Summarizes the plots of both The Green Years and
Shannon's Way.

33   ANON. Review of Shannon's Way. Christian Science Monitor,
5 August, p. 6.
The author displays his usual gift for "facile storytelling and characterization."

34   ANON. Review of Shannon's Way. Los Angeles Examiner, 24 July,
p. 5.
This novel will "arouse enthusiasm" equal to that accorded
The Citadel and The Keys of the Kingdom. Reprinted: 1948.35.

35   ANON. Review of Shannon's Way. San Francisco Examiner, 24 July,
p. 6.
Reprint of 1948.34.

36   ANON. Review of Shannon's Way. Sign, August, p. 11.

Finds this to be "the thinnest and most mechanical" of Cronin's novels. Comments on its conventional development, its predictable plot, its "overpowering" coincidences, and its stereotype characters.

37   ANON. "Shannon's Way Leads." Columbia (S.C.) State, 22 August, p. 4.
     Shannon's Way has sold the most copies of any Literary Guild selection in 1948.

38   ANON. "Shannon's Way: The August Selection by Dr. A.J. Cronin." Literary Guild Wings (August), pp. 1-3, 5-7.
     Includes plot summary, biographical background, and Cronin's comments on how he came to write the novel and how he developed his central characters. Also includes a comment by his wife on what it is like to live and travel with the writer. Excerpted: 1948.11, 22, 55, 106.

39   ANON. "Sure-Fire Cronin." Book-of-the-Month Club News (July), p. 4.
     Review of Shannon's Way. The combination of "medicine and true love is an effective formula for success, and results in a smooth, romantic novel which will please the Cronin public."

40   ANON. "The Bookseller's Almanac." Retail Bookseller, July, p. 15.
     Review of Shannon's Way. This novel "seems to have the qualities that make for success even in an unknown author, and A.J. Cronin is far from unknown."

41   B., M.H. Review of Shannon's Way. El Paso Times, 1 August, p. 3.
     "Mr. Cronin has a knack of taking his readers straight into [a story] with an honesty and insistence on detail that is most effective." But perhaps readers would like a bit less emphasis on uncertainty and hard times.

42   BEAUCHAMP, ELISE. "Literature and Less." New Orleans Times-Picayune, 18 July, p. 8.
     Review of Shannon's Way. Shannon is more confident here, in a way that makes us proud of him. Except for Jean Law, the women lack charm.

43   BELL, LISLE. "Books and Things." New York Herald-Tribune Books, 16 November, p. 4.
     Review of The Green Years. "The bridge of understanding between children and their environment--parents, assorted

1948

aunts and uncles, neighbors and teachers and what not--is
held only by saints and simpletons, by people so very old
that they are trusted by the very young, and by writers like
Dr. Cronin, whose novel is so sympathetic a link with childhood that it suggests--though this is merely a guess--chap-
ters of autobiography."

44   BERNE, HENRY. Review of Shannon's Way. Cincinnati Enquirer,
     17 July, p. 7.
       Calls this another "pleasant and readable" novel.

45   BILLINGS, F.T. "Selfless Life of Research." Nashville Banner,
     3 September, p. 9.
       Review of Shannon's Way. Cronin highlights "the discour-
agement, depressions, stresses and strains, and rare moments
of ecstasy" which are an inevitable part of the researcher's
life. Several of the minor characters are "unforgettable."
The novel will be read with sympathy and interest by "doctors who will perhaps remember some of their own earlier
aspirations, strivings and disappointments."

46   BLOOM, ELEANOR M. "Cronin's Dr. Shannon Takes Second Series
     of Hurdles." Minneapolis Tribune, 18 July, p. 10.
       Review of Shannon's Way. Lacks the "passion and compas-
sion" which made Hatter's Castle and The Stars Look Down
exceptional reading experiences, but Cronin has once again
"demonstrated his ability to take rather threadbare materials
and work them into a neat, often intriguing pattern."

47   BOND, ALICE DIXON. "The Case for Books." Boston Herald,
     21 July, p. 18.
       Review of Shannon's Way. Cronin's novel is refreshing.
It lacks the verbosity, introspection and vulgarity of so
much current fiction.

48   BONNER, WILLARD HALLAM. "Cronin Has a New Novel, Young Doctor
     Again the Hero." Buffalo Evening News, 31 July, p. 7.
       Review of Shannon's Way. Calls this an "out-and-out eye-
wash, but people seem to like it. And at least it can be
said that Cronin does no harm."

49   BREIT, HARVEY. "Books of the Times." New York Times, 19 July,
     p. 17.
       Review of Shannon's Way. Contains the ingredients of
both "good art and good commerce." The structure is "tried
and true," but the texture is "instinctive and very much Dr.
Cronin's own, and it is this that salvages Dr. Cronin's work,
as well as raises it above the level of the slickly

constructed, magnificently manufactured best-selling novel."
On one level, the novel offers an identical esthetic experience to reading Pluck and Luck or Work and Win or any Horatio
Alger tale. But there is also in the novel "an earnestness
in the author's narrative that gives it a sincere moral tone
and brings to the conflict of good and evil and concreteness,
a credibility, a sense that the narrator himself believes in
the momentousness of the conflict." His style is somewhat
reminiscent of Charles Dickens or Robert Louis Stevenson.
"Dr. Cronin's view is essentially romantic and idealistic."

50   BUCK, DORIS P. "Novel Moves with Speed of Comic Strip."
      Richmond Times-Dispatch, 1 August, p. 5.
            Review of Shannon's Way. The novel moves with the "speed
      and unfortunately the obviousness of a comic strip." The
      subplot itself could make an interesting novel.

51   BULLOCK, FLORENCE HAXTON. "Ambition Against Idealism." New
      York Herald-Tribune Books, 18 July, pt. vii, p. 4.
            Review of Shannon's Way. This is "a gentle book, sweetly
      conceived and written, designed to give a special, abiding
      joy to the pure in heart. To them I unreservedly commend
      it."

52   BURKE, HARRY R. "Hero's Way Lies through Morass of Self-Pity."
      St. Louis Globe-Democrat, 18 July, p. 6.
            Review of Shannon's Way. Finds missing in these pages
      the "warm humanism" of The Keys of the Kingdom. Says that
      "coincidence often serves as substitute for character. But
      a pleasingly readable style remains in a novel which will be
      widely read but is not likely to add to Dr. Cronin's reputa-
      tion."

53   BURKE, JAMES. "A.J. Cronin's Latest Novel Resembles The Green
      Years." Globe and Mail (Toronto), 17 July, p. 13.
            Review of Shannon's Way. This is the product of Cronin's
      highly popular, if simple, formula. "A young, sensitive,
      idealistic doctor with a passion for his science and a love-
      ly, wholesome girl with a real old-fashioned conscience are
      played against a rather depressing background." A bit of
      sex, a touch of spirituality is included. On reflection the
      reader realizes that Cronin has "dexterously avoided commit-
      ting himself on any of the very real issues raised. What he
      is trying to say is, let us be kind to one another."

54   BURNS, GEORGE V. "Cronin's New Novel Is Disappointing As Author
      Fails to Solve His Problem." Cleveland Press, 20 July, p. 7.
            Review of Shannon's Way. The story is unsatisfying because

1948

so many questions are left unanswered. "The ending gives
the impression that he decided to get it over with before
he got more involved."

55 BUTCHER, FANNY. "The Literary Spotlight." Chicago Tribune,
    18 July, p. 4.
        Biographical background. Cronin comments on the origin
    of Shannon's Way and his preoccupations as a writer. In-
    cludes excerpt from 1948.38.

56 CHRISMAN, LEWIS H. Review of Shannon's Way. Christian Advocate,
    26 August, p. 12.
        Cronin possesses "unusual skill both in depicting char-
    acter and in telling a story."

57 CLARAGE, ELEANOR. "Young Doctor Is Hero of New Cronin Novel."
    Cleveland Plain Dealer, 18 July, p. 5.
        Review of Shannon's Way. The hero's rejuvenation by the
    end of the novel seems implausible. However, this is pleas-
    ant summertime reading.

58 COMBA, MAY A. "New Books at the Town Library: Book Reviews."
    Milford (Mass.) News, 24 July, p. 6.
        Review of Shannon's Way. In this novel Cronin calls upon
    "his extraordinary abilities as a storyteller and his sympa-
    thetic understanding of human frailties and emotions."

59 COMMAGERE, RUTH. "The Book Corner." Crestline (Calif.) Courier,
    24 December, p. 3.
        Review of Shannon's Way. Cronin's characters are "realis-
    tic and believable." This is "a quiet and peaceful novel,
    although it is a story of struggle and discouragement before
    the end." But Shannon's persistence and courage carry him
    on.

60 COMPTON, NEIL M. "Exploited Myths." Gazette (Montreal),
    24 July, p. 8.
        Review of Shannon's Way. The novel is "a cliché, an ex-
    pertly manufactured product which does not contain one real
    character, one convincing scene, or one original idea."

61 CONNOLLY, FRANCIS X. "Literary Guild--August Selection."
    Best Sellers 8 (1 August):97-98.
        Review of Shannon's Way. Cronin's novel is obviously
    made for the screen. The themes are "simple, generous, ex-
    pansive." Add to them his powerful characters and vivid
    atmosphere, and it is not difficult to explain "why Dr.
    Cronin is a very popular novelist." His defects, however,

are easy to overlook. "The thinking of his main characters is an almost perfect reflection of popular moral sentiment." Noting that this is essentially a tragic story, we must conclude that Cronin has not "condoned immoral actions, but he has connived with a sentimental attitude in which human weakness is at once a forgivable evil and an artistic advantage."

62   CORCORAN, MARGUERITE PAGE. "New Books." Catholic World 167 (August):474-75.
     Review of Shannon's Way. "In Shannon's maturity the way is so dark and full of obstacles that only our admiration for his dogged perseverance justifies the journey at all."

63   COURNOS, JOHN. "Scotch Physician Has a Run of Hard Luck." Philadelphia Bulletin, 18 July, p. 5.
     Review of Shannon's Way. Its merits lie in the authentic experiences from real life and in Cronin's "ability to get the most out of touching human situations, fraught with drama."

64   CRUME, MARION. "Cronin's New Novel Has Doctor as Hero." Dallas News (18 July), p. 11.
     Review of Shannon's Way. Although not a challenging book, the novel does have its commendable qualities. It is "an unpretentious story, without literary ambitions, yet enjoyable and filled with action and suspense built around common, ordinary problems."

65   deC., R.M. "Manufactured Doctor." Providence Journal, 18 July, p. 5.
     Review of Shannon's Way. Unlike The Stars Look Down and The Keys of the Kingdom, this is a "manufactured" novel. Finds the style to be "stilted and somewhat old-fashioned." The romance has "a quality of Victorian sentimentality."

66   DEDMON, EMMETT. "Lonely Research Scientist Is Hero of New Cronin Novel." Chicago Sun, 18 July, p. 8.
     Review of Shannon's Way. Has all of the qualities that have made Cronin's previous novels so popular. The climax comes with the same drama and satisfaction that marks the conclusion of James Hilton's Random Harvest.

67   DERLETH, AUGUST. "Books of Today." Madison Capital Times, 3 September, p. 39.
     Review of Shannon's Way. This novel has all of the elements that have made Cronin's earlier works a success. Says Gregory Peck should play the hero.

1948

68   DEVER, JOSEPH. "Dr. Cronin's New Prescription." <u>Milwaukee
      Journal</u>, 18 July, p. 10.
            Review of <u>Shannon's Way</u>. Another "carefully plotted,
      melodramatic" novel in which we see Cronin at both his best
      and his worst. Praises the "gift of phrase," the Dickensian
      insight into character, and the compassion for the "unjustly
      exploited and underprivileged people." But criticizes
      Cronin's "facile sentimentality."

69   DORE, EDRIE VAN. "Humanness Saves Novel by Cronin." <u>Hartford
      Times</u>, 31 July, p. 4.
            Review of <u>Shannon's Way</u>. Cronin's novels are becoming
      "increasingly romantic, almost trite, but they have not the
      fairy-tale quality which makes some popular novelists hard
      to swallow." The novel is saved from banality, however, by
      "the freshness of its scenes and backgrounds, its obvious
      sincerity, and its delicate perception of the sympathies,
      motives and affections of its characters."

70   GARDINER, HAROLD C. "Books: Alger and/or Dickens?" <u>America</u>
      105 (31 July):15.
            Review of <u>Shannon's Way</u>. This is but an episode, for
      there are at least ten more books ahead "if Shannon's way
      is to lead to a rounded-tale of his life." The convincing
      sentiment we find in Dickens is just missed here. With his
      gifts as a storyteller, Cronin is "getting perilously close
      to Alger." Feels that "although all Cronin's stories are
      of a pattern--that of the hero against the universe, or at
      least any organized segments of it--this tale is his poorest
      to date."

71   GEISMAR, MAXWELL. "Books and Things." <u>New York Herald-Tribune
      Books</u>, 24 July, p. 17.
            Review of <u>Shannon's Way</u>. Says this is at least fifty
      years behind the times, "written out of the heart of the
      nineteenth century." Cronin's way is simply that of "Kings,
      Numbers, and Deuteronomy, of simple virtues and sparse plea-
      sures in an almost changeless environment of individual effort
      and immutable rewards." Cronin consistently substitutes
      "romance for reality." Although thinner than earlier novels,
      within its framework of values the book has both "insight and
      grace."

72   GRAY, JAMES. "Author Cronin's Bound to Make Hero Suffer."
      <u>Chicago News</u>, 28 July, p. 6.
            Review of <u>Shannon's Way</u>. Cronin seems to have written
      this novel in "a mood of fatalistic gloom." Finds the love
      affair to be "one of the most bleak and dismal in all the
      history of fiction." This is a "low water mark" for Cronin.

100

1948

73 GREEN, MARION A. "One Man's Fight Against Failure." Louisville
    Times, 6 August, p. 5.
        Review of Shannon's Way. A "somber book" filled with
    feeling for the weaknesses and triumphs of his protagonists.

74 H., D. Review of Shannon's Way. Telegram (Toronto), 27
    November, p. 2.
        As satisfying as the earlier novels, this work is written
    with strong characters and a sympathy for human frailties.

75 H., V.P. "'Sequel' to The Green Years Is a Distressingly Poor
    Novel." Omaha World Herald, 25 July, p. 18.
        Review of Shannon's Way. This is a synopsis for a novel,
    and a poor one at that. It is written "without humor, grace
    or saving honesty." The characters are one-dimensional and
    the background is "useless." The writing is cliché-ridden.

76 HANSEN, HARRY. "Brooklyn Plans Ballyhoo for Betty Smith's New
    Novel." Newark News, 8 August, p. 3.
        Brief mention that Cronin draws on his years in Scotland
    and writes in Connecticut.

77 H[ANSEN], H[ARRY]. "Cronin Extends Religious, Moral Issues in
    New Book." Indianapolis Times, 24 July, p. 10.
        Review of Shannon's Way. Cronin has always been aware
    of the importance of moral and religious themes. In this
    novel, he combines these themes with that of the doctor.

78 HARRIS, FOSTER. "Plot Is Old, Nicely Told." Oklahoma City
    Oklahoman, 29 August, p. 6.
        Review of Shannon's Way. Like James Hilton, this author
    knows "how to make the very seeming artlessness of his story
    telling carry a charm of its own." Certainly not one of
    Cronin's best efforts, however.

79 HORAN, KENNETH. "Book Marks: Very Dour Doctor: Fun with
    Titles." Dallas Times Herald, 22 August, p. 12.
        Review of Shannon's Way. Dislikes the overwhelming gloom
    in this novel. Recalls meeting Cronin at a luncheon in
    Chicago. Cronin explained how he hated America. He refused
    to sign any books until after he had his cup of tea. Calls
    him an "extremely reserved and cynical gentleman."

80 HYERS, FAITH HOLMES. "English Doctor Tries to Isolate Influenza
    Bug: Weird Tale of Secret Irish Army." Los Angeles News,
    31 July, p. 8.
        Plot summary of Shannon's Way.

1948

81 HYNES, BEATRICE. Review of Shannon's Way. Indianapolis Star,
      18 July, p. 13.
         His earlier works were Dickensian in flavor, but lately
      he has written with the screen in mind. He writes with
      "clarity and understanding of the work of the young research-
      er." This novel is a "rich tale in characterization and in-
      sight, but those who are forced to miss it can undoubtedly
      see an emasculated version at the neighborhood movie house
      soon."

82 JACKSON, KATHERINE GAUSS. "Books in Brief: Fiction." Harpers
      197 (September):126.
         Review of Shannon's Way. This is a "pleasant diversion,"
      thinner than his other novels. Contrasts the novel to Graham
      Greene's The Heart of the Matter and concludes: "Where Mr.
      Greene shows good and evil, love and hate, happiness and un-
      happiness for what they are, the complicated, un-simple mys-
      teries of the heart and spirit, in Mr. Cronin's hands they
      come out as smooth, one-dimensional, and sickeningly sweet
      to the taste."

83 JONES, CARTER BROOKE. "Dr. A.J. Cronin Rings the Bell for
      Hollywood." Washington (D.C.) Star, 18 July, p. 5.
         Shannon's Way moves easily along "tried-and-true" lines.
      Its closing is sentimental. It should make a most success-
      ful movie.

84 KIRBY, W.J. "New Cronin Novel." Rochester Democrat Chronicle,
      15 August, p. 5.
         Review of Shannon's Way. Wishes that Cronin had included
      "lovable qualities" in the hero. Misses the idealism found
      in the earlier characters. We are left with the feeling that
      by marrying the hero, Jean Law is headed for unhappiness.

85 M., W.J., Jr. "Literary Guild's August Selection." Montgomery
      Advertiser, 8 August, p. 1.
         Review of Shannon's Way. This is "a moving, completely
      satisfying novel and one worthy of taking its place along-
      side its illustrious Cronin predecessors."

86 McFEE, WILLIAM. "Cronin Novel about Doctor Is Finest Work of
      Author." Youngstown Vindicator, 25 July, p. 3.
         Review of Shannon's Way. Technically, this is Cronin's
      finest novel, but it "missed by a notch or two being the
      book this reviewer hopes Dr. Cronin will write. Like J.B.
      Priestley, he makes us admire his facility, and exasperates
      us because he is not better."

87 McGAREY, MARY. "Medical Researcher's Hard 'Way.'" Columbus
    (Ohio) Dispatch, 18 July, p. 4.
        Review of Shannon's Way. "His writing is compelling;
    his descriptions of persons, scenes and situations graphic
    and exciting."

88 MANNING, OLIVIA. "Fiction." Spectator 181 (15 October):506.
        Review of Shannon's Way. Cronin has nothing new to tell
    us. His characters lack anything to make them three-dimen-
    sional.

89 MARRIOTT, CHARLES. "Novels." Manchester Guardian, 15 October,
    p. 3.
        Review of Shannon's Way. Brief plot summary and focus
    on character delineation and atmosphere.

90 MEYERS, LAURA SCOTT. "The Book Shelf." El Paso Herald-Post,
    3 July, p. 3.
        Review of Shannon's Way. In this "sincere and arresting"
    novel, Dr. Cronin is concerned with the conflict in religious
    beliefs, but "only as it forms an impediment to happiness in
    marriage."

91 MILES, GEORGE. "Books." Commonweal 48 (27 August):479-80.
        Review of Shannon's Way. In this "unlikely tale," we
    find more "startled glances, involuntary gasps, slowly mount-
    ing blushes and sullen stares of defiance than you can find
    in forty-three motion pictures, 1920 style."

92 MUNN, L.S. Review of Shannon's Way. Springfield (Mass.)
    Republican, 25 July, p. 15A.
        Brief plot summary.

93 MURPHREE, ALEX. "The A.J. Cronin Phenomenon: Researcher and
    Medical Student Struggle Toward Final Reunion." Denver Post,
    1 August, p. 7.
        Review of Shannon's Way. Beyond his skills as a story-
    teller Cronin's success is a result of his selection of ma-
    terial. "His stories are built up of the universals of human
    living, of struggle, disappointment, love, success, failure--
    the quiet life stuff which everyone experiences."

94 N., R.D. "Shannon's Way." Lewiston (Maine) Sun, 4 August,
    p. 5.
        A "superbly written" novel with a sense of reality only
    a doctor could give to it. No character is comparable to
    Cadger Gow in The Green Years, however, although Jean Law
    is "the most piquant and charming of Cronin's heroes."

1948

95   NATHAN, PAUL S. "Books into Films." <u>Publishers Weekly</u> 153
(22 May):2175.
    Since <u>The Citadel</u>, Cronin has been popular with Hollywood
studios. Now <u>Shannon's Way</u> is getting a lot of attention.
<u>Jupiter Laughs</u>, however, was "something of a mistake" because
the play didn't offer much to build on. $300,000 is report-
edly being asked for <u>Shannon's Way</u>.

96   NAYLOR, PAULINE. "<u>Shannon's Way</u> Gripping Sequel to <u>The Green
Years</u>." <u>Fort Worth Star</u>, 1 August, p. 8.
    The Dickensian qualities noticeable in Cronin's earlier
novels are more than ever apparent in this novel of poverty,
burning ambition, and ineptness. As in <u>The Keys of the
Kingdom</u>, Cronin uses "heartbreak and adversity to tell an
absorbing story of human frailties."

97   NORTH, STERLING. "A.J. Cronin's Arrowsmith Has a Burr."
<u>Washington</u> (D.C.) <u>Post</u>, 18 July, p. 9.
    Review of <u>Shannon's Way</u>. In theme and plot, this novel
is similar to Sinclair Lewis's <u>Arrowsmith</u>. Cronin's work
"bears the quiet authority of a man who knows both medicine
and storytelling." Reprinted: 1948.98-99.

98   _____. "Scotch <u>Arrowsmith</u>." <u>Columbus</u> (Ohio) <u>Citizen</u>, 25 July,
p. 4.
    Reprint of 1948.97.

99   _____. "Today's Book: Dr. Cronin's Scotch <u>Arrowsmith</u>." <u>New
York Post</u>, 19 July, p. 10.
    Reprint of 1948.97.

100   O., O. "<u>Shannon's Way</u>." <u>Boston Post</u>, 25 July, p. 8.
    This novel is "less dramatic" than the others, and
"crowded with medical terms that may annoy some of his
readers." However, his wonderful characters, profound understanding of human nature, warmth and sincerity "was never
more evident." Calls Cronin "a solid bulwark in the chaotic
literary world."

101   O'DELL, SCOTT. "Publishers Go Down Fighting As Los Angeles
Comes of Age; Birds Grow Claws Like Badgers." <u>Los Angeles
News</u>, 14 August, p. 12.
    Brief mention of <u>Shannon's Way</u>. The pre-publication
printing was the largest for any novel in 1948.

102   P., A.H. Review of <u>Shannon's Way</u>. <u>Brockton</u> (Mass.) <u>Enterprise</u>,
3 August, p. 7.
    Cronin continues to be a "competent story teller," but
this novel fails to reach the heights of <u>The Citadel</u>.

103   P., F. "New Offerings in America: Cronin Scores New Success
        in Latest Novel." <u>Lewiston-Auburn</u> (Maine) <u>Journal</u>, 28 August,
        p. 11.
            Review of <u>Shannon's Way</u>. Finds in Cronin's work the "same
        sort of life" that one finds in the novels of Hardy and
        Galsworthy. Finds in his new novel "flesh-and-blood" people.

104   P., M. "The Doctor in Scotland." <u>Worcester</u> (Mass.) <u>Telegram</u>,
        18 July, p. 6.
            Review of <u>Shannon's Way</u>. Cronin draws on his life for
        background material in this novel, but the plot itself and
        the internal struggles of its main characters are fictional.
        This is a book of many characters with whom the reader can
        identify.

105   P., U. "A.J. Cronin's New Novel 'Not Up to Earlier Books.'"
        <u>Hollywood Citizen News</u>, 24 July, p. 5.
            Calls <u>Shannon's Way</u> "a mere pot-boiler tossed off by a
        writer who has done many superior jobs."

106   PASCONE, TERE. "A.J. Cronin, Who Gave Up Successful Career in
        Medicine So He Could Write <u>The Keys of the Kingdom</u>, Other
        Great Books, Now Lives in Beautiful New Canaan." <u>Bridgeport
        Post</u>, 11 April, p. 3.
            Review of <u>Shannon's Way</u>. This is Cronin's first romantic
        novel. Includes plot summary and excerpts from 1948.38.

107   PAULUS, JOHN D. "Cronin Combines Salesmanship with Art in
        <u>Shannon's Way</u>." <u>Pittsburgh Press</u>, 17 July, p. 4.
            Labels this "an entertaining, well-written, and well-
        constructed novel from the literary point of view." The
        fundamental theme is that people should be more tolerant of
        others.

108   PRAY, WALDO. "Another A.J. Cronin Novel of a Doctor."
        <u>Portland</u> (Maine) <u>Telegram</u>, 18 July, p. 7.
            Review of <u>Shannon's Way</u>. Complains about the tragic in-
        cidents and the sudden change of events at the end.

109   PRESSON, MARY EXLEY. "Oft-Wounded Knight: A.J. Cronin Creates
        More Masterly Misery." <u>Cleveland News</u>, 21 July, p. 4.
            Review of <u>Shannon's Way</u>. The only shortcoming of this
        book is "the uncommon piling on of disaster" that the hero
        experiences. The story is also "thin" compared to <u>Hatter's
        Castle</u>, <u>The Keys of the Kingdom</u>, and <u>The Citadel</u>.

110   REELY, MARY KATHERINE. "New Books: Fiction." <u>Wisconsin
        Library Bulletin</u> 44 (September):149.
            <u>Shannon's Way</u> will "probably be popular."

1948

111   ROACHE, MARY C. Review of Shannon's Way. Toledo Blade,
        16 July, p. 13.
            Notes parallels between this novel and The Citadel. Con-
        cludes that the former might well have been a short story.
        "It creates but one emotional impression, the characters are
        few, and the episodes are not involved." It also lacks even
        a hint of humor. The ideas, however, are "stimulating."

112   ROGERS, W.G. "Books in Review." Keene (N.H.) Sentinel,
        21 July, p. 3.
            Review of Shannon's Way. "You can always count on Cronin
        to write sponge-cake and buttermilk books, never graceless,
        never boorish, never badly dressed." Comments on Cronin's
        preference for "clichés and platitudes over original remarks
        and new situations." Reprinted: 1948.113-16.

113   [ROGERS, W.G.] "Cronin Takes Middle Road in New Novel about
        Doctor." Columbia (S.C.) State, 25 July, p. 3.
            Reprint of 1948.112.

114   _____. "Literary Guidepost." Wisconsin Rapids Tribune,
        24 July, p. 5.
            Reprint of 1948.112.

115   _____. "Of Sponge-Cake and Buttermilk." Tulsa World, 8 August,
        p. 4.
            Reprint of 1948.112.

116   R[OGERS], W.G. "Spongecake and Buttermilk: A New A.J. Cronin
        Homily." New Haven Register, 1 August, p. 7.
            Reprint of 1948.112.

117   ROTH, CLAIRE W. "New Books Appraised: Fiction." Library
        Journal 73 (July):1026.
            Review of Shannon's Way. Cronin's style is "easy and
        smooth, in spite of the overly long sentences. This new
        work does not advance Cronin's literary stature, but it does
        maintain the status quo."

118   RUSSELL, RICHARD M. "Cronin's Book Tells Tale of Young Doctor."
        Catholic Messenger, 4 November, p. 11.
            Review of Shannon's Way. Cronin was more concerned with
        the hero's problems than his readers might be. But the
        scenes between the hero and heroine are "tenderly done,"
        and his ideas are challenging.

119   S., H.L. Review of Shannon's Way. Telegram (Toronto), 17 July,
        p. 5.

1948

Once again Cronin's ending proves that "most things turn out for the best eventually."

120   SCOTT, KENNETH W. "Shannon's Way." Brooklyn Daily Eagle, 10 September, p. 8.
       Cronin blends his favorite subjects: science and religion. Praises his literary style, his warm characters, and his careful probing of man's scientific and spritual problems.

121   SEAVER, EDWIN. "Love Between Medics, and the CIC." Saturday Review of Literature 31 (24 July):13.
       Review of Shannon's Way. "Dr. Cronin remains the pale but legitimate inheritor of the Victorian storytellers, and his honest hero and heroine genuine if somewhat quaint--and rather late--children of Victorian times. If his story line and characterization go back to the horse-and-buggy days, it must be admitted that old Dobbin and the one-horse shay still get there in their own good time."

122   SENSABAUGH, MARY HOLMES. "All Set for the Movies." Birmingham (Ala.) News, 14 August, p. 5.
       Shannon's Way is a "straightforward, interest-compelling narrative" in which, until the last two pages, it seems that "artistic reason might win."

123   SHERMAN, THOMAS B. "Between Book Ends." St. Louis Post-Dispatch, 23 July, p. 9.
       Review of Shannon's Way. Cronin shows "a shrewd knowledge of storytelling craftsmanship. His main characters are engaging, the chief protagonist has a definite objective and the hazards he encounters in his eventful obstacle race are so arranged as to keep the narrative continuously active." Although Cronin does not deal with "powerful ideas" and does not invoke "profound emotions," he is interesting even to the "exacting reader."

124   STITH, LUCIA. "Story of Doctor's Progress." Nashville Tennessean, 25 July, p. 7.
       Review of Shannon's Way. Robert Shannon is the sort of hero with which every reader can identify. The love interest holds the reader's attention in this "smooth, surface-skimming narrative of conventional characters."

125   SYLVIA. "The Turning Point." Chelsea (Mass.) Record, 31 July, p. 3.
       Brief biographical background. Includes mention of Shannon's Way.

1948

126 TERRY, C.W. "Scotch Sour." New York Times, 18 July, p. 12.
Review of Shannon's Way. As a sequel to The Green Years,
this seems "a pale coda." Cronin follows his familiar formula throughout, "with no real variation in the monotony."

127 VOILES, JANE. "New Cronin Novel." San Francisco Chronicle,
18 July, p. 18.
Review of Shannon's Way. Lacks the "substantial characters" found in The Green Years and the depth found in The
Stars Look Down and The Keys of the Kingdom. Suggests that
this is "a transitional story that all writers who develop
are bound to write at one time or another."

128 W., A.J. "Shannon's Way." United Church Observer (Toronto),
1 September, p. 12.
This novel will not disappoint Cronin fans. Wishes the
author had written further, however, to reveal how Robert
and Jean's marriage worked out.

129 W., C.P. "Cronin's Novel is Depressing, Reviewer Says." New
Bedford (Mass.) Standard, 8 August, p. 6.
Review of Shannon's Way. The novel reminds one of the
troubles faced by many of Dickens's characters. But in
Cronin's work, it becomes "a chore to read on page after
page of the disappointment he meets, the penury of his ex-
istence and the catastrophes that seem to dog the footsteps
of his friends."

130 WALSH, ANNE. "A.J. Cronin on Doctors and Love." Dallas Times
Herald, 25 July, p. 4.
Review of Shannon's Way. Wonders if the title refers to
the "long and arduous path" chosen by the hero or to the
"dogged manner" in which he chooses to walk it. He is espe-
cially skilled in his portrayal of the "infectious atmosphere
surrounding those medical men and women who maintain rather
plush mental institutions."

131 WARE, HARLAN. "Shannon's Way Is Alive." Pasadena Star-News,
18 July, p. 8.
A "superior novel" with a story "complete, war polished,
warm-hearted." Cronin always knows what he is doing, and
he does it well. However, the novel may not create the excitement caused by The Keys of the Kingdom and The Green
Years.

132 WEINER, SAM. "Another Durable Story from A.J. Cronin."
Houston Post, 18 July, p. 6.
Shannon's Way is "admirable and light summer reading."

133 WHITFORD, R.C. "A New A.J. Cronin Opus." <u>Brooklyn Daily Eagle</u>,
    18 July, p. 10.
        Review of <u>Shannon's Way</u>. The strength in Cronin's writ-
    ings comes from "his sympathetic and detailed presentation
    of major characters whose dominant traits demand at once ex-
    planation and apology." The weakness in the novel is the
    same as that in <u>The Keys of the Kingdom</u>: the characters'
    motivations do not justify the plot complications. Concludes
    by calling this a "masterly piece" of sentimental fiction.

134 WILSON, KAY. "Dr. Robert Shannon's Career." <u>Raleigh Observer</u>,
    25 July, p. 7.
        Review of <u>Shannon's Way</u>. A good story, but lacking "the
    interest or excitement that is so often promised." Feels
    that the writer owes it to his public to "search a little
    deeper, work a little harder and bring to the reader some
    of the spirit that prevailed" in <u>The Citadel</u> and <u>The Keys
    of the Kingdom</u>.

135 ZWART, ELIZABETH CLARKSON. "Dr. A.J. Cronin's New Hero Is a
    Poor but Brilliant Scientist." <u>Des Moines Register</u>, 18 July,
    p. 5.
        Review of <u>Shannon's Way</u>. Its characters are "paperdolls";
    its plot is trite; and its style is "utterly undistinguished."
    All of this adds up to "exactly nothing, in the creative
    sense. What it may add up to in dollars and cents will be
    a tax expert's problem."

<u>1950</u>

1 A., J. "Domination Over Son Failed." <u>Minneapolis Tribune</u>,
    24 September, p. 9.
        Review of <u>The Spanish Gardener</u>. This is "a touching
    story" in which the scenes are "charming in their simplicity."

2 ADKINS, SAM. "Overextension by A.J. Cronin." <u>Louisville
    Courier-Journal</u>, 15 October, p. 5.
        Review of <u>The Spanish Gardener</u>. This is little more than
    an "over-extended short story."

3 ANON. "A.J. Cronin." <u>New York Herald-Tribune Books</u>, 17
    September, p. 21.
        Biographical background.

4 ANON. "Books." <u>Time</u> 56 (4 September):84.
        Review of <u>The Spanish Gardener</u>. This is "a minor effort,
    contrived and held together with unnaturally stilted dialogue."

1950

5   ANON. "Books: Fiction." Berlin (N.H.) Reporter, 14 September,
        p. 2.
            Brief plot summary of The Spanish Gardener.

6   ANON. "Cronin, A.J." Roanoke Times, 24 November, p. 10.
            Calls The Spanish Gardener a "melodramatic, neatly pack-
        aged tale."

7   ANON. "Cronin Takes New Tack in Story of Boy." San Diego
        Union, 27 August, p. 11.
            Review of The Spanish Gardener. Sees this as a departure
        from Cronin's novels: "no slow burns, no histrionics, no
        frustrated romances."

8   ANON. "Cronin's Latest." New York Post, 27 August, p. 13.
            Review of The Spanish Gardener. This "clumsy melodrama"
        has a trite plot and an unconvincing ending.

9   ANON. "Father and Son." New York Herald-Tribune Books,
        25 July, p. 7.
            Notices that The Spanish Gardener will appear in August.

10   ANON. "Fiction." Booklist 46 (1 July):326.
            The Spanish Gardener is "a melodramatic, neatly packaged
        tale."

11   ANON. "Fiction." Kirkus 18 (1 July):360.
            Review of The Spanish Gardener. This book will neither
        enhance nor detract from Cronin's reputation. The story is
        not totally convincing, and the characters are "somewhat
        wooden." Finds a "sense of anticlimax" at the end.

12   ANON. "Hillsboro Library More New Volumes." Hillsboro (Oreg.)
        Argur, 19 October, p. 5.
            Brief mention of The Spanish Gardener.

13   ANON. "Man Made Lonely by Egotism." Miami Herald, 27 August,
        p. 6.
            Review of The Spanish Gardener. A very different novel
        from its predecessors. Cronin has used his deep knowledge
        of human nature and psychology to picture a self-centered
        and insufferable American diplomat and his eight-year-old
        son.

14   ANON. "New Books." Kennebunk Star, 20 October, p. 5.
            Brief mention of The Spanish Gardener.

15   ANON. "New Cronin Is a Smoothie." Cleveland News, 30 August,

1950

p. 11.
Review of The Spanish Gardener. A reader of Cronin is
never confused as to which is the sympathetic character and
which is the villain. His latest novel is his "strongest
or most moving" and "deft to the point of virtuosity."

16   ANON. "Novels Revived." New York Herald-Tribune Books,
        5 November, p. 21.
        Cronin's novels entitled Shannon's Way and The Green Years
      have been reprinted by Grosset & Dunlap.

17   ANON. "Other Books." Newsweek 43 (28 August):83.
        Brief plot summary of The Spanish Gardener. This is
      another example of Cronin's "proficiency in the art of pop-
      ular fiction."

18   ANON. "Popular Novel Reissued." St. Louis Post-Dispatch,
        7 August, p. 11.
        The Green Years is reprinted and combined with Shannon's
      Way. This is "a gracious gesture the publishers have brought
      within the reach of a large circle of readers."

19   ANON. Review of The Spanish Gardener. Alhambra (Calif.) Post
        Advocate, 14 September, p. 3.
        Another simple plot, this novel has "moments of indescrib-
      able charm and humor." It does fall short of Cronin's previ-
      ous accomplishments, however.

20   ANON. Review of The Spanish Gardener. America 107 (26 August):
        10.
        This "convincing study of possessiveness" is a bit unusual
      for Cronin's style. "The death scene is on the melodramatic
      side and comes off a trifle too patly, but the other elements
      of the story are blended into a convincing whole." Says that
      the little boy is Cronin's "most deeply conceived character."
      The author's ability to handle young people's troubles is
      improving.

21   ANON. Review of The Spanish Gardener. America 107 (25
        November):6.
        Brief plot summary.

22   ANON. Review of The Spanish Gardener. Bookmark 47 (October):
        13.
        This is a "facile, not quite plausible novel." It was
      serialized in Collier's as The Prisoner.

23   ANON. Review of The Spanish Gardener. Chicago News,

111

1950

> 13 September, p. 5.
> This is "an inconsequential and scarcely believable yarn."

24   ANON. Review of The Spanish Gardener. El Paso Times, 23 July, p. 4.
> Calls this "a tense and tender novel." $20,000 has been spent on promotion prior to its release on 28 August.

25   ANON. Review of The Spanish Gardener. Farmington (Mass.) News, 4 November, p. 2.
> The tragedy and beauty of this tale will haunt the reader.

26   ANON. Review of The Spanish Gardener. Literary Guild Wings (November), p. 5.
> Somewhat difficult to believe in the boy's defiance of his father, but written with Cronin's "usual competence."

27   ANON. Review of The Spanish Gardener. Pomeroy East Washingtonian, 28 September, p. 3.
> A short novel told with economy and emotion.

28   ANON. Review of The Spanish Gardener. Providence Journal, 27 August, p. 4.
> Although readable, this novel "oozes with romantic sentimentality."

29   ANON. Review of The Spanish Gardener. San Francisco Chronicle, 24 September, p. 8.
> Cronin uses the same formula he used for the story of Shannon in The Green Years. Wonders if the story is worth "all of the woe and anguish which Dr. Cronin knows how to pile on."

30   ANON. Review of The Spanish Gardener. Syracuse Herald, 27 August, p. 7.
> This is "a fine example of what an artist can do creatively, with very little good material."

31   ANON. Review of The Spanish Gardener. Toppenish (Wash.) Review (12 October), p. 4.
> Cronin tells the story of Nicholas with the same "compassion and understanding" found in The Green Years.

32   ANON. Review of The Spanish Gardener. Vermont Free Press, 30 August, p. 5.
> "This is a haunting book with overtones of both beauty and tragedy."

33 ANON. "The Consul." Atlantic Monthly 186 (October):89.
    Review of The Spanish Gardener. There is nothing in this
    novel which has not been encountered before. It is "a 'well-
    made' novel, not an exceptional one."

34 ANON. "Undercover." San Francisco Argonaut, 28 July, p. 9.
    Brief mention of The Spanish Gardener.

35 B., A. Review of The Spanish Gardener. United Church Observer
    (Toronto), 15 December, p. 2.
    "Picking up the many-hued threads of life the author has
    woven one of those magic carpets that carries the reader into
    the hearts and homes of his people to become one of them."

36 B., D.B. "The Green Years in a New Edition." Springfield
    (Mass.) Republican, 3 September, p. 2.
    Notice of a reprinted edition of The Green Years. "Not
    only do his characters have personalities of their own, with
    their own frailties and emotions, but their problems and af-
    fairs, their fun and grief might be anybody's. This author's
    warm and understanding treatment, and the use he makes of the
    revealing incident have a way of bringing the whole thing
    home."

37 B., M.H. Review of The Spanish Gardener. El Paso Times,
    3 September, p. 4.
    A study of character is the dominant theme in this novel.

38 BARKHAM, JOHN. "Landscape with Figures." New York Times,
    27 August, p. 4.
    Review of The Spanish Gardener. Missing is Cronin's high
    emotions, large cast of characters, and busy plot. It could
    be argued that this is an extended short story. "What gives
    the story its unusual flavor is the kind of characters Dr.
    Cronin has chosen." But the "inner momentum" of the story
    stems from Cronin's narrative skill. Congratulates him for
    having "turned his back on formula fiction."

39 BARTLETT, ELIZABETH. "Sadistic Father, Criminal Butler, Mad
    Psychiatrist." Los Angeles News, 14 October, p. 16.
    Review of The Spanish Gardener. Comments on the solid
    plot, vivid characterization and emotional appeal. Although
    the theme may seem melodramatic, "there is tenderness and
    charm" to compensate for faults of style. "In short, it is
    a novel for those who like a swift, throbbing story."

40 BATES, GRAHAM. Review of The Spanish Gardener. Book-of-the-
    Month Club News (September), p. 11.

1950

"As a study of egotism, The Spanish Gardener may well
rank with the best in the field, while its more moving theme,
the terror and pity of childhood for the strange world of
adults, never understood, can leave few readers unshaken."

41 BECK, CLYDE. "Books of the Day: New Novels by A.J. Cronin and
Robert Nathan." Detroit News, 27 August, p. 10.
    Review of The Spanish Gardener. It is doubtful whether
some of Cronin's longer novels will measure up to this "brief
and compact novel of literature stature above the common."

42 BEDELL, W.D. Review of The Spanish Gardener. Houston Post,
27 August, p. 5.
    Says that Cronin's shallow writing "only adds to the de-
pressing effect of Brande's weaknesses."

43 BOARDMAN, TOM. "A.J. Cronin Scores Again." Indianapolis Times,
4 November, p. 9.
    Reprint of 1950.44.

44 _____. "New Cronin Novel Is Touching Story." Cleveland Post,
29 August, p. 6.
    Review of The Spanish Gardener. "The book is an engross-
ing series of small crises, moving rapidly along to a dramatic climax." Reprinted: 1950.43.

45 BOND, ALICE DIXON. "The New Books." Boston Traveler, 4
October, p. 8.
    Review of The Spanish Gardener. Unlike Cronin's previous
novels, this work is "a compact, incisive book, emotionally
tense and dramatically sparse." Moreover, it surpasses the
previous novels in "sensitivity and understanding."

46 BOWE, KAY. "Book Comment." Guilford (Conn.) Shore Line Times,
31 August, p. 3.
    Review of The Spanish Gardener. "It is a story that
clings to heart and to mind like a poignant song distilled
out of the shared experience of all mankind."

47 BRADY, CHARLES A. "Envoy to Spain Battling with Two 'Devils.'"
Buffalo Evening News, 25 August, p. 3.
    Review of The Spanish Gardener. Finds in this novel one
of Cronin's recurrent themes: "the power of Puritanism to
dry up the springs of human emotion." Because of his direct
approach to this material, Cronin is compelled to "sacrifice
complexity to power. But the power is there."

48 C., H.B. "Tense and Poignant Novel." Worcester (Mass.)

Telegram, 27 August, p. 7.
Review of The Spanish Gardener. "Dr. Cronin has once
more given to his admirers a tense novel, packed with pathos
and tender understanding, that can be classed as first-rate,
no matter what standard is used."

49   C., V. "Recent Fiction." Pasadena Star-News, 10 September,
p. 29.
As usual, Cronin handles an indelicate subject with
"delicate mastery." The psychiatric overtones are particularly fine.

50   D., E.V. "A Child's Mind Revealed in All Its Innocence."
Hartford Times, 26 August, p. 11.
Review of The Spanish Gardener. Finds once again Cronin's
"keen, almost clinical perception of a child's mind."

51   DEDMON, EMMETT. "Midweek Review of Books." Chicago Sun Times,
29 August, p. 5.
Review of The Spanish Gardener. In this slight novel,
the only distinction is "a well-drawn portrait of the vain
and cruel Harrington Brande." It is "a slender item of
quantity as well as quality."

52   DUNLAP, KATHERINE. "New Cronin Novel." Philadelphia Inquirer,
27 August, p. 6.
Review of The Spanish Gardener. Once again Cronin has
written a novel with "color, quick tempo and a quality of
characterization that compels the reader even as it inspires
him with the wish that the author had outlined his story with
less stress on the neurotic."

53   EELLS, CALVIN. "Cronin's Newest Novel Has Father and Son
Theme." Portland (Maine) Telegram, 3 September, p. 4.
Review of The Spanish Gardener. The characters are credible, the developments are "swift-paced." Finds it hard to
believe that "a man could write a whole book about an arro-
gant, stupid character, but Cronin has done it. And it's
worth reading."

54   ELWOOD, IRENE. "Cronin Book Cites Lesson of Gardener." Los
Angeles Times, 3 September, p. 21.
Review of The Spanish Gardener. Finds here "a surprising-
ly strong indictment of behavior and thoughts that are arro-
gant, unbending and vindictive." The climax is "as objec-
tively stated and creatively delivered" as in Clark's The
Oxbow Incident. Cronin fulfills the highest purpose of the
novelist in the character of Harrington Brande, for he "shows
the mind of man in the contemporary world of the writer."

1950

55 G., M. "Tragic Events Stem from Man's Vanity in New Cronin
    Tale." Spokane Chronicle, 12 October, p. 5.
        Review of The Spanish Gardener. "It isn't a pleasant
    theme, nor is it a happy book, but it does have some beauti-
    ful scenes and some shockingly unforgettable ones."

56 GANNETT, LEWIS. "Books and Things." New York Herald-Tribune
    Books, 29 August, p. 11.
        Review of The Spanish Gardener. Sees this as a combina-
    tion "pastiche of life" and psychological thriller. However,
    Cronin has gone beyond his depth. The villains are "prepos-
    terous. . . . Perhaps the answer is that Dr. Cronin under-
    stands virtue better than vice." Unfortunately, the villains
    overshadow the sensitive picture of the lonely, frightened
    small boy.

57 GRAUEL, GEORGE E. Review of The Spanish Gardener. Best Sellers
    (1 September), p. 6.
        This is "a rather thin narrative that depends for its
    effect chiefly on emotionally intense characterizations."
    José seems the most "humane and sympathetic." Dislikes the
    allusions to homosexuality.

58 GRIFFIN, DOROTHEA. "Swift-Moving Story." Nashville Banner,
    1 September, p. 4.
        Review of The Spanish Gardener. Although Cronin's writing
    has become "more facile," in this novel "the depth of pene-
    tration and the wealth of realistic detail which depicted the
    struggles of doctors in Scotland are much less evident."

59 H., C. "Too-Possessive Father." Nashville Tennessean, 10
    September, p. 2.
        Review of The Spanish Gardener. "The story is smooth,
    the characters straight out of an old-fashioned melodrama,
    plus a modern touch in the person of a sinister and fraudu-
    lent psychiatrist, and the whole somehow unsatisfying--unless
    you are a confirmed Cronin enthusiast."

60 H., M.J. "The Yoke of Father-Love." Newark Evening News,
    29 August, p. 5.
        Review of The Spanish Gardener. Once again, Cronin is
    "keen and able" as both medical man and novelist. The novel
    is shorter, and unusual in setting, plot, and characteriza-
    tions.

61 HAMILTON, E. "Bit of Croninizing: He Brings a Character to
    Life but Ends His Story Illogically." Boston Globe, 3
    September, p. 4.

Review of The Spanish Gardener. Like Hatter's Castle, this novel offers another excellent psychological study. Cronin captures the life and customs of the Spanish people. Finds it difficult to believe in the consul's son's turn-about at the end of the book.

62   HEWES, LYDIA. "Yet Another by Mr. Cronin." Hartford Courant, 3 September, p. 5.
Review of The Spanish Gardener. Harrington Brande is "one of the most objectionable fathers in fiction." None of the characters resembles a human being, however. "A certain aptitude for pictorial description is shown in passages that tell of the sights, sounds and smells of a small Spanish town. The other virtue of the book is its brevity."

63   HUGHES, ISABELLE. "Jealous Father." Globe and Mail (Toronto), 7 October, p. 7.
Review of The Spanish Gardener. Says that both the plot and the characterizations "are unfolded in an obvious, almost ingenious manner which makes each phase of the action very easy for the reader to anticipate--a strange fault to be found in the work of so experienced an author."

64   JONES, CARTER BROOKE. "Books in Review." Washington (D.C.) Star, 27 August, p. 11.
Review of The Spanish Gardener. This is a much better novel than Shannon's Way. It is "a tightly written psychological study of several characters, translated into swift action." The plot is plausible and the characters are credible.

65   KELLEY, JAMES E. "Cronin's Newest Novel Below Par--But Good." Denver Post, 27 August, p. 4.
Review of The Spanish Gardener. Compares this unfavorably with Cronin's previous novels. Although he once again demonstrates "his awareness of what makes the youthful mind tick," and although his portrayal of Brande is "ruthlessly efficient," unfortunately José is "rather woodenly-drawn."

66   KNICKMEYER, LOUISE. "Exciting, but Still a Bit Incredulous." Oklahoma City Oklahoman, 19 November, p. 4.
Review of The Spanish Gardener. Says that the believability of this novel is "somewhat strained."

67   LANE, VICTORIA A. "Cronin Slips Up on Latest Novel." Memphis Appeal, 10 September, p. 3.
Review of The Spanish Gardener. The gardener is the only memorable character. The book is "neither amusing nor satisfying." It ends "feebly."

1950

68 LAWRENCE, HENRY H. "New Cronin Novel Shows Tragic Family."
    San Antonio Express, 27 August, p. 12.
        Review of The Spanish Gardener. "It is a book in which
    beauty and tragedy move closely side by side, with some of
    Cronin's most sensitively modeled characters in operation."

69 M., J.W. "Books: Cronin Counts Vanity's Cost." New Haven
    Sunday Register, 3 September, p. 5.
        The Spanish Gardener is an interest novel, written in
    Cronin's "usual facile style."

70 McHUGH, MIRIAM. "Today's Books." Trenton Trentonian, 18
    November, p. 4.
        Review of The Spanish Gardener. Although the background
    is a bit mediocre, Cronin has created several outstanding
    characters. The book should attract reader interest because
    it emphasizes family relationships.

71 NAYLOR, PAULINE. "A.J. Cronin's New Novel: Story of Destruc-
    tive Force of One Man's Vanity and Jealousy." Fort Worth
    Star, 3 September, p. 5.
        Review of The Spanish Gardener. Cronin's "mastery of
    spiritual beauty and tragedy has never been better mani-
    fested." This novel demands to be read at one sitting. In
    spite of its tragic story, it does end on a note of hope for
    Nicholas.

72 [NORTH, STERLING.] "Cronin Novel Is Over Slick." St.
    Petersburg News, 17 September, p. 5.
        Reprint of 1950.74.

73 _____. Review of The Spanish Gardener. Buffalo Courier-Express,
    10 September, p. 10.
        Reprint of 1950.74.

74 NORTH, STERLING. "Sterling North Reviews the Books." New York
    World Telegram, 30 August, p. 12.
        Review of The Spanish Gardener. Like Maugham, this author
    writes books which are "virtually flawless in style and
    structure." Also like Maugham, his novels sometimes seem
    "too slick to be completely honest." Reprinted: 1950.72-73.

75 O., O. Review of The Spanish Gardener. Boston Post, 3
    September, p. 6.
        This novel is different from Cronin's other works because
    the writing is "exquisite" and the evil is more pervasive
    and "purer."

76   O'LEARY, THEODORE M. "Cronin's Jealous Father." Kansas City
      Star, 23 September, p. 5.
            Review of The Spanish Gardener. Cronin's story is too
      weak to overcome the superficial character protrayals. Also,
      his writing is monotonous. The reader always knows what's
      going to happen in advance.

77   PASCHALL, ALMA. "Over-Possessive Father Love Cronin Novel
      Tragic Theme." Toledo Blade, 27 August, p. 7.
            Review of The Spanish Gardener. Brande's suffering is
      deeply moving. The novel is "a depressing but powerful
      story."

78   PEARSON, FLAVAL. "Book Reviews." Chehalis Advocate, 7 December,
      p. 6.
            Brief plot summary of The Spanish Gardener.

79   PORTERSFIELD, WALDON. "The Spanish Gardener: A New Novel by
      Cronin Tells of a Doting Father's Evil Effect on His Son."
      Milwaukee Journal, 3 September, p. 4.
            In this fast-paced novel, the characters are "powerfully
      drawn" and Cronin has something significant to say.

80   PRESCOTT, ORVILLE. "Books of the Times." New York Times,
      27 August, p. 17.
            Review of The Spanish Gardener. Cronin is "a curious
      literary enigma. His work is uneven in quality and it never
      seems quite as good as it ought to be. But everything Dr.
      Cronin writes is stamped by his personality, his transparent
      sincerity, his direct concern with ethical issues, his seem-
      ingly instinctive knowledge of ordinary people and his great
      natural gifts for sheer story-telling." All of these quali-
      ties are apparent in his best work, including his latest nov-
      el. Not intended to shock or excite, the narrative is "a
      serious effort to write of the dangers which can threaten
      the helpless through weakness or corruption in the character
      of others." However, the novel lacks "the subtleties and
      power of major fiction." Perhaps this story would be more
      effective as a play or a movie.

81   PROVEN, GRACE. "Cronin Book Fascinating." Pittsburgh Press,
      27 August, p. 5.
            Review of The Spanish Gardener. The novel moves swiftly,
      it plays on the reader's emotions, and is uplifting in spite
      of the pathos.

82   RICE, JOAN. Review of The Spanish Gardener. Commonweal 52
      (8 September):540.

1950

Finds this resembles a modern Gothic melodrama in which
the climax is both "exciting dramatically and plausible psy-
chologically." The fact that the villains suffer from mental
strain "blends well into the malevolent shadows in the background."

83 RODRIGUEZ, J.S. "Tragedy in a Garden." Gazette (Montreal),
    16 September, p. 4.
        Review of The Spanish Gardener. "For some reasons [sic]
    the author has relapsed into a ponderous Victorian verbiage,
    recklessly sprinkled with clichés; and yet the tale itself
    is real and moving."

84 ROTHERMEL, J.F. "He Planted More than Just Seeds." Birmingham
    (Ala.) News, 3 September, p. 9.
        Review of The Spanish Gardener. Although this novel does
    not reach the level of The Citadel, The Keys of the Kingdom
    or Shannon's Way, it is not "an unmixed success." Cronin's
    portrait of the boy is not particularly skillful, however.
    The gardener's character "saves the book."

85 ROYER, DOROTHY PENCE. Review of The Spanish Gardener.
    Cincinnati Enquirer, 9 September, p. 5.
        Calls this "splendid reading."

86 SCHULBERG, LUCILLE. "Vanity Destroys Three Lives." Richmond
    Times-Dispatch, 3 September, p. 7.
        Review of The Spanish Gardener. Brande's vanity is simply
    "a crush around mediocrity." Hence, it is impossible to ac-
    cept his vanity. He has nothing to offer the world.

87 SCOTT, JAMES. "No Hope for the Sinner Is A.J. Cronin's View."
    Telegram (Toronto), 9 September, p. 7.
        Review of The Spanish Gardener. Because Cronin tells his
    tale of a super-inflated ego so remorselessly, it often slips
    into melodrama. It is hard to believe in the villain, there-
    fore. Finds it alarming that Cronin should write this kind
    of book. "Never too clear a thinker, his previous books at
    least had a compassion and understanding which many readers
    found helpful." But these qualities are missing here.

88 SCOTT, KENNETH W. "Shannon's Way by A.J. Cronin." Brooklyn
    Daily Eagle, 10 September, p. 8.
        Comments on the reprint edition. "His literate style,
    his warm characters, and his careful probing of man's scien-
    tific and spiritual problems have earned for him a vast audi-
    ence in Europe and America. This new reprint series should
    convert many more."

89 SHERMAN, THOMAS B. "Reading and Writing: A.J. Cronin Writes
    New Type of Novel." St. Louis Post-Dispatch, 27 August, p.
    5.
        Review of The Spanish Gardener. Finds that the author is
    more partisan in dealing with his central characters and more
    detached than he was in his previous novels. However, it is
    obvious where his sympathies lie. To some extent, Cronin has
    had to alter his style to fit the subject--a psychological
    study with a single character. Admirers of Cronin's are
    likely to feel that he has "sacrificed warmth of feeling--
    which played such an essential part in his other novels--
    without achieving a compensating depth of penetration."

90 SINKS, NAOMI BENDER. "Jealous Father Pays Penalty in New Cronin
    Novel." Cleveland Plain Dealer, 27 August, p. 2.
        Review of The Spanish Gardener. Comments on the excellent
    character portrayals, the tragic events themselves, and the
    "exciting maturity of a mastered art."

91 STOER, MARION WEST. "Mimosa and Miasma." Christian Science
    Monitor, 28 August, p. 14.
        Review of The Spanish Gardener. The title given to the
    serialized version of this novel--The Prisoner--was more
    appropriate than the current title. Cronin's portrayal of
    Nicholas is insightful and warm in this "closely knit, sus-
    penseful tale." The horror and tragedy of the tale frequent-
    ly overcomes any shafts of sunlight.

92 SUGRUE, THOMAS. "Smother Love of a Father." New York Herald-
    Tribune Books, 27 August, p. 6.
        Review of The Spanish Gardener. Because Cronin moves
    quickly, he has little time to develop the characters of
    Brande and José. That they are "insufficiently realized"
    detracts from the sympathetic Nicholas, "on which Doctor
    Cronin has expended considerable of his artistry."

93 TINKLE, LON. "Serpent in Eden." Saturday Review of Literature
    33 (9 September):20-21.
        Review of The Spanish Gardener. Cronin's moral is well
    worth restatement for our times: "simple, direct affections
    and honest acts can be corroded and destroyed by distrust
    and by too much introspection." The novel is reminiscent of
    Maugham's writings. The opening tone is "dry and detached,"
    but soon disappears. Cronin has "targets to scourge and no
    intention of remaining above the strife." Hence, his story
    is predictable. Most of the characters seem "mere puppets
    manipulated adroitly by Dr. Cronin's sure hand." Concludes
    that the relationship between Cronin and the novel "is not

1950

so much superficial as artificial. And in the end, the
freight of intended meaning is too heavy for such thin, pal-
lid creations."

94 WALBRIDGE, EARLE F. "New Books Appraised: Too Late for Last
     Issue." Library Journal 75 (1 September):1410.
          Review of The Spanish Gardener. As all too often, Cronin
     manipulates his characters. But the novel is "singularly
     appealing" in its depiction of the boy and the Spaniard.
     His craftsmanship is "expert" but marred by the "Grand
     Guignol" touches.

95 WENDT, LLOYD. "Cronin's New Novel Is Grim and Incredible."
     Chicago Sunday Tribune, 27 August, p. 3.
          Review of The Spanish Gardener. The Spanish scenes are
     the best. The other scenes "fade when you close the covers."
     Finds that the plot is more complex and more contrived than
     in his previous novels. "Yet, somehow, the good doctor's
     heart does not seem to be in this book." The characters
     seem to be caricatures, "completely incredible at times."

96 WILSON, KAY. "Cronin Novel of Father and Son." Raleigh
     Observer, 3 September, p. 9.
          Review of The Spanish Gardener. "A father-son relation-
     ship is tenderly treated with alternate overtones of beauty
     and tragedy."

97 WINN, ELIZABETH SMITH. Review of The Spanish Gardener. El
     Paso Herald-Post (26 August), p. 4.
          This is a psychological novel--something new for Cronin.
     Finds in it "a feeling of timelessness; . . . the characters
     seem unreal and more or less symbolic." Cronin's descrip-
     tions of anger are "precise and studied." He describes the
     anger in such a way that "the reader is always free to con-
     template the anger described rather than to partake [of] it."
     Hence, there is no catharsis for the reader.

1951

1   ANON. "Dr. A.J. Cronin." Philadelphia Inquirer, 5 August,
     p. 5.
          Notices that Cronin has completed his writing of a "spir-
     itual autobiography." Tentatively entitled Journey of
     Discovery, publication has been set for February 1952.

2   ANON. "Dr. A.J. Cronin." Pittsfield Berkshire Evening Eagle,
     4 August, p. 6.
          Mentions the upcoming publication of his autobiography.

3   ANON. "Nonfiction." Kirkus 19 (15 December):715.
        Review of Adventures in Two Worlds. Cronin's success
    story is extraordinary. Perhaps for today's less sentimental
    audience this may have some of the appeal that was felt two
    generations ago in the unforgettable Beside the Binnie Bear
    Bush (Ian Maclaren). Excerpted: 1952.18.

4   ANON. Review of The Spanish Gardener. Dayton (Wash.) Chronicle
    Dispatch, 1 January, p. 5.
        This novel may rate as Cronin's greatest triumph.

5   ANON. Review of The Spanish Gardener. Vancouver Teacher
    (February), p. 11.
        "The characterization is sometimes wooden, but the plot
    moves swiftly to an exciting climax."

6   WILLIS, MARIANNA. "Book Reviews." Glendora (Calif.) Press-
    Gleaner, 15 November, p. 4.
        Review of The Spanish Gardener. Cronin has been "sliding
    downhill rapidly" since The Keys of the Kingdom. This new
    novel is "obvious, told with an amazing lack of subtlety,
    and downright dull."

1952

1   AMES, A.C. Review of Adventures in Two Worlds. Chicago Sunday
    Tribune, 24 February, p. 3.
        Finds the book is "packed with vital characters and
    thrilling episodes. How it stirs the heart and lifts up the
    spirit! Without question, here is one of the great books in
    the English language."

2   ANON. "A.J. Cronin Tells His Story As Both Doctor and Writer."
    Fresno Bee, 6 March, p. 4.
        Review of Adventures in Two Worlds. Finds the reading
    pleasant and interesting in a book that runs "from quiet
    humor to gripping pathos."

3   ANON. "A.J. Cronin's Autobiography." Toledo Blade, 24
    February, p. 3.
        Review of Adventures in Two Worlds. This book is as in-
    teresting as any of Cronin's novels. His tribute to America
    "should gain him countless additional friends."

4   ANON. "About People." Wilson Library Bulletin 48 (April):92.
        Brief summary of Adventures in Two Worlds. Parts of the
    autobiography appeared in Collier's and Woman's Home
    Companion.

1952

5   ANON. "Books." <u>San Diego Union</u>, 24 February, p. C13.
     Review of <u>Adventures in Two Worlds</u>. "Being a practised
     novelist accustomed to probing the minds and hearts of his
     characters, Cronin must have found it a strange and perhaps
     disturbing experience to deal with himself in the same way."
     The experiences described are intensely dramatic; some of
     them are unforgettable.

6   ANON. "Books: Proud Soul v. Humble Soul." <u>Time</u> 59
     (25 February):98.
     Review of <u>Adventures in Two Worlds</u>. Finds the selections
     readable and, in most places, "charged with a strong dose of
     moral philosophy." First pre-publication press-run was
     75,000 copies.

7   ANON. "Bookstall Gossip." <u>Boston Post</u>, 2 March, p. 5.
     Brief biographical background. Describes Cronin's time
     spent during the winter months in New Hampshire and his pur-
     chase of some long underwear. Says that all of Cronin's
     fine novels reflect some phase of his life.

8   ANON. "Caduceus and Pen Each His Servant." <u>Memphis Appeal</u>,
     10 February, p. 6.
     Review of <u>Adventures in Two Worlds</u>. The book is in the
     fashion of short stories, "nonrelated but fairly integrated."
     Finds the tales "intriguing and written in crystal prose."
     However, Cronin becomes a bit too preachy toward the end.

9   ANON. "County Library News." <u>Hood River</u> (Oreg.) <u>News</u>,
     29 February, p. 2.
     Review of <u>Adventures in Two Worlds</u>. This book is sure
     to receive "a good deal of favorable comment and interest"
     from Cronin fans.

10   ANON. "Cronin Fascinates." <u>Indianapolis Times</u>, 2 March, p. 16.
     Review of <u>Adventures in Two Worlds</u>. Cronin tells his
     life's story "with the same sense of the dramatic that has
     won him thousands of loyal readers."

11   ANON. "Doctor and Novelist." <u>Newsweek</u> 39 (25 February):105-6.
     Review of <u>Adventures in Two Worlds</u>. This is an "extra-
     ordinary success story" of his double triumph in medicine
     and pop fiction. However, the book is "a little too expertly
     the work of a practiced novelist to be altogether convincing
     as autobiography."

12   ANON. "Doctor Gives Up Practice to Write." <u>Catholic Times</u>,
     13 June, p. 2.
     Brief mention of <u>Adventures in Two Worlds</u>.

13   ANON. "February Publication Planned for A.J. Cronin's First Non-Fiction." <u>Davenport Times</u>, 12 January, p. 3.
        Review of <u>Adventures in Two Worlds</u>. Quotes passages from the book and offers a brief biographical background.

14   ANON. "Fiction." <u>Lowell</u> (Mass.) <u>Sun-Telegram</u>, 24 February, p. 4.
        Review of <u>Adventures in Two Worlds</u>. Although not a novel, this book may appear as one to some readers. If it does, it is a tribute to Cronin's "engaging style of writing." Finds it a bit disorganized, however.

15   ANON. "General." <u>Booklist</u> 48 (15 February):189, 195.
        Review of <u>Adventures in Two Worlds</u>. Comments on the dramatic narrative and the sentimental stories. Finds that reader interest slackens as Cronin turns to the story of his later years.

16   ANON. "Life of Novelist." <u>Hartford Courant</u>, 24 February, p. 3.
        Review of <u>Adventures in Two Worlds</u>. Cronin relates "without concealment" his life to the present, "his hopes, fears, failures, artifices, and experiences." He is a man with "unusual talents."

17   ANON. "Non-fiction." <u>Berlin</u> (N.H.) <u>Reporter</u>, 24 April, p. 2.
        Review of <u>Adventures in Two Worlds</u>. This is a "skillful fusion of his experiences in the fields of medicine and literature, told in the most exciting narrative form." Finds the document to be perceptive in its revelations of the author.

18   ANON. "Nonfiction." <u>Kirkus</u> 20 (1 January):715.
        Brief review of <u>Adventures in Two Worlds</u>. "Anecdote and episode rather than continuous narrative, this makes good autobiography with a vocational slant." Includes excerpt of 1951.3.

19   ANON. Review of <u>Adventures in Two Worlds</u>. <u>Buffalo Evening News</u>, 23 February, p. 11.
        When Cronin writes fiction, he cannot help writing autobiography. Now he tries to write autobiography, but he can't help developing each chapter in the form of a short story. This is an "old-fashioned and oddly winning transcript of an old-fashioned and oddly winning life."

20   ANON. Review of <u>Adventures in Two Worlds</u>. <u>Burlington</u> (Vt.) <u>Free Press</u>, 27 November, p. 7.

1952

Notices that Cronin has arrived in Vermont en route to
Hollywood. Says that Cronin urges authors "to give their
work a definite social aim as a means of combatting 'the in-
creasing menace' of Fascism and dictatorship. Artists, now
he believes, have the chance to prove that the pen is might-
ier than the sword by spreading the truth, which dictators
are anxious to suppress."

21 ANON. Review of <u>Adventures in Two Worlds</u>. <u>Herald</u> (Calgary),
    26 April, p. 4.
       Finds this book "entertaining and beautifully written."
    Some of the episodes will sound familiar, since the author
    has used his life as background for his novels.

22 ANON. Review of <u>Adventures in Two Worlds</u>. <u>Columbia</u> (S.C.)
    <u>State</u>, 13 July, p. 5.
       This book has been on Columbia's best-seller list since
    its publication.

23 ANON. Review of <u>Adventures in Two Worlds</u>. <u>Horn Book</u> 11
    (August):15.
       The story reads like Cronin's novels. Although there
    are some grisly details and some clinical experiences, "his
    interest in people and his ability to tell a good story
    counterbalance them."

24 ANON. Review of <u>Adventures in Two Worlds</u>. <u>Kitchner Waterloo</u>
    (Canada) <u>Record</u>, 23 May, p. 11.
       Cronin has made his own story "as interesting and enter-
    taining as any of the fiction he has written."

25 ANON. Review of <u>Adventures in Two Worlds</u>. <u>Los Angeles Examiner</u>,
    17 February, p. 10.
       Finds surprising that Cronin is reticent about the details
    of his authorship. Except for the last few chapters, this
    book remains "a series of sketches rather than a sustained
    autobiography." But perhaps because of the limits he sets
    for himself, this book "weaves a spell as effectively as
    his novels do." Reprinted: 1952.28.

26 ANON. Review of <u>Adventures in Two Worlds</u>. <u>Los Angeles Times</u>,
    6 August, p. 18.
       Brief mention. Cronin calls <u>Adventures in Two Worlds</u>
    his "'spiritual autobiography.'"

27 ANON. Review of <u>Adventures in Two Worlds</u>. <u>Milwaukee Journal</u>,
    11 April, p. 4.
       "Extraordinary events occurred often in the life of the
    man and here he relates them in exciting, narrative form."

28   ANON. Review of <u>Adventures in Two Worlds</u>. <u>Milwaukee Sentinel</u>,
      17 February, p. 9.
         Reprint of 1952.25.

29   ANON. Review of <u>Adventures in Two Worlds</u>. <u>New Yorker</u> 28
      (1 March):95.
         "Like a skillful organist, [Cronin] knows just when to
      pull out the stops--tears, laughter, operations, bravery,
      pathos, success, God." Finds the writing to be "able and
      of a mesmeric flatness." Also finds a remarkable similarity
      between Cronin's personal experiences and those of his char-
      acters in the novels.

30   ANON. Review of <u>Adventures in Two Worlds</u>. <u>New York Times</u>,
      25 February, p. 19.
         Brief mention.

31   ANON. Review of <u>Adventures in Two Worlds</u>. <u>Pendleton East
      Oregonian</u>, 12 April, p. 7.
         This will please all those who like doctor stories.

32   ANON. Review of <u>Adventures in Two Worlds</u>. <u>San Francisco
      Call-Bulletin</u>, 23 February, p. 3.
         This book is certain to increase Cronin's "already con-
      siderable stature as a writer." Cronin reveals his usual
      "warmth and understanding" when describing the simple coun-
      try people of Scotland and the coal miners of Wales. Finds
      disappointing the account of his rapid literary climb and
      his return to faith.

33   ANON. "The Genuine Scot." <u>Atlantic Monthly</u> 189 (March):79.
         Review of <u>Adventures in Two Worlds</u>. Much of the auto-
      biography is predictable, since for two decades people have
      been reading about his life. He carries the reader forward
      "not by any compulsion of style, wit, or originality but by
      his genuine interest in men and women whom he doctored as
      best he could and whose problems and heartaches will appeal
      to many."

34   ANON. "Thoughts of A Novelist." <u>Times Literary Supplement</u>
      (London), 28 March, p. 219.
         Review of <u>Adventures in Two Worlds</u>. At times Cronin's
      reasoning seems "more dogmatic than persuasive; it will
      doubtless please the converted, but will it (as he hopes)
      convert the atheist? One suspects not, and that such a
      reader is the more likely to be won over when Dr. Cronin is
      recording, not commenting upon, incidents in his life." In
      truth, this book is "a novelist's by-product."

1952

35   ANON. "Vignettes." <u>Cincinnati Enquirer</u>, 2 March, p. 5.
          Review of <u>Adventures in Two Worlds</u>. This sentimental
      book is "impregnated with his own personal wisdom as a
      healer of men, and with his own optimism."

36   B., J. "Doctor Cronin Pens His Memoirs." <u>Hamilton Spectator</u>
      (Ont.), 29 March, p. 16.
          Review of <u>Adventures in Two Worlds</u>. Like most of his
      writings, Cronin entertains and educates, but toward the
      end the book is "little more than padding."

37   BARKHAM, JOHN. "Brief Reviews: A.J. Cronin on Himself."
      <u>Newark Star-Ledger</u>, 23 February, p. 4.
          Review of <u>Adventures in Two Worlds</u>. Says that "it is
      Cronin the doctor who makes this the best book Cronin the
      writer has yet produced."

38   BILLINGS, F. TREMAINE. "Doctor into Author." <u>Nashville Banner</u>,
      22 February, p. 7.
          Review of <u>Adventures in Two Worlds</u>. Cronin's writing is
      "smooth and quite readable." Feels that the first eighteen
      chapters are the best. In the later chapters, he becomes
      confused when trying to answer the question "'Why are we
      here?'" The book is similar to Alex Munthe's <u>The Story of
      San Michelle</u>. "Both authors are renegades from medicine,
      but Munthe from start to finish much more refreshingly ad-
      mits to clay legs."

39   BOND, ALICE DIXON. "The Case for Books: The Sum of a Life's
      Parts Makes a Colorful and Warmly Human Whole." <u>Boston
      Herald</u>, 24 February, p. 4.
          Review of <u>Adventures in Two Worlds</u>. The frame of Cronin's
      personal story is not unknown to readers of <u>The Green Years</u>
      and <u>Shannon's Way</u>. But in his autobiography, Cronin has
      given "the flesh of life to the picture."

40   BOOCHEVER, FLORENCE. "Recent Books: A Selection: Nonfiction."
      <u>Bookmark</u> 7 (February):104.
          <u>Adventures in Two Worlds</u> is an "absorbing tale."

41   BRAMAN, DON. "A.J. Cronin, Slaving for Success, Overwhelmed
      When He Caught It." <u>Minneapolis Tribune</u>, 24 February, p. 4.
          Review of <u>Adventures in Two Worlds</u>. Cronin reveals a
      "rare objective honesty about himself and his motives."
      Finds in this story reminiscences of Horatio Alger.

42   C., A. Review of <u>Adventures in Two Worlds</u>. <u>Daily Star
      Freeholder</u> (Cornwall, Canada) (29 March), p. 7.

The book is more than self-revelation. "It is an inter-
estingly-compiled narrative of an exciting and often enviable
life; and at the same time serves up a liberal helping of
faith and philosophy made easy to take because it is logical."

43 CADY, ERNEST. "Books: A.J. Cronin's Story Sure-Fire Candidate
    for Best Sellerdom." Columbus (Ohio) Dispatch, 24 February,
    p. 11.
        Review of Adventures in Two Worlds. "His reminiscences
    have a sturdy thread of continuity, but it is obvious that
    this is only the outline, embellished here and there, of
    the whole of an unusual and varied life." Hopes Cronin will
    share more of his life in future volumes.

44 CARROLL, TOM. "Dr. Cronin's Own History." Dayton News,
    24 February, p. 10.
        Review of Adventures in Two Worlds. The whole book is
    summed up in the final chapter in which he "offers a passion-
    ate plea for a universal moral regeneration." Fans of
    Cronin's novels will enjoy this book.

45 CULLIVAN, GERALD. "A.J. Cronin Recounts His Journey to Faith."
    Dallas Morning News, 16 March, pt. vi, p. 6.
        Review of Adventures in Two Worlds. Although this is an
    entertaining study, only in the final pages does it become
    "a very human, moving document."

46 D., W.A. "Scottish Novelist Writes of His Life As a Doctor."
    Globe and Mail (Toronto), 15 March, p. 10.
        Review of Adventures in Two Worlds. Calls this "charming
    and amusing." Hopes Cronin will complete the story in future
    volumes.

47 DANSKIN, HANNAH. "Drama Enlivens Doctor's Memoirs." Spokane
    Spokesman's Review, 1 May, p. 8.
        Review of Adventures in Two Worlds. Unlike a formal
    autobiography, this book is constructed of complete short
    stories from Cronin's own life. "Each incident is dramatic
    and persuasive. Each has suspense, sympathy and humor."

48 DAVENPORT, JOUETT. "Doctor Turned Writer: A.J. Cronin
    Adventures with Diagnosis of Life." Atlanta Constitution,
    24 February, p. 7.
        Review of Adventures in Two Worlds. Finds this "as rich
    in entertainment" as any of Cronin's novels. Enjoys the
    humor, the profound anecdotes, and the search for truth.

49 DUFFEY, FELIX D. Review of Adventures in Two Worlds. Notre

1952

Dame Ave Maria (March), p. 14.
In this "moving narrative," Cronin's style is free of af-
fection. His tone is warm and conversational. Although
some of these pieces appeared earlier, "in their proper setting as parts of a variegated whole life's pattern they have
even a greater charm and significance than when they first
appeared." Enjoys Cronin's character portrayals and philosophy. There is not a dull page in the book.

50   FARQUHARSON, R.A. "Books: Man, Medicine, Literature."
Saturday Night (Toronto), (29 March), p. 62.
Review of Adventures in Two Worlds. To this book Cronin
brings the techniques of a fiction writer. Therefore, "the
characters have the reality of the good novelist rather than
the more prosaic reality of fact." Cronin leaves plenty of
room for another volume.

51   FORD, ANNE. "Lucky Dr. Cronin Had a Wife to Brag To." Boston
Globe, 30 November, p. 8.
Brief summary of Adventures in Two Worlds.

52   G., M.D. "Cronin on Cronin: Good; Cronin on World: So-So."
Colonist (Victoria, B.C.), 30 March, p. 7.
Review of Adventures in Two Worlds. The book is fresh
and interesting because "it reveals a mind sensitive to and
familiar with the tragic-comic possibilities or aspects of
almost every phase of human experience." The final chapters
are a bit too anecdotal in style, however.

53   GRADY, R.F. S.J. Review of Adventures in Two Worlds. Best
Sellers 31 (March):22.
This account is as fascinating as any novel Cronin has
written. Perhaps the material might be rewritten into a
collection of stories, similar to Maugham's Quartet and Trio.

54   H., H. "Popular Author Tells Own Story." Springfield (Mass.)
Republican, 23 March, p. 219.
Review of Adventures in Two Worlds. None of Cronin's novels is "more gripping, or richer in fundamental values" than
this account of his own experiences.

55   H., R. "A Doctor Who Turned Writer." Portland (Maine) Telegram,
23 March, p. 5.
Review of Adventures in Two Worlds. Finds in this book
the "pace, the narrative interest, and the fine touches of
human sympathy" which are found in his novels.

56   HEYERDAHL, ANNA. "On the Shelf at Clarkston." Lewiston (Idaho)

130

Tribune, 9 March, p. 11.
 Adventures in Two Worlds is "exciting and dramatic."

57 HILL, HARRIET. "Books of the Day: Physician and Writer."
     Gazette (Montreal), 15 March, p. 8.
      Review of Adventures in Two Worlds. This is not only
     absorbing reading but also "a testament to force and up-
     rightness of character."

58 J., R.E. "Cronin's Non-Fiction." Tucson Star, 19 April, p. 5.
      Review of Adventures in Two Worlds. Comments on the sus-
     pense and power of description in this Horatio Alger story.
     Unless the reader is a Cronin fan, it might be better to
     read this book a little at a time.

59 JANEWAY, ELIZABETH. "To the Top in 90 Days." New York Times,
     24 February, p. 6.
      Review of Adventures in Two Worlds. Cronin avoids answer-
     ing in depth many questions about his work as a writer as
     well as about internal events of his personal life. Thus,
     it is not autobiography but "a series of episodes which might
     have happened to any of his characters." Finds the early epi-
     sodes to be the best. In the later ones, Cronin is less lik-
     able. He moralizes too much and has little use for Londoners.
     "Without the warmth of friendship to give them a glow Dr.
     Cronin's stories get a little tricky and a little sticky,
     too."

60 JOHNSON, BLANCHE. "Doctor Yearned to Be Novelist." Tulsa
     World, 20 April, p. 6.
      Brief summary of Adventures in Two Worlds.

61 JOHNSTON, MARGUERITE. Review of Adventures in Two Worlds.
     Houston Post, 16 March, p. 11.
      Cronin's experiences as a youth have given "color, real-
     ism and body" to his novels. So many of these episodes are
     recognizable to readers of The Citadel.

62 JORDAN-SMITH, PAUL. "Cronin's Life Story Has Powerful Appeal."
     Los Angeles Sunday Times, 24 February, pt. iv, p. 6.
      Review of Adventures in Two Worlds. In this very moving
     autobiography, Cronin does not disappoint his expectant read-
     ers. The dramatic tales, the character portrayals, and the
     religious philosophy at the end contribute to a powerful
     story.

63 JOYCE, MARGARET. "Leaves from the Library." Quincy (Mass.)
     Patriot Ledger, 12 March, p. 18.

1952

Review of <u>Adventures in Two Worlds</u>. Cronin tells his
story with "disarming simplicity and in fast moving narrative form."

64   KILCOYNE, FRANCIS P. Review of <u>Adventures in Two Worlds</u>.
      <u>Brooklyn Eagle</u>, 9 March, p. 7.
           Cronin has set down some of the most interesting experi-
      ences of his life. Each chapter is a story in itself.

65   LAVERY, EMMET. "Books." <u>Commonweal</u> 55 (29 February):523.
           Review of <u>Adventures in Two Worlds</u>. As a born storyteller,
      Cronin writes about his own life "with gusto and a lavish use
      of color." In spite of the "heart-warming" character por-
      trayals, however, the book is "more dogmatic than persuasive."
      Although "the style is a little rich, [Cronin's] heart is in
      the right place."

66   LAWRENCE, HENRY H. "A.J. Cronin's Own Life Is Colorful Story."
      <u>San Antonio Express</u>, 9 March, p. 7.
           Review of <u>Adventures in Two Worlds</u>. For a fuller summa-
      tion of Cronin's life, one should read his novels.

67   M., J.J. "Prescription." <u>Catholic Times</u>, 8 February, p. 7.
           Review of <u>Adventures in Two Worlds</u>. Reading all of these
      episodes at one sitting is "mental gluttony." But they should
      be read. The book is characterized by the "chivalry of Frank
      Merriwell and the sustained suspense of O. Henry."

68   M., N.B. "Double Success: Physician-Novelist Recalls Dual
      Career." <u>Oakland Tribune</u>, 11 May, p. 33.
           Review of <u>Adventures in Two Worlds</u>. "As a raconteur
      Cronin ranks with the best. He brings feeling, vividness
      and a sure sense of climax to every incident."

69   MURPHY, WALLACE. "Dr. A.J. Cronin's Essays Cover Life, Medicine,
      Faith." <u>Dallas Times Herald</u>, 30 March, p. 6.
           Review of <u>Adventures in Two Worlds</u>. Compares Cronin's
      career to that of Lloyd Douglas, retired pastor turned novel-
      ist. Both men had a greater impact on the public during their
      second careers. Both have written "moral fiction" which has
      been made into movies and translated into many languages.
      Yet Cronin is certainly "the better craftsman, better artist
      in words and better philosopher." But his autobiography is
      not his best book. It lacks continuity and "explicit char-
      acterization." Its spiritual lessons, however, are needed
      more than ever.

70   N., G.L. "Dr. A.J. Cronin and His Two Worlds." <u>New Bedford</u>

Standard, 31 March, p. 10.
Review of *Adventures in Two Worlds*. This is "a beautiful and inspiring story of faith in the goodness and godliness of mankind."

71   N., S. Review of *Adventures in Two Worlds*. *Vancouver Sunday Sun* (B.C.), 8 March, p. 7.
Comments on Cronin's character portrayals (better than when he is writing about himself) and his love for human beings.

72   NAYLOR, PAULINE. "Hobnails and Guineas: Two Worlds of Spirit and Flesh in Cronin Life Story." *Fort Worth Star*, 24 February, p. 7.
Review of *Adventures in Two Worlds*. Cronin expresses "a simple faith and concern for humankind." His character portrayals are "magnificent."

73   NEUMAN, IRENE F. "Book of the Week." *Gloucester* (Mass.) *Times*, 9 April, p. 3.
Review of *Adventures in Two Worlds*. This is a "perceptive document of self-revelation, a fast-moving narrative of an exciting life, and a stirring adventure in the realm of faith and philosophy."

74   O., O. "A Proud Man Who Found His Happiness in Humility." *Boston Post*, 2 March, p. 16.
Review of *Adventures in Two Worlds*. "This is a lovely book, nourishing to more than the mind. Robust and old-fashioned in its moral courage, timeless in its human appeal to the heart, superb in its power to entertain and delight."

75   O'LEARY, MARY C. "Doctor Who Turned Author." *Worcester* (Mass.) *Telegram*, 24 February, p. 6.
Review of *Adventures in Two Worlds*. This is as lively reading as his novels. "Medicine's loss was the literary world's gain."

76   O'NEILL, FRANK. "Books in the News: A.J. Cronin Writes Glowing Memoir but Part of the Story Is Missing." *Cleveland News*, 26 February, p. 12.
Review of *Adventures in Two Worlds*. Missing in the title of the book is reference to Cronin's third world--"the world of the author's spiritual self-discovery and revival."

77   P., D.T. "Ex-Agnostic Cronin Sees the Importance of Faith." *New Haven Register*, 24 February, p. 8.
Review of *Adventures in Two Worlds*. Finds in this book

1952

the same "warmth of feeling and vivid characterization" that
is found in Cronin's novels.

78   PATTERSON, WILLIAM D. "Literary Medico Popular Among Readers
      Now." Santa Barbara News, 18 May, p. 3.
          Review of Adventures in Two Worlds. "As a novelist, the
      author has the skill to raise or depress us with the story
      of himself as he once was." Many of these episodes are hard
      to forget.

79   PAULDING, GOUVERNEUR. "The Old-Fashioned Success Story of A.J.
      Cronin, Doctor-Novelist." New York Herald-Tribune Books,
      24 February, p. 3.
          Review of Adventures in Two Worlds. These memoirs are
      "unashamedly moral, sentimental, clean and hopeful. They
      are written with disarming simplicity."

80   PEARSON, R.N. ·"Cronin's Autobiography Has Appeal of His
      Novels." Windsor Daily Star (Ont.), 15 March, p. 24.
          Review of Adventures in Two Worlds. For those readers
      looking for a day-by-day chronology of Cronin's life, this
      book will be a disappointment. Revealed is the author's
      faith in the goodness of mankind. "His mastery of English
      is deft and leaves his reader with a crystal-clear picture
      of character and scene."

81   REED, LOIS. "Writings on Readings." Hudson (Ohio) Times,
      29 February, p. 11.
          Review of Adventures in Two Worlds. Readers of Cronin's
      fiction will find in this book "equal interest, adventure
      and faith."

82   ROTHERMEL, J.F. "Book Suggests Underlying Spiritual Integrity
      Apparently Motivates Cronin's Writing." Birmingham (Ala.)
      News, 24 February, p. 9.
          Review of Adventures in Two Worlds. In spite of its "lack
      of connectedness," this book will appeal to all Cronin fans.
      A third "world" of Cronin's is spiritual.

83   S., R.I. Review of Adventures in Two Worlds. Cleveland Plain
      Dealer, 23 March, p. 2.
          A modest book without "a dull line." Finds disappointing
      the lack of details about Cronin's life after Hatter's Castle.

84   S., T. "Stethoscope and Stylus." Nashville Tennessean, 6 April,
      p. 4.
          Adventures in Two Worlds has all the drama of the usual
      "rags-to-riches recital."

1952

85   SHERMAN, THOMAS B. "Reading and Writing: A.J. Cronin's Memoirs
      Recall His Novels." St. Louis Post-Dispatch, 24 February,
      p. 3.
          Review of Adventures in Two Worlds. Readers of Cronin's
      fiction will recognize many of these episodes. Speculates
      that in some of these scenes, Cronin must have allowed him-
      self the license of the artist. In style, material and basic
      philosophy, much is the same in both fact and fiction.

86   SLAUGHTER, FRANK G. "Physician-Novelist." Saturday Review
      (London) 35 (1 March):11.
          Review of Adventures in Two Worlds. Admires Cronin's
      "flair for suspense and crisis" as well as his ability to
      write bits of a detective story. Finds here the "emergence
      of a more mature, more philosophical talent, which . . . may
      yet herald A.J. Cronin's most important field of work."

87   SMITH, HENRY H. "Dr. A.J. Cronin and a Critic from Mars."
      Providence Journal, 24 February, p. 5.
          Review of Adventures in Two Worlds. Never has autobiog-
      raphy revealed so little and enjoyed "so many baroque adjec-
      tives doing so." Unfortunately, too, Cronin says little
      about his literary triumphs.

88   SPRY, DICK. "Cronin." Des Moines Register, 17 February, p. 3.
          Review of Adventures in Two Worlds. Cronin must have led
      a Horatio Alger life.

89   STARR, JIMMY. Review of Adventures in Two Worlds. Los Angeles
      Herald Express, 27 February, p. 5.
          Cronin writes about his life as an author with "annoying
      nonchalance," but his story is filled with warmth.

90   TAYLOR, PAMELA. Review of Adventures in Two Worlds. Book-of-
      the-Month Club News (April), p. 4.
          "His gift for catching the excitement, unexpected twists,
      humorous overtones and frequent tragic endings of human situ-
      ations makes this autobiography as readable and entertaining
      as his fictions."

91   THEALL, D. BERNARD. Review of Adventures in Two Worlds.
      America 103 (8 March):8.
          It is unclear whether the two worlds of the title refer
      to the worlds of medicine and literature or to those of the
      flesh and the spirit. The later chapters "seem to be in-
      creasingly fictional in nature, and reminiscent of the in-
      spirational episodes so dear to the Reader's Digest." All
      in all, this is disappointing as autobiography.

1952

92   THOMAS, A.M. "Cronin Story Covers Two Career Success."
     Victoria Times (Canada), 12 April, p. 7.
            Review of Adventures in Two Worlds. Cronin telescopes
     his chronology for dramatic effect. After reading the book,
     one will think "the world a better and a safer place in spite
     of everything."

93   THOMPSON, B.J. Review of Adventures in Two Worlds. Catholic
     World 175 (April):76.
            "It is difficult to recount one's own triumphs, small or
     great, with becoming modesty; but Dr. Cronin has succeeded
     admirably, focusing the reader's attention upon the drama,
     the pathos, and the glory of human existence as seen through
     the eyes of a doctor."

94   VOILES, JANE. Review of Adventures in Two Worlds. San
     Francisco Chronicle, 30 March, p. 18.
            Cronin's writing is simple, "using the manner of a genera-
     tion ago." The book is more entertaining than his last two
     novels. As in his fiction, here he attacks "the great mass
     of indifference and materialism in the world today."

95   WALBRIDGE, EARLE F. "General: New Books Appraised." Library
     Journal 77 (1 February):208.
            Review of Adventures in Two Worlds. Although lacking
     clear organization, "it is crisply told, always interesting,
     and filled with life, like his fiction." Cronin is an in-
     variable storyteller. Notes that the chapters covering the
     writing of Hatter's Castle appeared years ago in John O'
     London's Weekly.

96   WARE, HARLAN. "Dr. Cronin's Own Story." Pasadena Star-News,
     2 May, p. 10.
            Review of Adventures in Two Worlds. As with his fiction,
     here Cronin writes with "clarity and restraint, with honesty
     and imagination. His work is well organized, soundly con-
     structed, always intact." He knows how to use the tools of
     his trade without fumbling.

97   WILSON, WILLIAM E. "A.J. Cronin Recalls His Medical Days:
     Books in Review." Baltimore Evening Sun, 25 February, p. 2.
            Review of Adventures in Two Worlds. This is pleasurable
     reading. Cronin once again draws on his talent for narrative.

98   WOOD, JAMES PLAYSTED. "Author-Physician Cronin Reviews His Dual
     Career." Philadelphia Inquirer Magazine, 24 February, p. 37.
            Review of Adventures in Two Worlds. "It is the kind of
     readable, pleasant, not very profound but not too commonplace,

easily dramatic story one would expect from the author of
The Citadel and The Keys of the Kingdom." Finds that every
episode is "carefully wrought with balanced ingredients of
drama."

99 WORKS, CHARLES. "Keeping Up." Mesa (Ariz.) Daily Tribune,
      12 April, p. 4.
          Calls Adventures in Two Worlds Cronin's "stirring" adven-
      tures in "the realm of faith and philosophy."

1953

1 ADAMS, ELIZABETH. Review of Beyond this Place. Providence
      Journal, 26 July, p. 5.
          Says that no one can define good and evil as clearly as
      Cronin. His narrative skill saves this book from "a patent
      slickness." Finds that his formula for success is still
      working.

2 ANON. "A False Conviction." Hamilton Spectator (Ont.),
      15 August, p. 6.
          Review of Beyond this Place. This is a story that has
      been told many times. Cronin does a fair job with it, "but
      only because he is a practised storyteller." He uses the
      plot to destroy yet another citadel--the whole body of the
      British judiciary. However, "the righteous wrath that comes
      at the end, with the triumph of virtue, loses much of its
      force because we do not believe in its justification."

3 ANON. "A.J. Cronin Novel Is Guild Selection." Indianapolis
      Times, 29 March, p. 11.
          Notes that Beyond this Place, to be published 20 July,
      is the Literary Guild's selection for August.

4 ANON. "A Physician Sails the Sea." St. Louis Post-Dispatch,
      29 March, p. 4.
          Comments on the paperback edition of Grand Canary--a
      "popular romance," one of the best.

5 ANON. "Book Club Choices." New York Herald-Tribune Books,
      24 March, p. 11.
          Literary Guild has chosen Beyond this Place for its
      August selection.

6 ANON. "Books." Time 62 (27 July):92.
          Review of Beyond this Place. "Author Cronin's British
      memories seem to have got confused by his 14 years of

1953

residence in the U.S., so that his book is like a game of
baseball played by somebody who thinks it is cricket."
Questions the believability of the following characters:
Sir Matthew Sprott, Wortley's police chief, and Wortley's
newspapermen.

7   ANON. "Books: Briefly Noted: Fiction." New Yorker 29
(1 August):59.
    Review of Beyond this Place. In this slow, "rather in-
tense" novel, Cronin tries to make the conspiracy against
Burgess "very evil, but is unconvincing because of the small
stature of the people involved in it." He is sincere, however, and therefore "the occasional descents into melodrama
are touching."

8   ANON. "Cronin Novel Choice of Literary Guild." Bridgeport
Post, 22 March, p. 3.
    Beyond this Place is the August selection of the Literary
Guild.

9   ANON. "Dr. Cronin's Search for Justice." Boston Sunday Herald,
19 July, p. 10.
    Review of Beyond this Place. Calls this search for the
truth "a suspenseful, many peopled, attention engaging tale
which holds much implicit information about the pitfalls for
justice in the system of trial by jury." However, this novel
lacks the depth and vitality found in his best work.

10 ANON. "Fiction." Booklist 50 (1 September):13.
    Review of Beyond this Place. "What might have been a
routine detective story becomes an absorbing novel, with
convincing characterization and sensitivity to ethical values."

11 ANON. "Fiction." Bookmark 12 (July):231.
    Review of Beyond this Place. This will make "absorbing,
somewhat melodramatic reading." A shorter version appeared
in Collier's under the title, To Live Again.

12 ANON. "Fiction." Kirkus 21 (15 May):309.
    Review of Beyond this Place. Notes that this novel is
an expansion of the serialized To Live Again (Collier's).
Although mystery stories are not Cronin's forte, "his gift
for spinning a yarn stands him in good stead and keeps the
reader interested."

13 ANON. Review of Beyond this Place. Albuquerque Journal,
11 October, p. 5.
    This is "a very human and enthralling story."

14 ANON. Review of <u>Beyond this Place</u>. <u>Idaho Tribune</u>, 4 October,
    p. 3.
       Brief plot summary.

15 ANON. Review of <u>Beyond this Place</u>. <u>Manchester</u> (N.H.) <u>News</u>,
    26 July, p. 6.
       Cronin's story holds the reader's attention throughout.
    "Yet I find it hard to believe I can be so gripped, and I
    am but red-faced about it, too, when the story is so obvious,
    and the style and vocabulary so trite."

16 ANON. Review of <u>Beyond this Place</u>. <u>Monetary Times</u> (Toronto)
    (November), p. 10.
       This novel is memorable because of "the dark glimpses it
    offers of life behind prison walls." Cronin offers "no sub-
    tle colors" in this novel. Everything is "harsh, ironical,
    and overcast with a thick Puritanical gloom."

17 ANON. Review of <u>Beyond this Place</u>. <u>New York Times</u>, 7 April,
    p. 16.
       Brief notice of its publication date and adoption by the
    Literary Guild for August. Reprinted: 1953.18.

18 ANON. Review of <u>Beyond this Place</u>. <u>New York Times</u>, 15 June,
    p. 18.
       Reprint of 1953.17.

19 ANON. Review of <u>Beyond this Place</u>. <u>Trenton Times</u>, 28 June,
    p. 13.
       Quotes Cronin's comments on the novel. "'I felt I must
    write this book because the present system of trial by jury,
    which has remained unchanged for many centuries, does not
    represent the best or the fairest method of judiciary pro-
    cesses, especially in capital charges. The system is liable
    to grave errors, particularly when, as so often happens, the
    case for the prosecution is presented by a strong and capable
    advocate and that for the defense by someone less competent
    and with less ability to play upon the emotions of the jury,
    who, incidentally, may be uninformed and, in some cases, un-
    intelligent individuals.'"

20 ANON. Review of <u>Beyond this Place</u>. <u>Washington Post</u>, 12 July,
    p. 3.
       "A novel about a youth who was able to reverse the unjust
    conviction of his father."

21 ANON. Review of <u>Beyond this Place</u>. <u>Waterloo Record</u> (Ont.)
    1 August, p. 6.

1953

> This is "a moving story of a man's love for his father whom he had not seen for fifteen years."

22 ANON. "The Book Review." San Francisco Call-Bulletin, 25 July, p. 7.
> Review of Beyond this Place. Cronin's new novel is saved because it is a "whodunit." The hero is recognizable to Cronin readers, but his fortunes "fail to evoke the same emotional response and deep sympathy as previous prototypes." Comments on the suspense, the stereotype characters, the co-incidental plot, and the unsatisfying solution.

23 B., D.B. "Beyond this Place: A.J. Cronin's Novel of Loyalty and Injustice an Indictment of the Jury System." Springfield (Mass.) Republican, 19 July, p. 7D.
> "Even with the social importance of the theme, it takes a writer of Mr. Cronin's talent for drama and characterization to make a story of this kind convincing. And he keeps getting on with it, without undue preaching."

24 BARKHAM, JOHN. "Even the Judge Was a Conniver." New York Times, 19 July, p. 5.
> Review of Beyond this Place. Calls this an "old-fashioned melodrammer of the kind popular circa Ouida and Marie Corelli." Cronin has elected to write a suspenseful tale "without regard for people or probabilities."

25 C., D.H. "Books and Authors." Lewiston-Auburn (Maine) Sun, 21 July, p. 4.
> Review of Beyond this Place. In what is perhaps Cronin's most dramatic tale, the theme speaks to both the heart and the mind of the reader. "This book will appeal to all who would champion the underdog; to all who believe in a true and equitable justice; and to all who despise public officials who promote their own careers at the expense of anyone who stands in their way."

26 COMANS, GRACE P. "Search for Justice." Hartford Courant, 18 July, p. 9.
> Review of Beyond this Place. Once again Cronin has proved himself "a master contriver of plot and atmosphere." The story is "rich in its emotional content."

27 CULHANE, ELEANOR F. "Books to Read: A Son's Efforts--New Cronin Novel Tells Story of English Family Drama." Boston Sunday Globe, 19 July, p. 21.
> Review of Beyond this Place. Other writers have handled crime reconstruction and trial procedure "far more

penetratingly;" however, this is a "reasonably exciting story, in which the most vital and credible character turns out to be the convict Mathry."

28   ELLIOTT, J.K. Review of Beyond this Place. Evening Free Press (London), 3 October, p. 9.
        This novel is likely to "ruffle the law courts." It is different from the autobiographical novel which preceded it.

29   HILL, HARRIET. "Miscarriage of Justice." Gazette (Montreal), 8 August, p. 7.
        Review of Beyond this Place. "Putting aside the question of fairness, the story has a fine suspense that guarantees its reading to be a 'one session' job." Avid detective story fans will enjoy this, as will those who, "like the Victorians before them, only appreciate a villain when he consistently acts the villain. After all, a world of black and white is a comfortable world. You know exactly where you're at!"

30   HOLDEN, THEODORE L. "Cronin Novel a Human Study." Hartford Times, 18 July, p. 4.
        Review of Beyond this Place. Calls this "another potent mixture of fast-paced narrative and perceptive study of human reactions." Cronin's people stand out "sharply."

31   HOLZHAUER, JEAN. "The Price of Reticence." Commonweal 58 (17 July):374.
        Review of Beyond this Place. Cronin's latest novel is "a rather flat and mechanical tale." The outcome is predictable and the atmosphere is "oppressive with contrived mystification." His authentic touches when describing local scenes are lost "in the elaborate forest of stereotype."

32   HUTCHENS, JOHN K. "Book Review." New York Herald-Tribune Books, 20 July, p. 6.
        Review of Beyond this Place. "It is really hard to remember when a novelist last filled a book with so many one-dimensional characters, rich, verdant clichés and generally implausible conversations." Ever since Hatter's Castle, Cronin has written in support of "honest hearts, willing hands, troubled heroes who surmount their problems, and forthright plots that have a better than even chance of turning successfully into celluloid."

33   KEEFER, CLAIRE. "Novel of the Week." Journal (Ottawa), 15 August, p. 5.
        Review of Beyond this Place. Although the story begins slowly, Cronin's narrative builds to a climax. "An exciting but meretricious novel."

1953

34   LEE, CHARLES. "Fraying Margins of Error." <u>Saturday Review of
     Literature</u> 36 (25 July):14.
          Review of <u>Beyond this Place</u>. Quotes Cronin who said about
     this novel: "'It is probably the most exciting novel I have
     ever written.'" Feels, however, that Cronin's nine previous
     novels are "better proportioned and more intelligent." Finds
     the major fault here as having been "'constructed' . . . to
     fit a crusade." The characters are stereotyped. The book
     reads like "badly diluted Dickens, passionate urgency all
     but gone and humor totally absent."

35   McQUAID, ESTHER. "Notes about New Books and Libraries."
     <u>Medford</u> (Mass.) <u>Mercury</u>, 25 August, p. 2.
          Review of <u>Beyond this Place</u>. Praises the novel for its
     "smooth dramatic plot, its intense writing, and its skillful
     characterization." Its theme adds to the novel's "social
     importance."

36   MILLER, LOUISE R. "New Books Appraised: Fiction." <u>Library
     Journal</u> 78 (15 June):1148.
          Review of <u>Beyond this Place</u>. "A sure best seller, this
     is unexpectedly a mystery. But in smooth dramatic plot, in-
     tense writing, and skillful characterization, it equals the
     famous novelist's early successes." Reminiscent of Dickens.

37   N., G.L. "Convict's Son Seeks the Truth." <u>New Bedford Standard</u>,
     16 August, p. 5.
          Review of <u>Beyond this Place</u>. Although not up to the stan-
     dards of Cronin's earlier novels, this sentimental book is
     "a good subject for a night of cozy reading."

38   NORTH, STERLING. "Sterling North Reviews the Books." <u>New York
     World Telegram</u>, 20 July, p. 7.
          Review of <u>Beyond this Place</u>. Finds a number of similari-
     ties between this book and Cronin's earlier novels: it is
     "smooth melodrama"; there is a "strong, triangular love in-
     terest, contrast between life of the rich and the poor, white
     virtue and black villainy, suspense action, excellent pace
     and unexpectedly perceptive relationship between father and
     son"; and there is to the story some social significance.
     In this protest against injustice, however, the prose is un-
     distinguished, the contrasts are often "too violent."

39   O., O. "A World-Famous Novelist Attacks the English Court."
     <u>Boston Post</u>, 26 July, p. 7.
          Review of <u>Beyond this Place</u>. Calls this an "exciting,
     important, and satisfying" novel. The ending, however, is
     anticlimactic. "It is a pity that Dr. Cronin's editors let

1953

Lena walk out of the story ages before the finale, only to
appear as a shadowy after-thought on the last page." Also,
the real murderer's monologue reads like "a takeoff of itself." All in all, the novel is "robust and old-fashioned
in its moral courage, timeless in its human appeal to the
heart, superb in its power to entertain."

40   P., D.T. "Novel of Suspense." Worcester (Mass.) Telegram,
       19 July, p. 5.
            Review of Beyond this Place. Finds the first half of the
       novel better than the latter half. Little depth of interpre-
       tation suggests that Cronin may be at his best when he is not
       dealing with "crime and degradation."

41   PIPPETT, ROGER. Review of Beyond this Place. Book-of-the-Month
       Club News (August), p. 4.
            "Like a latter-day Dickens, Cronin is moved to indignation
       by the callousness of the law and its workings, and the
       frightening change that imprisonment has wrought in Paul's
       father is most movingly conveyed." Finds "a Hardyish note
       of irony and mischance."

42   PRESCOTT, ORVILLE. "Books of the Times." New York Times,
       20 July, p. 15.
            Review of Beyond this Place. This latest novel--detective
       story as well as a tale of legal and police corruption and a
       young man's struggle against heavy odds--seems one of Cronin's
       least successful. The writing is at times careless and awk-
       ward. There are many improbabilities. However, "the essen-
       tial drama of its story and the steady march of its action
       do much to atone for its shortcomings and to insure that Dr.
       Cronin's readers will be entertained."

43   PROVEN, GRACE. "Book Marks." Pittsburgh Press, 3 May, p. 4.
            Review of Beyond this Place. Cronin appears headed for
       another "'hour of glory'" with his latest novel.

44   ROSS, MARY. "Pattern of Murder." New York Herald-Tribune
       Books, 19 July, p. 6.
            Review of Beyond this Place. As usual, Cronin pleads for
       "understanding of the poor and unsuccessful and does not hesi-
       tate to show up callousness and worse in high places where he
       finds it." But this story fails to hold the reader's atten-
       tion. The outcome is obvious from the beginning. "Neither
       as a 'whodunit' nor as a tale of passion and character does
       the story become sufficiently important to the reader."

45   SMITH, HARRISON. Review of Beyond this Place. Evening Citizen

1953

(Ottawa), 18 July, p. 7.
Calls this a "powerful and moving indictment." Wonders
why Cronin has abandoned his romantic and "often prodigious-
ly successful themes" for this "angry book."

46 SULLIVAN, RICHARD. Review of Beyond this Place. Chicago Sunday
Tribune, 19 July, p. 3.
Comments on Cronin's simple characterizations, unpreten-
tious and plain phrasing, and the "surge of feeling" which
dominates the narrative. "Expertly handled melodrama and
lavishly evoked emotion--these are elements upon which Cronin
relies for his effects. And for what he wants to do they
serve him well."

47 WALKER, JOAN. "Melodrama." Globe and Mail (Toronto), 12
September, p. 5.
Review of Beyond this Place. Calls this "a pseudo who-
dunit which reads like an early Victorian melodrama and is
peppered with clichés from first to last."

48 WEDMAN, LES. Review of Beyond this Place. Vancouver Province
(B.C.) 3 October, p. 10.
"Cronin is one of the most straightforward writers in the
business so there's no guesswork as to what's behind his
words. They all add up to a good story, well told and worth
an evening's attention."

1956

1 ANON. "Fiction." Booklist 52 (15 April):325-26, 384.
Review of A Thing of Beauty. "An excellent picture of
an artist and a man obsessed." The condensed version appeared in Cosmopolitan under the title The Pride of Beauty.

2 ANON. "Fiction." Kirkus 24 (15 March):217.
Review of A Thing of Beauty. "This is the best thing
Cronin has done since Shannon's Way."

3 ANON. "Mr. Cronin Returns." Hamilton Spectator (Ont.), 18 May,
p. 5.
Review of A Thing of Beauty. This novel is rewarding to
read. In it Cronin puts "sham and artifice where they be-
long." It will undoubtedly confirm Cronin's position in the
front rank of contemporary writers.

4 ANON. Review of A Thing of Beauty. Chelsea (Mass.) Record,
11 July, p. 8.

This is unquestionably one of Cronin's major works. It
is "a mature and thoughtful novel with a big theme, rich in
character and event, colorful in detail and powerful in its
emotional impact." Its success is its universality. One
doesn't have to know about art to enjoy the story.

5   ANON. Review of A Thing of Beauty. Knoxville News-Sentinel,
    10 June, p. 4.
       Brief mention of the story of "a dedicated artist who
    gave up all else, family included, for art."

6   ANON. Review of A Thing of Beauty. New York Times, 2 May,
    p. 18.
       Notices that this novel will be published by Little, Brown
    on 21 May and that it has been selected by the Literary Guild
    for its June distribution.

7   ANON. Review of A Thing of Beauty. Peterborough (N.H.)
    Transcript, 12 July, p. 4.
       Comments on the beautifully sketched characters and set-
    tings.

8   BARKHAM, JOHN. "Persecuted for His Art." New York Times Book
    Review, 20 May, p. 4.
       Review of A Thing of Beauty. Calls this Cronin's best
    novel since The Citadel. It is, to begin with, "an object
    lesson in the power a writer can infuse into a story when
    he becomes deeply involved with its theme." Unlike his last
    book, Beyond this Place, in which Cronin was "the profession-
    al storyteller," here he writes with "a crusading fervor that
    makes this one of the most moving novels of the year." Every
    word reveals character or advances the plot. In its best
    passages he reaches "heights of real eloquence."

9   BULLOCK, FLORENCE HAXTON. "Cronin Novel of an Artist." New
    York Herald-Tribune Books, 20 May, p. 7.
       Review of A Thing of Beauty. Cronin writes of his hero
    with typical "warmth and appreciation of natural and cultural
    beauty." Because of its sympathetic insight into the life of
    an artist and because of its good story line, it belongs with
    Thomas Craven's Lust for Life and Paint.

10 BUTCHER, FANNY. Review of A Thing of Beauty. Chicago Sunday
    Tribune, 20 May, p. 1.
       Includes plot summary and commentary on the characters
    and conflicts.

11 CONROY, JACK. "Good Reading but No Thing of Beauty." Chicago

1956

Sun Times, 20 May, p. 7.
Review of A Thing of Beauty. Calls this pleasant reading,
in spite of its "hackneyed theme and frequently platitudinous
or banal language." Finds that some of the episodes are
"forcefully written."

12   COONS, PHYLLIS W. "Aristocrats and Artists: Enduring Popular
      Formula Followed Again by A.J. Cronin." Boston Globe,
      27 May, p. 10.
          Review of A Thing of Beauty. "If all the details worked
      out for this enduringly popular formula don't captivate as
      many readers as did Hatter's Castle and The Keys of the
      Kingdom then a revolution will have taken place on the best
      seller lists."

13   FYTTON, FRANCIS. "Dr. Cronin: An Essay in Victoriana."
      Catholic World 183 (August):356-62.
          Discusses the man behind Cronin's novels and his religious
      thinking since his return to the Faith. His works may be di-
      vided into two groups: those before The Keys of the Kingdom
      and those after. The first category grows in quality, and
      the second descends with The Keys of the Kingdom as a peak.
      "And the descent exactly corresponds with the author's growth
      in religious conviction." What is needed of him today is
      "more intellectual purpose, more sense of the Catholic Church
      as a living organism, as the Church Militant and the Church
      Suffering, rather than the Church Triumphant which can seldom
      be the sphere of the novelist with a sense of religion." Re-
      fers to Beyond this Place, The Keys of the Kingdom, Hatter's
      Castle, Shannon's Way, The Green Years, The Spanish Gardener,
      Adventures in Two Worlds, A Thing of Beauty, Grand Canary and
      Crusader's Tomb.

14   H., J. "Dedicated Artist." Boston Post, 20 May, p. 7.
          Review of A Thing of Beauty. Finds that this novel reads
      like "a carefully compiled biography of a good and sincere
      man." It is the story of a man who gave his life for an
      ideal, told against the background of two forces that have
      always existed: "the conservatives and those who strive to
      break through the existing boundaries of self-expression."

15   HENDERSON, ROBERT W. "Fiction." Library Journal 81 (15 April):
      911.
          Review of A Thing of Beauty. Calls this a "magnificent
      picture on a vast canvas." The Spanish episodes remind one
      of Don Quixote.

16   HOWE, MARJORIE. "Marjorie Howe." Burlington (Vt.) Free Press,

146

25 July, p. 4.
Review of A Thing of Beauty. Finds this similar to Noble Savage, a story about Paul Gaugin. Says this is Cronin's "finest book."

17   McL., P. "From Dr. Cronin's Heart." Free Press (Winnipeg), 26 May, p. 7.
Review of A Thing of Beauty. This is Cronin's "most sat-isfying" novel since The Citadel. In spite of its cliché-ridden language, its familiar plot, it is an "absorbing story." Finds the reason for this in Cronin's comment on the book: "'While it is difficult for an author to appraise his own work, I can say in all honesty that this book, more than any other, was written from the heart.'"

18   MERAS, PHYLLIS. "No Joy Forever." Providence Journal, 15 July, p. 10.
Review of A Thing of Beauty. Cronin writes with his ex-pected "agility and polish." Although neither his charac-terization nor his philosophy is memorable, it is enjoyable reading. Wishes, however, that he had expressed a more "powerful feeling." Instead, what one gets is "a most read-able but superficial tale."

19   MINARD, RALPH. "Artist's Story by Cronin Has Unusual Twist." Hartford Times, 19 May, p. 8.
Review of A Thing of Beauty. Cronin's twist at the end is different from some of the recent novels about Van Gogh and Gaugin. Calls this "a fine novel, and an understanding one, in which Cronin provides us with a sort of counterpart of the French artists of a generation ago who suffered while they broke new ground." However, the book is not memorable, for it is the life of "a concocted man."

20   NORTH, STERLING. "Sterling North Reviews the Books." New York World Telegram, 21 May, p. 21.
Review of A Thing of Beauty. Comments on the similarities and differences between this novel and Maugham's Of Human Bondage. Says this is one of Cronin's best works ever writ-ten. Like Maugham, he knows the art of France and Spain. He, too, is an "exceedingly skilled popular story teller." Both books present a tragic theme, too.

21   PRESCOTT, ORVILLE. "Books of the Times." New York Times, 8 June, p. 23.
Review of A Thing of Beauty. This novel ranks below The Stars Look Down and The Citadel, "whose crude power and in-tensity of personal emotion" made them memorable, and well

1956

above his last three novels, "which were sadly disappointing." In spite of his clumsy, old-fashioned prose, and his
flat characters, Cronin always writes with "commendable narrative power." When his feelings are involved, he can make
the reader share those feelings.

22   REDMAN, BEN RAY. "A Painter's Peregrinations." Saturday Review
of Literature 89 (2 June):12.
Review of A Thing of Beauty. Cronin gives his readers "a
carefully constructed story, carefully described characters,
and carefully evoked landscapes. What he does not give them,
on many pages, is the breath of life."

1957

1   M. "Latest Bantams." Montgomery Advertiser, 14 July, p. 2.
Brief mention that A Thing of Beauty is one of the "outstanding titles" released as a Bantam paperback.

1958

1   ANON. "Books: Mixed Fiction." Time 71 (9 June):102-3.
Review of The Northern Light. Cronin's "muscles of . . .
indignation have sagged." Page is a "noble but dull character."

2   ANON. "Fiction." Booklist 54 (15 April):465.
Review of The Northern Light. "The story dramatizes
Page's stubborn fight against the financial power, unscrupu-
lous methods, and sensational appeal of a large London tab-
loid."

3   ANON. "Fiction." Booklist 54 (1 June):561.
Brief mention of The Northern Light.

4   ANON. "Fiction." Bookmark 17 (May):198.
Brief mention of The Northern Light.

5   ANON. "Fiction." Kirkus 26 (15 March):245.
Review of The Northern Light. A somewhat "contrived"
story not likely to win the reader's "emotional acceptance."
Says that it is "slick reading, a time passer, but little
more."

6   ANON. "Fiction." Wisconsin Library Bulletin 54 (May):214.
Review of The Northern Light. "In spite of moments of

suspense, this is a quiet story." The characters are not quite as realized as in previous novels, however.

7   ANON. "More of the Same." Fall River (Mass.) Anchor, 12 June, p. 4.
       Review of The Northern Light. Cronin writes as if Joyce, Mailer, or James Jones had never existed. "Art means nothing to him, and his single objective appears to be to give people 'a good long read' as melodramatic as the stage plays of the turn of the century." Calls this novel "genuine mediocrity, and eminently salable."

8   ANON. "Newspaper Battlefield for Cronin." Bridgeport Post, 18 May, p. 6.
       Review of The Northern Light. Plot summary and brief commentary. Even if this novel were written by an unknown, it would be "an event."

9   ANON. "Paper Goes On." Boston Herald, 1 June, p. 4.
       Review of The Northern Light. "It is a compelling and exciting story which builds steadily and adroitly to its unforeseen climax."

10   BUTCHER, FANNY. Review of The Northern Light. Chicago Sunday Tribune, 1 June, p. 1.
       Finds in this novel Cronin's favorite and always success-ful theme: "a man whose faith in the right is impregnable." Comments on the narrative pressure, the lack of humor, and the characterization. "From this reader's point of view this isn't Cronin's masterpiece, but his second best is so much better than most storytellers' best that The Northern Light is destined for best sellerdom."

11   CRABBE, KENNETH C. "Previewing Books: Dr. Cronin Retells a Newsman's Saga." Augusta (Ga.) Chronicle, 23 September, p. 4.
       Review of The Northern Light. Like Cronin's previous novels, this one concerns a dedicated man. But in writing about a newspaperman, Cronin has strayed away from his ac-customed themes of medicine and religion.

12   FULFORD, ROBERT. "Dr. Cronin at Work." Telegram (Toronto), 7 June, p. 3.
       Review of The Northern Light. When he was writing this novel, Cronin remarked to an interviewer from a British news-paper, "'There is nothing new to write about, only a new way to write about the old things. That is the gimmick.'" The Northern Light demonstrates this thesis. "It is a gimmick

1958

book, with a skillfully twisted plot but not a hint of character." Calls it "a silly, sentimental bore."

13   GIRVIN, PETER. "But the Paper Came Out." New York Herald-
     Tribune Books, 25 May, p. 5.
          Review of The Northern Light. Calls this "a skeleton
     Cronin novel." Missing is the "richness of detail, the
     solidly woven warp and woof of living that have been so
     typically Cronin in previous novels."

14   HAVIGHURST, WALTER. "First-Rate Fourth Estater." Saturday
     Review (London) 41 (24 May):16.
          Review of The Northern Light. "As the plot intensifies
     in threat, resistance, and blackmail, the novel diminishes
     into one-dimensional storytelling." Henry Page reacts to
     the crisis in "terms of his own character and convictions."

15   HENDERSON, ROBERT W. "Fiction." Library Journal 83 (1 June):
     1784.
          Review of The Northern Light. This is a story of "mount-
     ing tension and highly dramatic incident." Although not
     Cronin's best ("Page is much too perfect a man"), it is
     nevertheless "a gripping story and a strong plea for an in-
     dependent press."

16   HUGHES, RILEY. "Books: Novels Reviewed by Riley Hughes."
     Catholic World 187 (June):229.
          Review of The Northern Light. "No doubt the issues and
     problems involved in Dr. Cronin's theme are more complicated
     than he makes them appear to be here, but nobody can deny
     that The Northern Light is that rare thing in a novel today,
     a satisfying and exciting novel."

17   KINNAIRD, CLARK. "Books: An Editor Sticks to his Guns." New
     York Journal-American, 18 May, p. 6.
          Review of The Northern Light. Points out that there
     really is a newspaper called "The Northern Light." It is
     published in the British Isles, Belfast, by "'the Ulster
     Anti-Prohibition Council.'" Predicts that the novel will
     not enhance Cronin's reputation.

18   MUNN, L.S. "An Owner-Editor Meets the Test." Springfield
     (Mass.) Republican, 13 July, p. 5C.
          Review of The Northern Light. "Dr. Cronin has availed
     himself of all the excesses of very, very black and pure,
     pure white in the unrolling of his story and his character
     delineations. Usually an expert in his heavy-handed field
     of personal suffering, Dr. Cronin has missed his mark in

<u>The Northern Light</u>, a novel likely to disappoint even his most ardent admirers."

19 NORMANDIN, FERN. "From the Library." <u>Wakefield</u> (Kans.) <u>Sun</u>, 28 October, p. 7.
     Review of <u>The Northern Light</u>. As the tension rises in this novel, the reader is carried along on "a rushing tide of emotions and events, rising to a breathtaking climax of the kind that only Dr. Cronin can create."

20 O., M.J. "Books." <u>Providence Sunday Journal</u>, 25 May, p. 6.
     Review of <u>The Northern Light</u>. Cronin tells "an old-fashioned story in an old-fashioned manner and reminds us all that truth, honor and integrity will somehow shine through in an imperfect world, in the midst of death, destruction, violence, and general woe."

21 P., D.T. "Idealistic Editor Is Hero of Latest Cronin Novel." <u>New Haven Register</u>, 25 May, p. 8.
     Review of <u>The Northern Light</u>. "Once again A.J. Cronin writes a dramatic and moving story about a man who fights against overwhelming odds to defend his integrity." This might well be one of Cronin's most exciting novels; however, the melodrama is a bit heavy and the villains are not totally convincing. "Yet Cronin's theme rings strong and true and it is satisfying to encounter a plea for idealism after reading books by so many defeatists and cynics."

22 PIPPETT, ROGER. "Facing the Final Deadline." <u>New York Times Book Review</u>, 25 May, p. 4.
     Review of <u>The Northern Light</u>. Says that Cronin has found in Harry Page "a crusader worthy of his talent and his narrative flair." The story line "loops out in near-melodrama in the closing scenes, but it holds."

23 POORE, CHARLES. "Books of the Times." <u>New York Times</u>, 24 May, p. 4.
     Review of <u>The Northern Light</u>. In this "dourly melodramatic" novel, Cronin shows that "righteousness, after a formidable battering, may at least hope to emerge with a share of victories over evil." As readers, we share the struggles of Cronin's characters and of Cronin himself as he wrestles with the plot.

24 RAVEN, SIMON. "Maiden Voyage." <u>Spectator</u> 200 (5 December):835.
     Review of <u>The Northern Light</u>. As usual, Cronin succeeds in making the reader "a partisan over a grossly simplified issue of exaggerated urgency which has been presented in terms of nursery morality."

1958

25 RUDKIN, MARION. "Marion Rudkin's Book Review." Marblehead
    (Mass.) Town Crier, 4 June, p. 2.
        Review of The Northern Light. "May this novel reach out
    across our land with its needed challenge!"

26 SHRAPNEL, NORMAN. Review of The Northern Light. Manchester
    Guardian, 2 December, p. 4.
        Because of its "excessive readability," this novel will
    fail to interest many readers. "All the same it is admirably
    done in its way, and will make large numbers of the more pas-
    sive sort of reader, not to mention the booksellers, happy
    enough."

27 VOILES, JANE. Review of The Northern Light. San Francisco
    Chronicle, 1 June, p. 24.
        As a popular novelist, Cronin is more concerned with what
    he has to say than with how he says it. But his latest novel
    "ranks with his better novels, maintaining a dignity and a
    generous tone throughout."

28 WINSHIP, ELIZABETH C. "Cronin Doesn't Know Newspapers."
    Boston Globe, 1 June, p. 8.
        Review of The Northern Light. Although readable, this is
    a disappointing novel. Henry Page is the same type of hero
    we've found in the earlier novels. "He is a professional
    man, honorable and sensitive, fighting a lonely battle for
    his principles." But he does not seem as real as the hero
    of The Citadel or The Keys of the Kingdom. In spite of the
    timely topic and the "engrossing" story, it hardly seems
    credible that a big newspaper would resort to blackmail.

                              1959

1   ANON. "Fiction: Rooted in Unreality." Times Literary
    Supplement (London), 2 January, p. 5.
        Review of The Northern Light. Cronin's novel is readable
    and the northern industrial background is "plausible." How-
    ever, the characters are "cardboard cut-outs, crudely black
    or white. Page's wife and daughter are too stupid and friv-
    olous to come alive and his daughter-in-law, with her golden
    heart and her guilty past, is a figure of melodrama."

2   DAVIES, DANIEL HORTON. "Pilgrims, Not Strangers." In A Mirror
    of the Ministry in Modern Novels. New York: Oxford
    University Press, pp. 113-28.
        Compares and contrasts the portrayal of a Protestant mis-
    sionary in Maugham's "Rain" and Cronin's Grand Canary and

The Keys of the Kingdom. "If Maugham's is the story of a
believer turned skeptic, Cronin's is that of a skeptic con-
verted."

1960

1   ANON. Review of The Northern Light. Charleston Gazette,
        7 February, p. 7.
        This is yet another of Cronin's "slick woman's magazine-
    type fiction."

1961

1   ANON. Review of The Judas Tree. Adrian (Mich.) Telegram,
        1 July, p. 5.
        Brief comment on a novel about "a man beset by a supreme
    egoism which affects his entire life, particularly his rela-
    tionship with women."

2   ANON. Review of The Judas Tree. Bangor News, 9 October, p. 3.
        This is Cronin's "most probing character study" in some
    time. The author treats his hero with compassion; hence,
    "one would not grace him with the classification of villain."
    Calls the novel "smooth and readable, rich in background as
    always."

3   ANON. Review of The Judas Tree. Minneapolis Tribune, 2 July,
        p. 7.
        Brief mention.

4   BOND, ALICE DIXON. "A.J. Cronin's Judas Tree Conveys His
        Spiritual Values." Boston Sunday Herald, 26 November, p. 17.
        Calls this "a tour de force in which the author gives evi-
    dence, understanding and impact to the ethical problem of an
    individual who will not face up to himself or to the obliga-
    tions he incurs." Comments on Cronin's "strong spiritual
    values" and compassion.

5   DOWNEY, HUGH F. "Books: The Judas Tree Unworthy of Author."
        Lowell (Mass.) Sunday Sun, 29 October, p. 11.
        "The plot is pat, the whole material very trite" and the
    characters are real stereotypes. Expresses regret that
    Cronin has done little in recent years to warrant much at-
    tention.

6   HEALEY, ROBERT C. "A Suave Egoist and His Guilty Past." New

1961

York Herald-Tribune Books, 8 October, p. B4.
Review of The Judas Tree. This is more of a "straight character study" than is expected from Cronin. "He places much less emphasis on melodrama and external action, much more on introspection and psychological development." This technique tends to "minimize his virtues and magnify his vices as a writer." In spite of the clichés, stilted dialogue, flat characters, and uncomplicated emotions, however, his novels are "somehow immensely readable." Says that the hero's metamorphosis is "too complete, too decisive to be credible."

7   KEESE, PARTON C. "Storyteller of Finesse." Worcester (Mass.)
     Telegram, 8 October, p. 11.
     Review of The Judas Tree. The hero should be looked upon with sympathy in this "circumspective" novel. "He lacks good judgment especially. He also lacks a sense of consideration for others. He is particularly a pawn at the hands of women and persons with unscrupulous designs." Yet we feel deeply for Moray through Cronin's magical storytelling ability. From this novel it is easy to see Cronin's preference for "the opulent and the well-bred, culture with altruistic streaks, the conservatism and warmth of the good old days." Obviously he is disenchanted with modern living.

8   LUKER, ELLEN WILLIAMS. "Fiction." Library Journal 86
     (1 October):3298.
     Review of The Judas Tree. Cronin fulfills once again "the promise of great skill in writing and great enjoyment in reading."

9   P., F. "Judas Tree New A.J. Cronin Book." Lewiston (Maine)
     Journal, 16 December, p. 8.
     David Moray lacks the qualities which made the priest in The Keys of the Kingdom such an outstanding and sympathetic character. "But the drawing of Moray is every bit as realistic, even if he is far less appealing as a person."

10   PIPPETT, AILEEN. "Memory of Love." New York Times Book Review,
     15 October, p. 46.
     Review of The Judas Tree. "The mixture of romance and realism is adroit; the reports on life among the ignorant poor and the cultured rich are convincing; the different notes of moral fervor and elegant sophistication are appropriately struck." But too much is contrived. "The sudden changes in situation which would be suitable for comedy turn tragedy into melodrama." David Moray is a flat character whose actions at times are implausible.

11   S., M. "Cronin's Latest Is Slick-Paper Story." Durham (N.C.)
         Herald, 24 December, p. 5.
            Review of The Judas Tree. In spite of Cronin's experience
         as a skillful writer, Moray is not a convincing character.
         His final escape is not well motivated. Only Kathy is real.
         Her fate is "more credible than Moray's own ignoble end."

12   W., A.M. "Cronin Novel Is Study in Tragedy." Hartford Times,
         9 December, p. 6.
            Review of The Judas Tree. In this novel Cronin is "an
         able craftsman, sure of his medical settings and equally
         sure of his story's dramatic content."

1962

1   MATTHEW, CHRISTOPHER. "With Pen and Scalpel." Milwaukee
         Journal, 2 March, p. 4.
            Review of Adventures in Two Worlds. Like an artist,
         Cronin transforms routine case histories into "breathless
         dramas" and reveals a lot about human nature at the same
         time. His chapters on faith will seem oversimplified to
         many readers, yet for others "it will mean a glorious affir-
         mation of their own faith by a distinguished writer."

1963

1   KUNKEL, FRANCIS L. "The Priest As Scapegoat in the Modern
         Catholic Novel." Ramparts 1 (January):72.
            Brief reference to explain the recurrence of the archetype
         of "the priest as a Christ-like scapegoat" in The Keys of the
         Kingdom. Like G.K. Chesterton, Bruce Marshall, Giovanni
         Guareschi and Henry Morton Robinson, this author focuses on
         "exterior struggles and pen portrayals of the priesthood,
         ecclesiastical and anthropocentric, that are concerned with
         compassionate moral integrity, and service. By imitating
         the ethical ideal of the Master, by bearing natural witness,
         and by mediating little," Cronin's hero can show that life
         without God can at least be comfortable, though without
         beauty. In contrast, Georges Bernanos, Graham Greene,
         François Mauriac, Sven Stolpe, and Morris West concentrate
         on "interior crises and sweat protrayals of the priesthood,
         theological and theocentric, that ooze the mystery of grace
         and sin. By imitating the sacrificial ideal of the Master,
         by bearing supernatural witness, and by meditating much,"
         their heroes show that life with God can be frightening.

1964

1 ANON. "Books for Young Adults." <u>Library Journal</u> 89
   (15 October):3505.
       Review of <u>A Song of Sixpence</u>. Wonders if this is an auto-
   biographical novel. "Another acceptable work by a recognized
   author."

2 ANON. "Briefly Noted: Fiction." <u>New Yorker</u> 40 (3 October):
   222-23.
       Review of <u>A Song of Sixpence</u>. This is "a simple, grace-
   fully written domestic story."

3 ANON. "Other New Novels." <u>Times Literary Supplement</u> (London),
   27 August, p. 769.
       Review of <u>A Song of Sixpence</u>. Finds the story sluggish
   because of its "Victorian paraphernalia." Laurence's experiences remind one of David Copperfield's. Nevertheless,
   this is "a pleasant, competent book, and only slightly dull."

4 BOND, ALICE DIXON. "Books: A.J. Cronin at His Best." <u>Boston
   Sunday Herald</u>, 20 September, sec. vi, p. 5.
       Review of <u>A Song of Sixpence</u>. Finds many characters, all
   "sharply etched," but the boy's journey and realization gives
   the novel "power and depth."

5 BURNS, ROBERT. "Another Key, Another Kingdom." <u>Critic</u> 23
   (October):74-75.
       Review of <u>A Song of Sixpence</u>. "On one level it is a
   pleasant if superficial novel for people with nostalgia for
   old-fashioned drug stores and band concerts in the park. On
   another, it may be escapist fare for some."

6 CAZAMIAN, LOUIS, and Las VERGNAS, RAYMOND. "The Twentieth
   Century (1914-1963): Chapter I: The Novel and the Short
   Story." In <u>A History of English Literature: Book VIII</u>.
   New York: The Macmillan Company, p. 1411.
       As a "prolific storyteller," Cronin delighted many readers
   with <u>The Citadel</u>. He also "touched their hearts" with his
   Dickensian <u>The Green Years</u>, and he "stirred their souls"
   with <u>The Keys of the Kingdom</u>. "All this does not go very
   far; it is a pity, because at the outset he had a natural
   and powerful talent for storytelling."

7 FLANIGAN, MARION. "A Scotch Horatio Alger." <u>Providence Journal</u>,
   18 October, p. 9.
       Review of <u>A Song of Sixpence</u>. Cronin maintains a "certain
   politeness" in this novel by means of "detachment from human

1964

agony, and by his deliberately Victorian style." The style,
however, is "alternately beguiling and nerve-wracking." Also
troublesome is Cronin's point of view, in that "the scope of
the novel as a whole" contracts as Laurence's fortunes rise.

8   GORDAN, JOHN D. "Doctors As Men of Letters: Archibald Joseph
     Cronin." Bulletin of the New York Public Library 68
     (November):600-601.
          Brief biographical mention.

9   GRAUEL, G.E. "Fiction." Best Sellers 24 (1 October):258.
          Review of A Song of Sixpence. Finds satisfying Cronin's
     "unaffected warmth and human genuineness." Although not as
     suspenseful as his earlier novels, "the very simplicity of
     the narrative is part of its charm." His portrait of the
     young hero is successful because it apparently contains
     autobiographical details. "The book deserves recommendation
     to the adult public [to] which it is addressed."

10   HENDERSON, ROBERT W. "New Books Appraised: Fiction." Library
     Journal 89 (15 September):3334.
          Review of A Song of Sixpence. Much of the interest is
     found in the characters. "It is told with Cronin's expert
     professional skill."

11   LEVIN, MARTIN. "A Reader's Report." New York Times Book Review,
     18 October, p. 43.
          Review of A Song of Sixpence. Finds it difficult to read
     a Cronin novel without seeing it as a movie out of Hollywood's
     golden era. The hero's success in spite of his humble sur-
     roundings is predictable to those familiar with Cronin's
     previous novels.

12   MacMANUS, PATRICIA. "A Pocketful of Wry." Sunday Herald-
     Tribune Book Week, 25 October, p. 21.
          Review of A Song of Sixpence. In both subject matter and
     style, Cronin's novel echoes an earlier era. But the work
     does reinforce his reputation as a storyteller.

13   MURRAY, J.G. "Fiction." America 111 (17 October):458.
          Review of A Song of Sixpence. This is a second-rate novel
     that "does not meet the requirements of its lower estate."
     Cronin lacks "the talent to manage a genuine autobiographical
     novel."

14   SALVESON, CHRISTOPHER. "Et in Somalia Ego." New Statesman 68
     (31 July):155.
          Review of A Song of Sixpence. In this "pure stretch of

157

1964

storytelling," the characters are oversimplified. "Since
there is no continuity, the young Carroll is more patronised
than self-pitying."

1967

1   ANON. "Cronin, A(rchibald) J(oseph)." In Contemporary Authors.
    Edited by James M. Ethridge and Barbara Kopala. Detroit:
    Gale Research Company, pp. 215-16.
        Includes biographical background and brief listing of
    critical sources through 1964.

1968

1   TEMPLE, RUTH Z., and TUCKER, MARTIN. "A.J. Cronin." In
    Twentieth Century British Literature: A Reference Guide
    and Bibliography. New York: Frederick Ungar Publishing
    Company, p. 150.
        Lists selective reviews from Hatter's Castle through A
    Song of Sixpence.

1969

1   ANON. "Book Reviews: A Pocketful of Rye." Lafayette (Calif.)
    Mid-Week, 24 December, p. 7.
        Finds the same "authenticity" in this hero as Cronin gives
    to all of his doctors. It is surprising that the author is
    able to write so forcibly about the current scene, consider-
    ing his age. Carroll's sexual mores would have been unthink-
    able for his earlier heroes. "That in itself doesn't credit
    the author as much as it proves his flexibility." The chap-
    ter recounting the mystical experience is unnecessary.

2   ANON. "Brief Reviews." Critic 28 (November):106-7.
        Review of A Pocketful of Rye. "The pious novel is alive
    --and dreary as ever--thanks to Mr. Cronin who is offering
    the 1969 model featuring a wee bit of sex."

3   ANON. Review of A Pocketful of Rye. Nashville Tennessean,
    9 November, p. 6.
        "It will be a miracle if any reader can identify with
    Carroll. He cannot feel emotion therefore we do not. The
    novel is largely based on misunderstandings between the main
    characters."

4   B., J.A. "Another Laurence Carroll Story: Conversion Episode
      Fails to Convince." Columbia (S.C.) State & Record,
      28 October, p. 11.
          Review of A Pocketful of Rye. Although in one sense this
      is a continuation of A Song of Sixpence, those who missed it
      can read the new novel with no feeling of any loss. The
      characters are alive and the story is readable, but the doc-
      tor's conversion at the end "somehow fails to convince."

5   DIORIO, PAT. Review of A Pocketful of Rye. El Paso Times,
      12 October, p. 6.
          Praises Cronin's daring in writing a novel about sexual
      perversion. Moreover, Cronin actually tells "a sensitive,
      poignant story with a terse, simple style that breathes a
      bit of freshness through the rolling fumes of smut which
      seems to have polluted the sophisticated novel of today."
      Dr. Carroll is plagued with indecision.

6   ENNIS, STARLING. "Cronin's New Novel Again Shows His Skill."
      Birmingham News, 28 October, p. 5.
          Review of A Pocketful of Rye. This novel demonstrates
      Cronin's "remarkable ability to convey and to celebrate the
      drama, the pathos and the glory of human existence."

7   LACEY, MAYBELLE. "New Books Appraised: Fiction." Library
      Journal 94 (1 September):2953.
          Review of A Pocketful of Rye. "Characterization and at-
      mosphere are good in one of Cronin's lighter-weight novels."

8   LINEHAN, J. "Fiction." Best Sellers 29 (1 November):285.
          Review of A Pocketful of Rye. Although the happy ending
      reminds one of a soap opera, Cronin is "a man of style and
      the novel can stand on its own as a good, tight little tale
      which encourages all of us to face ourselves a bit more hon-
      estly." It is "solid entertainment."

9   POUDER, G.H. "Books: Some Suggestions of the Macabre."
      Baltimore Sunday Sun, 5 October, p. 5D.
          Review of A Pocketful of Rye. Finds in this novel "the
      same touch, the same sardonic humor, and the same broad sym-
      pathy with man's weakness and struggle with conscience."
      Cronin's gift for characterization improves as he gets older.

10   WASHER, JANE DENNIS. "Just Pleasant Reading from the Pen of
      Cronin." Richmond Times-Dispatch, 28 October, p. 7.
          Review of A Pocketful of Rye. Although Cronin has not
      lost his flair for writing "wonderful description" and cre-
      ating "interesting characters," this novel lacks the sub-
      stance found in his earlier works.

1970

1   ANON. "Language & Literature: English and American." Choice
6 (February):1752.
Review of A Pocketful of Rye. Characters remind one of
a Harold Robbins novel. The hero is a bore and the situa-
tion is "preposterous."

2   GIBSON, TEDDI. "Cronin Still Having a Medicine Ball."
Cleveland Press, 8 May, p. 12.
Review of A Pocketful of Rye. "Despite the predictable
rather melodramatic plot, the story still has a kind of readable fascination. And one must certainly admire Cronin's
energy and ability to weave together the strands of a good
yarn."

3   JONES, BRYNMOR. "A.J. Cronin." In A Bibliography of Anglo-
Welsh Literature: 1900-1965. The Wales and Monmouthshire
Branch of the Library Association, pp. 14, 115.
On The Citadel, gives publication dates, translations and
their dates. Includes brief bibliographical entry for this
novel, too.

4   MYERS, ROBIN, ed. "A.J. Cronin." In A Dictionary of Literature
in the English Language from Chaucer to 1940. Vol. 1.
Oxford and New York: Pergamon Press, pp. 217-218.
Brief biographical background and bibliographic listing
of primary sources to 1964.

5   VALENTINE, DAN. "M.D. Authors 'Corny,' Imaginative Novel."
Salt Lake Tribune, 11 January, p. 5.
Review of A Pocketful of Rye. Although the plot is "somewhat corny," Cronin continues to write with "vitality and integrity." Finds, as usual, an "undercurrent of sadness" even
when the characters try to be happy.

1971

1   ERDOS, ELIZABETH. "Paperbacks: Fiction." Publishers Weekly
199 (11 January):64.
Review of A Pocketful of Rye. Finds the novel "contrived
and unconvincing." Notes that it was a poor seller in hard-
cover edition.

1972

1   ADELMAN, IRVING, and DWORKIN, RITA. "Cronin, (A)rchibald
    (J)oseph, 1896-." In The Contemporary Novel: A Checklist
    of Critical Literature on the British and American Novel
    Since 1945. Metuchen, N.J.: The Scarecrow Press, p. 106.
        Brief listing of secondary sources for Grand Canary and
    The Keys of the Kingdom.

1975

1   ANON. "Fiction." Booklist 72 (1 October):220.
        Review of Desmonde. "Cronin's latest effort suffers from
    stereotyped characters and situations and more than a hint
    of misogyny. It is a relic of outdated modes which may nev-
    ertheless ride through on his past reputation."

2   ANON. "Fiction." Kirkus 43 (1 June):620.
        Review of Desmonde. In this sentimental tale, Cronin's
    narration is both "premeditated and foreordained." Notes
    that the author himself appears in a novel which "might well
    be one of his old novels," taking place in the best of both
    possible worlds--"spiritual and physical, ancient . . . and
    modern."

3   BANNON, BARBERA A. "Fiction." Publishers Weekly 203 (2 June):
    46, 48.
        Review of Desmonde. Finds in this novel "elegant descrip-
    tions, leisurely revealed character studies and a dose of
    'old morality.'" Recommended only to readers who want an
    old-fashioned tale.

4   GOODFELLOW, PATRICIA. "Book Reviews: Fiction." Library
    Journal 100 (15 September):1651.
        Review of Desmonde. Comments on Cronin's "easy story-
    telling art." Desmonde's character, and Cronin's universe
    of black and white, Catholic orthodoxy, and social assump-
    tions of fifty years ago. "Desmonde is an enjoyable narra-
    tive of a half-rogue, half-saint which should please tradi-
    tionalists."

5   SHUCARD, ALAN R. "Cronin, A(rchibald) J(oseph)." In
    Contemporary Novelists. Edited by James Vinson. 2d ed.
    London: St. James' Press; New York: St. Martin's Press,
    pp. 327-29.
        Lists Cronin's publications through 1975, and traces his
    reputation and career. "That A.J. Cronin has succeeded in

1975

entertaining a massive audience throughout the English-
speaking world for over four decades is testimony both to
the public appetite for tripe and to his adroitness at ren-
dering it palatable, even absorbing." Hatter's Castle and
Three Loves showed promise, but they were tainted by "a certain dullness and unpolished style," offset only by the characterization of the women. Grand Canary gave evidence that
Cronin was beginning to edit his work with care. But the
superficiality of characters and their relationships limits
this work's value. Grand Canary marks the beginning of two
tendencies in his writing: it introduces the doctor hero,
and it "demonstrates his inability to create characters suf-
ficiently complex or plausible to render his treatment of
serious themes." Frequently, his works are "novels of escape disguised as novels of substance." His writing parodies
itself in "Victorian quaintness."

6   WARD, A.C. "Cronin, A.J." In Longman Companion to Twentieth
     Century Literature. 2d ed. London: Longman Group, pp.
     151-52.
         Brief biographical background.

1977

1   CASSIS, A.F. "A.J. Cronin." In The Twentieth-Century English
     Novel: An Annotated Bibliography of General Criticism. New
     York and London: Garland Publishing Co., 413 pp. passim.
         Lists secondary sources up to 1976.

1978

1   ANON. "A.J. Cronin." In Who Was Who Among English and European
     Authors: 1931-1949. Vol. 1. Detroit: Gale Research
     Company, p. 365.
         Brief biographical background.

2   ARMES, ROY. "The 1930s Sound Film." In A Critical History of
     the British Cinema. New York: Oxford University Press, pp.
     79, 91-92.
         Comments on The Citadel as an example of realistic cinema
     of the 1930s. According to J.A.P. Taylor, Cronin, Priestley
     and Louis Golding offered "'chunks of ordinary life, usually
     in drab surroundings.'" Includes a brief description of
     working with Robert Donat, star of The Citadel.

1981

1 ANON. "Author A.J. Cronin Dies at Age 84." San Francisco
    Chronicle, 10 January, p. 4.
      Obituary notice and biographical background.

2 ANON. "Author Cronin of The Citadel Renown Is Dead." Chicago
    Sun-Times, 10 January, p. 11.
      Brief biographical background and events surrounding his
    passing.

3 ANON. "Novelist A.J. Cronin Dies At 84 In Switzerland." San
    Diego Union, 10 January, p. 2.
      Obituary notice.

4 ANON. "Obituary: A.J. Cronin." Washington Post, 10 January,
    p. 10.
      Obituary notice.

5 ANON. "Obituary: Dr. A.J. Cronin: Doctor Who Became Graphic
    Novelist." Times (London), 10 January, p. 14.
      Biographical background and review of his literary repu-
    tation. Calls Cronin "a prodigiously fast and methodical
    worker."

6 ANON. "Scottish-Born Author A.J. Cronin Dies at Age 84."
    Chicago Tribune, 10 January, sec. 2, p. 11.
      Obituary notice.

7 CRONIN, VINCENT. "Recollection of a Writer." Tablet 235
    (21 February):175-76.
      An appreciation of Cronin written by one of his surviving
    sons. Includes biographical background. His novels were
    both "indictments of social injustice" and expressions of "a
    deep religious faith." From the latter stemmed "the warm
    humanity which gave his novels a worldwide appeal." Includes
    a brief discussion of Hatter's Castle, The Green Years, The
    Keys of the Kingdom, Dr. Finlay's Casebook, The Citadel, The
    Spanish Gardener, and quotes from two messages of sympathy
    sent to the family.

8 MITGANG, HERBERT. "A.J. Cronin, Author of Citadel and Keys of
    the Kingdom, Dies." New York Times, 10 January, p. 16.
      Biographical sketch and brief discussion of The Citadel,
    The Keys of the Kingdom, and The Stars Look Down. Reprinted:
    1981.9.

9 [_____.] "A.J. Cronin, Author of The Citadel, Dies." Los

1981

Angeles Times, 10 January, p. 3.
Reprint of 1981.8.

10   TEBBEL, JOHN. "The Boston Twins: Houghton and Little, Brown."
In A History of Book Publishing in the United States: The
Great Change, 1940-1980. New York and London: R.R. Bowker
Company, p. 229.
The Keys of the Kingdom was the best seller of 1941 with
Little, Brown.

Index

A., C., 1935.1

A., J., 1950.1

"A.J. Cronin," (Anon.), 1931.1;
1937.3; 1947.1; 1950.3;
1978.1; (A. Cassis), 1977.1;
(J. Frederick), 1941.101;
(B. Jones), 1970.3; (A.
McIntyre), 1941.126; (R.
Myers), 1970.4; (R. Temple),
1968.1; (M. Tucker), 1968.1

"A.J. Cronin Again Proves His
Story Telling Ability,"
1937.103

"A.J. Cronin, Author of The
Citadel, Dies," 1981.8-9

"A.J. Cronin Creates Robert
Shannon," 1944.73

"A.J. Cronin Himself a Physician,
Vivisects the Medical
Profession," 1937.76

"A.J. Cronin Mixes Religion with
Science in New Novel," 1944.58

"A.J. Cronin Novel Is Guild
Selection," 1953.3

"A.J. Cronin on Doctors and Love,"
1948.130

"A.J. Cronin Phenomenon:
Researcher and Medical Student
Struggle Toward Final Reunion,
The," 1948.93

"A.J. Cronin Plans Visit in
November," 1937.4

"A.J. Cronin Recalls His Medical
Days: Books in Review,"
1952.98

"A.J. Cronin Recounts His Journey

to Faith," 1952.45

"A.J. Cronin Scores Again," 1950.43

"A.J. Cronin Scores Triumph in The
Keys of the Kingdom," 1942.4

"A.J. Cronin Slaving for Success,
Overwhelmed When He Caught
It," 1952.41

"A.J. Cronin Tells His Story As
Both Doctor and Writer,"
1952.2

"A.J. Cronin Turns to the Field
of the Spirit," 1941.32

"A.J. Cronin, Who Gave Up
Successful Career in Medicine
So He Could Write The Keys of
the Kingdom, Other Great Books,
Now Lives in Beautiful New
Canaan," 1948.106

"A.J. Cronin Writes of a Man's
Regeneration through New
Love," 1933.25

"A.J. Cronin Writes One of Season's
Better Books in The Green
Years," 1944.1

"A.J. Cronin's Arrowsmith Has a
Burr," 1948.97

"A.J. Cronin's Autobiography,"
1952.3

"A.J. Cronin's Judas Tree Conveys
His Spiritual Values," 1961.4

"A.J. Cronin's Latest Novel,"
1941.135

"A.J. Cronin's Latest Novel Is
Outstanding Book of Month,"
1941.84

"A.J. Cronin's Latest Novel Is
Shannon's Way," 1948.5

165

"A.J. Cronin's Latest Novel
Resembles The Green Years,"
1948.53
"A.J. Cronin's Moving Novel Tells
Story of Scotch Priest,"
1941.79
"A.J. Cronin's New Novel 'Not Up
to Earlier Books,'" 1948.105
"A.J. Cronin's New Novel: Story
of Destructive Force of One
Man's Vanity and Jealousy,"
1950.71
"A.J. Cronin's Own Life Is
Colorful Story," 1952.66
"A.J. Cronin's Somber Portrait
of Knight in White," 1948.8
"ABA Awards Book Honors for
1937," 1938.1
Abelard, Peter, 1933.1
"About People," 1952.4
Adams, Elizabeth, 1953.1
Adelman, Irving, 1972.1
Adkins, Sam, 1948.1; 1950.2
Adventures in Two Worlds, 1951.3;
1952.1-6, 8-96, 98-100;
1956.13; 1962.1. See also
Journey of Discovery
Ahearne, Daniel E., 1948.2
Albright, Letty, 1948.3
"Alien in Scotland . . . A New
Cronin," 1945.12
Allen, Leroy, 1936.1
Allred, Pearl O., 1941.64
"All Set for the Movies," 1948.122
"Ambition Against Idealism,"
1948.51
"American Scene Dominates in Best
Fiction for August," 1941.3
Ames, A.C., 1952.1
"Among the Publishers," 1938.2
"An Analysis of The Citadel,"
1938.13
Anderson, Bett, 1948.4
"Another A.J. Cronin Novel of a
Doctor," 1948.108
"Another Cronin Book to Provoke
Discussion," 1944.2
"Another Durable Story from A.J.
Cronin," 1948.132
"Another Key, Another Kingdom,"
1964.5

"Another Laurence Carroll Story:
Conversion Episode Fails to
Convince," 1969.4
"Another Novel," 1948.3
Appel, David H., 1938.9; 1941.65;
1944.39
Appleby, John T., 1941.66
"Archibald Joseph Cronin," 1947.2
"Aristocrats and Artists: Enduring
Popular Formula Followed Again
by A.J. Cronin," 1956.12
Armes, Roy, 1978.2
"Artist's Story by Cronin Has
Unusual Twist," 1956.19
"Atlantic Bookshelf, The," 1941.74
"At the Library," 1937.44
"At York Harbor," 1940.1
"Author A.J. Cronin Dies at Age
84," 1981.1
"Author Cronin of The Citadel
Renown Is Dead," 1981.2
"Author Cronin's Bound to Make
Hero Suffer," 1948.72
"Author of The Citadel Has New
Tale," 1944.72
"Author of The Citadel Writes His
Greatest Novel, The," 1941.150
"Author of the Week: Cronin
Polishes Up Religion in His
Best Novel," 1941.70
"Authors and Books: Doctors in
Literature," 1939.4
"Autobiographical Work," 1940.2

B., A., 1950.35
B., D.B., 1950.36; 1953.23
B., E.M., 1944.40
B., H., 1937.41; 1941.67
B., J., 1952.36
B., J.A., 1969.4
B., L.B., 1941.68
B., M., 1941.69
B., M. duQ., 1941.70
B., M.H., 1937.42; 1941.71;
1945.7; 1948.41; 1950.37
"Back of Books," 1941.104
"Balancing the Books," 1941.82
Bander, Naomi, 1937.43
Bannon, Barbara A., 1975.3
Barish, Mildred, 1941.72
Barkham, John, 1950.38; 1952.37;

1953.24; 1956.8

Bartlett, Elizabeth, 1950.39

Bates, Graham, 1950.40

Battle, Nell G., 1937.44

Beals, Helen, 1941.73

Beauchamp, Elise, 1948.42

Beaufort, John, 1940.8

Beck, Clyde, 1950.41

Becker, Charlotte, 1937.45

Bedell, W.D., 1950.42

"Beginning the Next Hundred Years: At 35," 1937.93

Bell, Herbert C.F., 1941.74

Bell, Lisle, 1948.43

Bennett, Alice Kizer, 1941.75

Bentley, Florence R., 1935.22

Berne, Henry, 1948.44

Berry, Lee, 1937.46; 1941.76

"Best Best Seller," 1941.4

"Best Sellers," 1938.3

"Between Book-Ends," (Anon.), 1945.1; (T. Sherman), 1948.123

"Between the Covers," 1937.88

"Between the Lines," 1938.4

Beyond This Place, 1953.1-3, 5-48; 1956.8, 13. See also To Live Again

"Beyond This Place: A.J. Cronin's Novel of Loyalty and Injustice an Indictment of the Jury System," 1953.23

Bihn, Hazel E., 1941.77

Billings, F.T., 1948.45

Billings, F. Tremainer, 1952.38

Binsse, H.L., 1941.78

"Bit of Croninizing: He Brings a Character to Life But Ends His Story Illogically," 1950.61

"Bitter Novel--But One of the Best 1935 Has Seen, A," 1935.26

Bloom, Eleanor M., 1948.46

Boardman, Tom, 1950.43-44

Bond, Alice Dixon, 1941.79; 1944.41; 1948.47; 1950.45; 1952.39; 1961.4; 1964.4

Bonner, Willard Hallam, 1948.48

Boochever, Florence, 1952.40

"Book a Day," 1935.27

"Book Chats," 1937.98

"Book Chatter," 1937.8

"Book Club Choices," 1953.5

"Book Comment," 1950.46

"Book Corner, The," (R. Commagere), 1948.59; (R. Duncan), 1944.46

"Book Ends," 1937.94

"Bookman Gallery: A.J. Cronin, The," 1933.34

"Bookman's Notebook, A," 1938.11

"Book Mark, The," 1944.59

"Book Marks," 1953.43

"Book Marks: Very Dour Doctor: Fun with Titles," 1948.79

"Book News," 1937.74

"Book Nook, The," 1941.60

"Book Notes," 1937.9; 1946.1

"Book Notes, Fiction," 1932.2

"Book of the Day, The," 1941.125

"Book of the Day: A.J. Cronin's New Novel Will Please His Audiences, The," 1945.13

"Book of the Month," 1941.5

"Book-of-the-Month Club Dividend," 1945.2

"Book of the Summer--and Autumn," 1941.110

"Book of the Week," (P. Allred), 1941.64; (C. Lee), 1944.50; (I. Neuman), 1952.73

"Book of the Week, The," 1935.18

"Book of the Week: A.J. Cronin's Fine Novel of a Priestly Career," 1941.114

"Book of Youth," 1944.50

"Book Parade: One of Best Novels of Year, The," 1935.44

"Book Prods Medical Profession," 1937.83

"Book Review," (Anon.), 1935.10; 1941.6; 1944.3; 1953.22; (B. Catton), 1935.28; (M. Fletcher), 1945.10; (J. Hutchens), 1953.32; (C. MacDonald), 1935.43; (E. Wilson), 1938.16

"Book Review of New Books at the Eustis Memorial Library," 1938.5

"Book Reviews," (F. Pearson), 1950.78; (F. Simms), 1935.61; (M. Willis), 1951.6

"Book Reviews: A Pocketful of
Rye," 1969.1
"Book Reviews by Westlake
Pastor," 1945.11
"Book Reviews: Fiction," 1975.4
"Books," (Anon.), 1935.2;
1937.11; 1941.7-8; 1950.4;
1952.5; 1953.6; (D. Appel),
1938.9; (H. Bihn), 1941.77;
(K. King), 1938.12; (E.
Lavery), 1952.65; (G. Miles),
1948.91; (M. O.), 1958.20;
(M. Rinker), 1945.16; (J.
Selby), 1941.140; (K.
Tooill), 1937.102; (C.
Wagner), 1937.106; 1941.156
"Books Abroad: London Letter,
June," 1931.21
"Books: Adolescence a la
Cronin," 1944.4
"Books: A.J. Cronin at His
Best," 1964.4
"Books: A.J. Cronin's Story
Sure-Fire Candidate for Best
Sellerdom," 1952.43
"Books: Alder and/or Dickens?"
1948.70
"Books and Authors," (D.C.),
1953.25; (V. Walker),
1939.107
"Books and Book-Makers," 1941.9
"Books and Bywords," 1935.40
"Books and the Arts: A Good
Doctor's Story," 1937.109
"Books and Their Writers: Cronin
Makes You Angry," 1941.89
"Books and Things," (L. Bell),
1948.43; (R. Feld), 1941.97;
(L. Gannett), 1950.56; (M.
Geismar), 1948.71; (I.
Paterson), 1937.85
"Books and Writers," 1937.12
"Books: An Editor Sticks to His
Guns," 1958.17
"Books: Books in Brief," 1931.2
"Books: Briefly Noted: Fiction,"
1948.37; 1953.7
"Books: Cronin Counts Vanity's
Cost," 1950.69
"Books: Cronin: The Stars Look
Down on Life and Death in the
Mines," 1935.3
"Books: Doctor: England's New
Dickens Reports on Former
Profession," 1937.13
"Books: Dr. Cronin's New Novel,"
1935.4
"Books: Dr. Cronin's New Novel
Full of 'Incredible Hokum,'"
1941.58
"Books: Dr. Cronin's Study in
Sanctity," 1941.66
"Bookseller's Almanac, The,"
1948.40
"Books: Fiction," 1950.5
"Books for Young Adults," 1964.1
"Books: Goodness Made Readable,"
1941.10
"Bookshelf," 1937.50
"Bookshelf, The," 1935.34
"Book Shelf, The," (Anon.),
1935.19; (L. Meyers), 1948.90
"Bookshelf: Blue Ribbons,"
1938.10
"Book Shelf: Late Book Reviews
and Literary Criticism, The,"
1941.100
"Books in Brief: Fiction,"
1948.82
"Books in July," 1941.11
"Books in Review," (C. Jones),
1950.64; (W. Rogers), 1948.112
"Books: Inside a Nazi--Dr.
Cronin's Saint," 1941.96
"Books in the News: A.J. Cronin
Writes Glowing Memoir but Part
of the Story Is Missing,"
1952.76
"Books into Films," (R. Mealand),
1944.61; (P. Nathan), 1948.95
"Books: Man, Medicine, Literature,"
1952.50
"Books: Mixed Fiction," 1958.1
"Books: Novels Reviewed by Riley
Hughes," 1958.16
"Books of the Day: New Novels by
A.J. Cronin and Robert Nathan,"
1950.41
"Books of the Day: Physician and
Writer," 1952.57
"Books of the Times," (H. Breit),
1948.49; (R. Gelder), 1935.35;

(C. Poore), 1958.23; (O.
Prescott), 1944.70; 1950.80;
1953.42; 1956.21; (R.
Thompson), 1937.101; 1941.153
"Books of the Week," 1945.17
"Books of the Week: Cronin's New
Hero A Priest," 1941.120
"Books of the Week: Cronin's
Novel Points Value of
Ordinary Human Kindness,"
1941.108
"Books of Today," 1948.67
"Books Old and New," 1941.152
"Books: Proud Soul v. Humble
Soul," 1952.6
"Books: Public Library:
Fiction," 1948.8
"Books: Some Suggestions of the
Macabre," 1969.9
"Bookstall Gossip," 1941.133;
1952.7
"Books: The Judas Tree Unworthy
of Author," 1961.5
"Books to Read: A Son's Efforts
--New Cronin Novel Tells
Story of English Family
Drama," 1953.27
"Book Suggests Underlying
Spiritual Integrity Apparent-
ly Motivates Cronin's Writ-
ing," 1952.82
"Book Trends of the Hour,"
1941.12
"Book World, The," 1937.43
"Boston Twins: Houghton and
Little, Brown, The," 1981.10
"Bound To Be Read," 1937.14-15;
1941.13
Bouwhuis, Rev. Andrew L., S.J.,
1941.80
Bowe, Kay, 1950.46
"Boy Against the World," 1944.5
"Boy's Courage Theme of Tale,"
1944.6
"Boy's Story," 1944.74
Bradshaw, Michael, 1941.81
Brady, Charles A., 1950.47
Braman, Don, 1952.41
Brégy, Katherine, 1945.8
Breit, Harvey, 1948.49
Brickell, Herschel, 1935.23;

1936.2
"Briefly Noted: Fiction," 1944.7;
1964.2
"Brief Reviews," 1969.2
"Brief Reviews: A.J. Cronin on
Himself," 1952.37
Brighouse, Harold, 1937.47
Britton, Beverley, 1941.82
"Broadway in Books," 1940.13
"Brooklyn Plans Ballyhoo for Betty
Smith's New Novel," 1948.76
Brown, Violet J., 1937.48
"Browsings from Parlin Library,"
1948.9
Buck, Doris P., 1948.50
Bullett, Gerald, 1932.8
Bullock, Florence Haxton, 1944.42;
1948.51; 1956.9
Burcher, Dorothy Gray, 1941.83
Burgard, August C., 1941.84
Burke, Harry R., 1948.52
Burke, James, 1948.53
"Burns Club of London: Dr.
Cronin's Tribute," 1932.1
Burns, George V., 1948.54
Burns, Robert, 1964.5
Butcher, Fanny, 1935.24; 1937.49;
1948.55; 1956.10; 1958.10
"But the Paper Came Out," 1958.13

C., A., 1952.42
C., D.H., 1953.25
C., H.B., 1950.48
C., J.A., 1941.85
C., V., 1950.49
"Caduceus and Pen Each His
Servant," 1952.8
Cady, Ernest, 1952.43
"Calls Cronin Book 'Most Rewarding'
of All His Novels," 1944.75
"Calvinism and Scant Fare," 1944.8
"Canisius Reader," 1941.80
Cantwell, Robert, 1935.25
Carpenter, H.A., 1941.86
Carroll, Tom, 1952.44
"Case for Books, The," 1944.41;
1948.47
"Case for Books: The Sum of a
Life's Parts Makes a Colorful
and Warmly Human Whole,"
1952.39

Cassis, A.F., 1977.1
Caswell, Wilbur Larremore,
1941.87
"Catholic Missionary Is Hero of
A.J. Cronin's Latest Novel,"
1941.138
Catton, Bruce, 1935.26-28
Cazamian, Louis, 1964.6
"Challenge to Skeptics, A,"
1937.1
"Change, A," 1933.36
Chapman, Gladys D., 1937.50;
1938.10
"Chasing Balloons," 1932.9
"Check List, The," 1937.40
Cheney, Robert J., 1941.88
"Child's Mind Revealed in All Its
Innocence, A," 1950.50
Chrisman, Lewis H., 1948.56
"Christmas Shopping List,"
1941.14
Citadel, The, 1937.1-15, 17-25,
27-88, 90-98, 100-109;
1938.1-3, 5-16; 1939.4;
1940.7; 1941.9, 57, 61, 101,
107, 113-14, 116, 126, 136,
139, 150-54, 157, 159; 1942.1;
1944.3, 5, 40, 72; 1948.4, 9,
17, 26, 28, 34, 95, 102, 109,
111, 134; 1950.84; 1952.61,
99; 1956.8, 17, 21; 1958.28;
1964.6; 1970.3; 1978.2;
1981.8-9. See also Manson,
M.D.
"Citadel by A.J. Cronin, The,"
1941.61
"Citadel by A.J. Cronin Powerful
Story of Medicine, The,"
1937.63
"Citadel Brings Another
Arrowsmith, The," 1937.97
Clarage, Eleanor, 1948.57
Clarke, Alan Burton, 1931.8
"Clash of Capital and Labor,
The," 1935.41
"Close to Heaven and Earth,"
1941.157
Cobb, Sue, 1937.51
Comans, Grace P., 1953.26
Comba, May A., 1948.58
"Comedy Opening: Broadway in
Review," 1940.11
Commagere, Ruth, 1948.69
"Communications," 1941.90
Compton, Neil M., 1948.60
"Conflict at the Mines," 1935.36
Connolly, Francis X., 1948.61
Conroy, Jack, 1956.11
"Consul, The," 1950.33
"Convict's Son Seeks the Truth,"
1953.37
Coolidge, Christine, 1941.89
Coons, Phyllis W., 1956.12
Corcoran, Marguerite Page, 1948.62
Cort, John C., 1941.90
Cosulich, Bernice, 1937.52
"County Library News," 1952.9
Cournos, John, 1948.63
Crabbe, Kenneth C., 1958.11
Craig, 1942.4
"Cronin," (Anon.), 1941.15; (D.
Spry), 1952.88
"Cronin, A.J.," (Anon.), 1950.6;
(A. Ward), 1975.6
Cronin, A.J.
-Bibliography, 1942.1; 1967.1;
1968.1; 1970.3-4; 1972.1;
1975.5; 1977.1
-Biography, 1931.1; 1935.47;
1937.4, 10, 14, 16, 65, 106;
1938.6; 1939.1; 1940.3;
1941.9-10, 32, 35, 37, 62, 126,
133; 1942.1; 1944.4, 35, 38,
50, 83; 1947.1-2; 1948.9, 19,
38, 55, 76, 104; 1951.3;
1952.1-100; 1956.13; 1967.1;
1970.4; 1975.5-6; 1978.1-2;
1981.1-9
-Interview, 1932.1; 1937.19;
1939.2; 1941.33, 106, 126;
1944.38; 1947.79; 1953.19, 34
"Cronin Almost Missed Becoming
Famous Author," 1948.10
"Cronin, Archibald Joseph," (Anon.),
1942.1; 1967.1; (A. Shucard),
1975.5
"Cronin, Archibald Joseph, 1896--,"
1972.1
"Cronin Book Cites Lesson of
Gardener," 1950.54
"Cronin Book Fascinating," 1950.81
"Cronin Book Has Great Sales

Record," 1941.16
"Cronin Book Lives Up to His
    Promise," 1937.95
"Cronin Combines Salesmanship
    with Art in Shannon's Way,"
    1948.107
"Cronin Doesn't Know Newspapers,"
    1958.28
"Cronin Extends Religious, Moral
    Issues in New Book," 1948.77
"Cronin Fascinates," 1952.10
"Cronin Forced to Rest, Becomes
    Great Author," 1941.17
"Cronin Has a New Novel, Young
    Doctor Again the Hero,"
    1948.48
Cronin, J.F., 1944.43
"Cronin Not First Doctor-Author,"
    1937.17
"Cronin Novel about Doctor Is
    Finest Work of Author,"
    1948.86
"Cronin Novel a Human Study,"
    1953.30
"Cronin Novel Choice of Literary
    Guild," 1953.8
"Cronin Novel Is Over Slick,"
    1950.72
"Cronin Novel Is Study in
    Tragedy," 1961.12
"Cronin Novel of an Artist,"
    1956.9
"Cronin Novel of Father and Son,"
    1950.96
"Cronin Novel Should Please His
    Followers," 1935.24
"Cronin on Cronin: Good; Cronin
    on World: So-So," 1952.52
"Cronin on His Methods," 1948.11
"Cronin Raps Evil Practices in
    Medicine," 1937.79
"Cronin's Autobiography Has Appeal
    of His Novels," 1952.80
"Cronin's Book Tells Tale of
    Young Doctor," 1948.118
"Cronin's Citadel Indicts a
    System," 1937.17
"Cronin's Dr. Shannon Takes
    Second Series of Hurdles,"
    1948.46
"Cronin's Enchanting Novel of a

Boy's Life," 1944.42
"Cronin's First Romance Promises
    New Audience," 1933.19
"Cronin's Genius Creates Beautiful
    Tale of Youth," 1944.9
"Cronin's Green Years Merits Few
    Laurels," 1944.44
"Cronin's Jealous Father," 1950.76
"Cronin's Latest," 1950.8
"Cronin's Latest Doesn't Ring the
    Bell," 1944.10
"Cronin's Latest Falls Below
    Earlier Works," 1944.55
"Cronin's Latest Is Dramatic
    Story," 1941.160
"Cronin's Latest Is Slick-Paper
    Story," 1961.11
"Cronin's Latest Novel Gleams with
    Integrity," 1944.82
"Cronin's Latest Novel Immensely
    Readable," 1941.81
"Cronin's Life Story Has Powerful
    Appeal," 1952.62
"Cronin Slips Up on Latest Novel,"
    1950.67
"Cronin's New Book Greatest,"
    1941.67
"Cronin's New Book Long, Rich
    Study of Real Men and Women
    Written Without Artificiality,"
    1935.23
"Cronin's New Doctor Story,"
    1948.12
"Cronin's Newest Novel Below Par
    --But Good," 1950.65
"Cronin's Newest Novel Has Father
    and Son Theme," 1950.53
"Cronin's Newest Novel Strikes
    Vital Note, Creates Strong
    Figure," 1941.112
"Cronin's New Novel Again Shows
    His Skill," 1969.6
"Cronin's New Novel Has Doctor As
    Hero," 1948.64
"Cronin's New Novel Is Disappoint-
    ing as Author Fails to Solve
    His Problem," 1948.54
"Cronin's New Novel Is Grim and
    Incredible," 1950.95
"Cronin's Non-Fiction," 1952.58
"Cronin's Novel Is Depressing,

Reviewer Says," 1948.129
"Cronin's Novel, Tale of Youth
    and Idealism," 1944.53
"Cronin's Orphan Grows Up,"
    1948.1
"Cronin's Powerful Story of
    Doctor," 1937.82
"Cronin Still Having a Medicine
    Ball," 1970.2
"Cronin Story Covers Two Career
    Success," 1952.92
"Cronin Takes Middle Road in New
    Novel about Doctor," 1948.113
"Cronin Takes New Tack in Story
    of Boy," 1950.7
"Cronin Uses Vivid Characters to
    Flay English Medical Prac-
    tices," 1937.91
Cronin, Vincent, 1981.7
"Cronin Writes in Maine Cottage,"
    1939.1
"Cronin Writes Worthy Defense of
    Catholic Priest in New Vol-
    ume," 1941.69
"Cruise of the Aureola and What
    Followed," 1933.31
Crume, Marion, 1948.64
Crusader's Tomb, 1956.13. See
    also A Thing of Beauty and
    The Pride of Beauty
Culhane, Eleanor F., 1953.27
Cullivan, Gerald, 1952.45

D., E.V., 1950.50
D., W.A., 1952.46
Dancoke, Charles, S.J., 1944.44
Dangerfield, George, 1931.9;
    1935.29
Danskin, Hannah, 1952.47
Davenport, Basil, 1932.9; 1933.18;
    1941.91
Davenport, Jouett, 1952.48
Davies, Daniel Horton, 1959.2
Davies, Joe, 1937.53
Davis, Elizabeth B., 1933.19
Dean, Mary Scott, 1937.54
"Death and Rebirth of Ideals,"
    1937.78
"Death, Destruction, and Power,"
    1931.20
deC., R.M., 1948.65

DeCasseres, Benjamin, 1941.92
"Decisive Decade of Man's Life
    Depicted by Cronin," 1944.62
"Decline and Fall," 1931.9
"Dedicated Artist," 1956.14
Dedmon, Emmett, 1948.66; 1950.51
"'Deeply Significant Today,'"
    1941.113
Derleth, August, 1948.67
"Descent into Harley Street: Dr.
    Cronin's Novel," 1937.18
Desmonde, 1975.1-4
Dever, Joseph, 1948.68
"Dickens Characters in Tale of
    Miners," 1935.5
"Dickensesque Touch in The Stars
    Look Down, A," 1935.66
Diorio, Pat, 1969.5
Dittermore, Eldon, 1942.5
"Doctor and Novelist," 1952.11
"Doctor Cronin Drops Tragedy,"
    1933.32
"Doctor Cronin Pens His Memoirs,"
    1952.36
"Doctor Discovers That He Has a
    Soul, A," 1933.2
"Doctor Finds a Way Back to Life,
    A," 1933.3
"Doctor Gives Up Practice to
    Write," 1952.12
"Doctor in Scotland, The," 1948.104
"Doctor into Author," 1952.38
"Doctor Looks at Doctors, A,"
    1937.71
"Doctor Pens Novel Based on His
    Own Profession," 1937.89
"Doctors As Men of Letters:
    Archibald Joseph Cronin,"
    1964.8
"Doctor's Dilemma," (Anon.),
    1937.21; (M. Ulrich), 1937.104
"Doctors, Nurses Inspire New Cronin
    Novel," 1937.22
"Doctors' Smugness Flayed by
    Novelist A.J. Cronin," 1937.100
"Doctor's Story about Doctor Points
    to Evils of Profession,"
    1937.23
"Doctor's Story of Doctor's Life
    in Fine Novel," 1937.92
"Doctor's Title for Professional

Integrity, A," 1937.2
"Doctor Turned Writer: A.J.
Cronin Adventures with
Diagnosis of Life," 1952.48
"Doctor Understands the Soul,
A," 1935.56
"Doctor Who Turned Author,"
1952.75
"Doctor Who Turned Writer, A,"
1952.55
"Doctor Yearned To Be Novelist,"
1952.60
"Domination Over Son Failed,"
1950.1
Dore, Edrie Van, 1948.69
Doren, Carl Van, 1937.55
Dottin, Paul, 1933.20; 1934.2
"Double Success: Physician-
Novelist Recalls Dual Career,"
1952.68
Downey, Hugh F., 1961.5
"Do You Know Your Authors?"
1937.65
"Dr. A.J. Cronin," 1951.1-2
"Dr. A.J. Cronin and a Critic
from Mars," 1952.87
"Dr. A.J. Cronin and His Two
Worlds," 1952.70
"Dr. A.J. Cronin Has Written a
Powerful and Revealing Novel
and of the Less Pleasant Side
of Medicine," 1937.87
"Dr. A.J. Cronin on Doctors,"
1937.19
"Dr. A.J. Cronin Rings the Bell
for Hollywood," 1948.83
"Dr. A.J. Cronin's Essays Cover
Life, Medicine, Faith,"
1952.69
"Dr. A.J. Cronin's New Hero Is a
Poor but Brilliant Scientist,"
1948.135
"Dr. A.J. Cronin Writes Story of
Catholic Church," 1941.141
"Dr. Cronin: An Essay in
Victoriana," 1956.13
"Dr. Cronin and Family in U.S.,"
1940.3
"Dr. Cronin at Work," 1958.12
"Dr. Cronin Dramatizes Virtue in
His New Best-Selling Novel,"

1941.151
"Dr. Cronin Frowns on His Medical
Brothers," 1937.59
"Dr. Cronin Invades the Church,"
1941.118
"Dr. Cronin Pays His Respects to
the Doctors," 1937.20
"Dr. Cronin Popular," 1944.11
"Dr. Cronin Proves His Pen Power,"
1935.30
"Dr. Cronin Scores Again,"
1941.155
"Dr. Cronin Writes Story about
Church and Life," 1941.124
"Dr. Cronin's Gift for Narrative,"
1933.22
"Dr. Cronin's New Book Is about
Missionary," 1941.85
"Dr. Cronin's New Novel," 1941.111
"Dr. Cronin's New Novel Is Story
of a Catholic Priest," 1941.142
"Dr. Cronin's New Novel One of Life
and Realism," 1935.6
"Dr. Cronin's New Prescription,"
1948.68
"Dr. Cronin's Novel about the
Medical Profession," 1937.72
"Dr. Cronin's Own History," 1952.44
"Dr. Cronin's Own Story," 1952.96
"Dr. Cronin's Portrait of a
Stubborn Woman," 1932.11
"Dr. Cronin's Search for Justice,"
1953.9
"Dr. Cronin's Sixth Success,"
1941.130
"Dr. Robert Shannon's Career,"
1948.134
"Drama Enlivens Doctor's Memoirs,"
1952.47
"Drama: Fun in a Hospital,"
1940.12
"Drama: Jupiter Laughs, The,"
1940.16
DuBois, William, 1944.45
Duffey, Felix D., 1952.49
DuFour, Stuart, 1937.56
Dukes, Ashley, 1940.9
Duncan, Robert, 1944.46
Dunlap, Katherine, 1950.52
Dunton, Edith K., 1941.93
"Dusting the Library Shelves,"

1944.12
Dworkin, Rita, 1972.1

Eastman, Elizabeth, 1937.57
Eaton, Walter Prichard, 1940.10
Edgett, E.F., 1931.11
Edgett, Edwin Francis, 1937.58
"Editor's Choice: What of the
    Dry?" 1944.13
Eells, Calvin, 1950.53
Elliott, Dorothy, 1935.30-31
Elliott, J.K., 1953.28
Elwood, Irene, 1950.54
"Enchanting, Unforgettable New
    Novel Already Among Best-
    Seller Lists," 1944.48
"English Arrowsmith," (D.
    Ahearne), 1948.2; (Anon.),
    1937.24
"English Doctor Tries to Isolate
    Influenza Bug: Weird Tale
    of Secret Irish Army," 1948.80
"Engrossing and Fine Story,"
    1948.13
Ennis, Starling, 1969.6
"Enter a He-Man," 1933.4
"Envoy to Spain Battling with
    Two 'Devils,'" 1950.47
Erdos, Elizabeth, 1971.1
Erskine, John, 1944.47
"Escape," 1941.98
"Et in Somalia Ego," 1964.14
"Even the Judge Was a Conniver,"
    1953.24
"Ex-Agnostic Cronin Sees the
    Importance of Faith," 1952.77
"Exciting, But Still a Bit
    Incredulous," 1950.66
"Exploited Myths," 1948.60

F., B.W., 1941.94
F., M., 1945.9
F., R.B., 1941.95
F., W.H., 1937.59
"Facing the Final Deadline,"
    1958.22
Fadiman, Clifton, 1941.96
"False Conviction, A," 1953.2
Farquharson, R. A., 1952.50
"Father and Son," 1950.9
"February Publication Planned for

A.J. Cronin's First Non-
    Fiction," 1952.13
Feld, Rose, 1941.97
Ferguson, Otis, 1937.60
Ferguson, Mrs. Walter, 1941.98
"Fiction," (Anon.), 1931.3;
    1932.3; 1933.5; 1935.7;
    1937.25; 1941.18-19; 1942.2;
    1944.14; 1948.14-16; 1950.10-
    11; 1952.14; 1953.10-12;
    1956.1-2; 1958.2-6; 1975.1-2;
    (B. Bannon), 1975.3; (H.
    Binsse), 1941.78; (F. Butcher),
    1937.49; (A. Clarke), 1931.8;
    (G. Gravel), 1964.9; (G.
    Greene), 1933.21; (R.
    Henderson), 1956.15; 1958.15;
    (J. Linehan), 1969.8; (E.
    Luker), 1961.8; (O. Manning),
    1948.88; (H. Miles), 1937.77;
    (J. Murray), 1964.13; (W.
    Plomer), 1935.53; (L. Strong),
    1932.14
"Fiction: The Rough and the
    Smooth," 1931.19
"Fiction: Rooted in Unreality,"
    1959.1
"Fine and Warmly Human Story of
    an Old Man and a Lad," 1944.47
"Fine New Novel by A.J. Cronin,
    A," 1944.79
"Fine Novel of Piety by A.J.
    Cronin," 1941.115
"First-Rate Fourth Estater,"
    1958.14
"First Reader," 1935.37; 1937.67;
    1944.49
"First Reader: Dr. Cronin Pits
    Kindness and Generosity Against
    Violence and Hate in His New
    Book, The Keys of the Kingdom,
    The," 1941.107
"First Reader (The Best of the New
    Books), The," 1935.38
"Fisherman, Scots Priest: Cronin's
    Story of an Old Man's Wisdom,"
    1941.109
Fitt, Frank, 1941.99
Flanigan, Marion, 1964.7
Fletcher, Marie, 1945.10
Flint, Doris, 1941.100

Ford, Anne, 1952.51
Fox, Sue Mac, 1935.32
Frame, Alexander, 1935.33
"Fraying Margins of Error,"
    1953.34
Frederick, John T., 1941.101
Freer, Rev. Harold Wiley,
    1945.11
"From Dr. Cronin's Heart,"
    1956.17
"From My Book Shelf," 1941.83
"From the Library," 1958.19
Fulford, Robert, 1958.12
Fytton, Francis, 1956.13

G., F., 1937.61
G., J.T., 1937.62
G., M., 1950.55
G., M.D., 1952.52
Gannett, Lewis, 1950.56
Gardiner, H.C., 1941.102
Gardiner, Harold C., 1948.70
Garrard, Maxine, 1937.63
Gay, R.M., 1935.34
Geismar, Maxwell, 1948.71
Gelder, Robert Van, 1935.35
"General," 1952.15
"General: New Books Appraised,"
    1952.95
"Genuine Scot, The," 1952.33
Gibson, Teddi, 1970.2
Gilder, Rosamond, 1940.11
Girvin, Peter, 1958.13
"Good Enough but Too Late,"
    1948.17
Goodfellow, Patricia, 1975.4
"Good Reading," 1941.123
"Good Reading but No Thing of
    Beauty," 1956.11
Gordan, John D., 1964.8
"Gossip of the Book World,"
    1937.26
Gould, Ray, 1944.48
Govan, Gilbert E., 1937.64;
    1941.103
Grady, R.F., S.J., 1952.53
Grand Canary, 1933.1-2, 4-19,
    21-37; 1934.1; 1935.55;
    1941.101, 156; 1942.1;
    1953.4; 1956.13; 1959.2;
    1972.1; 1975.5

"Grand Canary," 1933.26
"Grand Canary Fine Regeneration
    Yarn," 1933.6
"Grand Canary: A Novel by A.J.
    Cronin," 1933.37
Gravel, George E., 1950.57;
    1964.9
Graver, Otto C., 1941.104
Gray, James, 1948.72
"Great New Novel Written by
    Cronin," 1937.81
"Great Novel of English Coal Mines
    Surprises," 1935.49
Greene, Gladys, 1937.65
Greene, Graham, 1933.21
Green, Marion A., 1948.73
Green Years, The, 1944.1-2, 4-74,
    76-84; 1945.1-2, 3-17;
    1946.1-4; 1948.1, 6, 14, 18,
    32, 43, 75, 94, 96, 126-27,
    131; 1950.16, 18, 29, 31, 36;
    1952.39; 1956.13; 1964.6;
    1981.8
"Green Years Again," 1948.18
"Green Years by Dr. A.J. Cronin,
    The," 1944.76
"Green Years Described As Best
    A.J. Cronin Novel, The,"
    1944.57
"Green Years Given Praise by
    Reviewer," 1944.69
"Green Years Goes into Sixth
    Printing," 1944.15
"Green Years in a New Edition,
    The," 1950.36
"Green Years Is Affecting Tale of
    a Scotch Family, The," 1944.36
Griffin, Dorothea, 1950.58
"Growth of Character," 1944.43
"Guild Chooses Cronin," 1948.19

H., C., 1950.59
H., C.P., 1941.105
H., D., 1948.74
H., G., 1935.36
H., H., 1952.54
H., J., 1956.14
H., M.J., 1950.60
H., P., 1937.66
H., R., 1952.55
H., V.P., 1948.75

Hamilton, E., 1950.61
Hansen, Harry, 1935.37–38;
    1937.67; 1941.106–7; 1944.49;
    1948.76–77
Harris, Foster, 1948.78
Harris, W.E., 1935.39
Hart, Evelyn, 1941.108
Hart, Philomena, 1941.109
Harwood, H.C., 1931.12; 1932.10
Hatcher, Harlan, 1941.110
Hatter's Castle, 1931.1–9, 11–22;
    1932.2–5, 11; 1933.2, 5, 9–
    10, 18, 22, 27, 34; 1935.18,
    42, 46, 64; 1937.25, 31, 45,
    67, 76, 79; 1941.17, 24,
    101, 113, 116, 125; 1942.1;
    1944.34, 69; 1945.13;
    1948.46, 109; 1950.61;
    1952.83, 95; 1953.32; 1956.12–
    13; 1968.1; 1975.5; 1981.8
"Hatter's Castle, a Novel in the
    Great Tradition," 1931.14
Havighurst, Walter, 1958.14
Hawthorne, Hazel, 1931.13
Hayes, Sibyl C., 1941.10
Healey, Robert C., 1961.6
Henderson, Robert W., 1956.15;
    1958.15; 1964.10
"He Planted More than Just
    Seeds," 1950.84
"Hero, in Varied Practice, Is a
    British Arrowsmith," 1937.55
"Heroic Priest Is Protagonist in
    New Novel by A.J. Cronin,"
    1941.75
"Hero's Way Lies through Morass
    of Self-Pity," 1948.52
Hewes, Lydia, 1937.68; 1950.62
Heyerdahl, Anna, 1952.56
"Highlights from New Books,"
    1944.16
"Highlights of 100 Years,"
    1937.99
"Highly Praised," 1937.27
Hill, Harriet, 1952.57; 1953.29
Hill, Victor, 1944.50
"Hillsboro Library More New
    Volumes," 1950.12
Hillyer, Dorothy, 1944.51
"His 'Mortal Sin,'" 1944.17
"Hobnails and Guineas: Two

Worlds of Spirit and Flesh in
    Cronin Life Story," 1952.72
Holden, Theodore L., 1953.30
Holle, William Stanley, 1935.40
Hollis, C.E., 1937.69
Hollis, Eva E., 1941.112; 1945.12
Holzhauer, Jean, 1953.31
Hoole, William Stanley, 1935.40
Horan, Kenneth, 1948.79
Houseboat for Heaven, 1938.6
"How Author Feels When He Sees
    Film Version of His Book,"
    1941.106
Howe, Marjorie, 1956.16
Hudson, Thomas Franklyn, 1944.52
Hughes, Isabelle, 1950.63
Hughes, Riley, 1958.16
"Humanness Saves Novel by Cronin,"
    1948.69
Hutchens, John K., 1953.32
Hutchinson, Percy, 1931.13;
    1932.11; 1933.22; 1935.41
Hyers, Faith Holmes, 1948.80
Hynes, Beatrice, 1948.81

"Idealistic Editor Is Hero of
    Latest Cronin Novel," 1958.21
"Ideals of Adolescence Stormed by
    Adults," 1944.83
"Illness Proved Boon," 1948.20
"Important Novel about the Medical
    Profession," 1937.28
"In a Dramatic Novel of Great
    Human Interest, Dr. A.J.
    Cronin Reveals the Illnesses
    of the Medical Profession,"
    1937.64
"In Brief," 1941.20
"Indictment," 1937.54
"In New Novel, A.J. Cronin Tells
    Colorful and Inspiring Life
    of a Scottish Missionary,"
    1941.103
"Innkeeper's Wife, The," 1945.6
"Interesting, Fine Novel," 1935.33
"In the Great English Tradition,"
    1931.16
"In the Library," 1941.21
"An Irish Child in Scotland,"
    1944.84
"Irish Youth in Family of Scotch
    Miser," 1944.68

J., R.E., 1952.58

Jackson, Joseph Henry, 1935.42; 1938.11

Jackson, Katherine Gauss, 1948.82

Janeway, Elizabeth, 1952.59

"Jealous Father," 1950.63

"Jealous Father Pays Penalty in New Cronin Novel," 1950.90

Jessup, Lee Cheney, 1941.113

Johnson, Blanche, 1952.60

Johnston, Marguerite, 1952.61

Jones, Brynmor, 1970.3

Jones, Carter Brooke, 1948.83; 1950.64

Jordan-Smith, Paul, 1952.62

Journey of Discovery, 1951.1. See also Adventures in Two Worlds

Joyce, Margaret, 1952.63

"Jubilant Praise Greets The Keys of the Kingdom!" 1941.22

Judas Tree, The, 1961.1-12

"Judas Tree New A.J. Cronin Book," 1961.9

Julka, Lucile, 1944.53

Jupiter Laughs, 1939.2; 1940.4-6, 8-16; 1941.29; 1942.1; 1948.95

"Just Pleasant Reading from the Pen of Cronin," 1969.10

K., E.C., 1937.70

Kaleidoscope in K., 1933.34

Kaplan, Cora L., 1937.71

Kazin, Alfred, 1937.72

Keefer, Claire, 1953.33

"Keeping Up," 1952.100

Keese, Parton C., 1961.7

Kelley, James E., 1950.65

Kelly, Fred C., 1937.73

Kendrick, Alexander, 1941.114

Keys of the Kingdom, The, 1941.1-28, 30-60, 62-123, 125-32, 134-39, 141, 149-60; 1942.1-8; 1944.10, 22, 34, 41, 64, 81; 1947.2-3; 1948.17, 34, 52, 65, 96, 106, 109, 127, 131, 133-34; 1950.84; 1951.6; 1952.99; 1956.12-13; 1958.28; 1959.2; 1961.9; 1963.1; 1964.6;

1972.1; 1981.8-10

"Keys of the Kingdom: In His Third Best Seller Scotland's Writing Doctor Takes Faith for His Theme, The," 1941.62

Kiessling, E.C., 1941.115

Kilcoyne, Francis P., 1952.64

Kimball, Frederick H., 1939.4

King, Kathleen, 1938.12

Kingsbury, William, 1941.116

Kinnaird, Clark, 1958.17

Kirby, W.J., 1948.84

Kirsch, Paul, 1933.23

Knapp, Valerie, 1942.6

Knickmeyer, Louise, 1950.66

Knight, Elizabeth B., 1944.54

Kolstad, Freddie, 1937.74

Krutch, Joseph Wood, 1940.12

Kunkel, Francis L., 1963.1

L., A.F., 1941.117

Lacey, Maybelle, 1969.7

LaMont, William H. F., 1938.13

"Landscape with Figures," 1950.38

Lane, Victoria A., 1950.67

"Language and Literature: English and American," 1970.1

"Lappin, Henry A., 1941.118; 1944.55

Las Vergnas, Raymond, 1964.6

"Latest Bantams," 1957.1

Lavery, Emmet, 1952.65

Lawrence, Henry H., 1950.68; 1952.66

Laycock, Edward A., 1941.119

"Leading Critics Pick Best Books in Annual Poll," 1941.23

"Leaves from the Library," 1952.63

Lee, Charles, 1941.120; 1944.56; 1953.34

Lemon, Mary Dyer, 1933.24

Levin, Martin, 1964.11

Lewis, R.J., Jr., 1941.121

"Library of the Quarter: Outstanding Novels, The," 1931.15

"Life Before the War," 1935.57

"Life of Novelist," 1952.16

Linehan, J., 1969.8

"Literary Guidepost," 1948.114

"Literary Guidepost, The," 1941.145

"Literary Guild--August Selection," 1948.61
"Literary Guild's August Selection," 1948.85
"Literary Landscape: Proletarian, The," 1936.2
"Literary Lantern, The," 1937.52
"Literary Medico Popular among Readers Now," 1952.78
"Literary Parade," 1935.63
"Literary Spotlight, The," 1948.55
"Literature and Less," 1948.42
"Literature: English and American," 1941.86
"littérature anglaise en 1932, La," 1933.20
"littérature anglaise en 1933, La," 1934.2
"London Scene: Midwinter View, The," 1940.9
"Lonely Research Scientist Is Hero of New Cronin Novel," 1948.66
"Love and Climate," 1933.29
"Love Between Medics, and the CIC," 1948.121
Lowrey, Jacob H., 1944.57
"Lucky Dr. Cronin Had a Wife to Brag To," 1952.51
"Lucy Moore's Three Loves," 1932.4
Luening, Muriel Luise, 1938.14
Luker, Ellen Williams, 1961.8

M., 1957.1
"M.D. Authors 'Corny,' Imaginative Novel," 1970.5
M., J.J., 1952.67
M., J.W., 1950.69
M., N.B., 1952.68
M., W.J., 1937.75
M., W.J., Jr., 1948.85
MacAfee, Helen, 1931.15
McCabe, Ward, 1941.122
McCleary, Dorothy, 1941.123
McD., M.I., 1933.25
MacDonald, Claire, 1935.43-44
McFee, William, 1935.45; 1937.76; 1941.124-25; 1944.58; 1945.13; 1948.86

McGarey, Mary, 1948.87
McHugh, Miriam, 1950.70
McIntyre, Alfred, 1941.126
McL., P., 1956.17
MacManus, Patricia, 1964.12
McNeill, Alex, 1933.26
McQuaid, Esther, 1953.35
McSorley, Joseph, 1941.127
McVicker, Daphne Alloway, 1944.59
"Magnificent Novel Acts As Scathing Indictment of Certain Aspects of British Medical Profession," 1937.45
"Maiden Voyage," 1958.24
"Man Made Lonely by Egotism," 1950.13
Manning, Olivia, 1948.88
Manson, M.D., 1937.26, 58. See also The Citadel
"Manufactured Doctor," 1948.65
Man Who Came Back, The, 1933.23
Marchand, Lafayette, 1941.128
"March of Events, The," 1941.92
"Marion Rudkin's Book Review," 1958.25
"Marjorie Howe," 1956.16
Marriott, Charles, 1948.89
Marsh, Fred T., 1931.16; 1932.12
Martin, Gertrude A., 1944.60
Martin, Rosalind Ewing, 1935.46
"Mary Paige Reports," 1945.14
Matthew, Christopher, 1962.1
Meade, Gilbert W., 1933.27
Mealand, Richard, 1944.61
"Medical Dilemma," 1937.29
"Medical Researcher's Hard 'Way,'" 1948.87
"Medicine and Morals," 1948.21
"Medic's Career in Coming Novel," 1948.22
"Melodrama," 1953.47
"Melodrama Fills New Cronin Novel," 1941.95
"Memory of Love," 1961.10
"Men at Work," 1937.60
"Men Who Hold Our Lives," 1937.62
Meras, Phyllis, 1956.18
Merlin, Milton, 1944.62
Meyers, Laura Scott, 1948.90
Middletown, May Carney, 1935.47
"Midweek Review of Books," 1950.51

Miles, George, 1948.91
Miles, Hamish, 1937.77
Miller, Louise R., 1953.36
Miller, Margaret, 1941.129
Miller, Mary Thomas, 1937.78;
    1941.130
Minard, Ralph, 1956.19
"Mimosa and Miasma," 1950.91
"Miscarriage of Justice," 1953.29
Mitgang, Herbert, 1981.8-9
"Modern St. Francis As Seen by
    A.J. Cronin, A," 1941.1
"Modern St. Francis: Hero of
    Cronin Novel Is Catholic
    Priest Who Preaches Toler-
    ance, Goodwill, A," 1941.2
"Modern Saint Is the Hero of
    A.J. Cronin's Novel, A,"
    1941.159
"More of the Same," 1958.7
Morley, Christopher, 1941.131;
    1944.63
Morris, Marvin L., 1953.47
"Most Appealing and Memorable
    Book: Cronin's New Novel
    Will Be the Subject of Wide
    Discussion, A," 1941.139
"Mostly Trade," 1948.23
"Mr. Cronin Returns," 1956.3
"Mr. Cronin Scores with Another
    Winner in Grand Canary,"
    1933.28
"Msgr. T.V. Shannon Calls The
    Keys of the Kingdom Catholic
    Book of the Year," 1941.149
Munn, L.S., 1948.92; 1958.18
Murgatroyd, M., 1933.28
Murphree, Alex, 1948.93
Murphy, Spencer, 1937.79
Murphy, Wallace, 1952.69
Murray, J.G., 1964.13
Myers, Robin, 1970.4
"Myself When Young," 1944.77

N., C., 1937.80
N., G.L., 1952.70; 1953.37
N., R.D., 1948.94
N., S., 1952.71
N., W., 1933.29
Nathan, Paul S., 1948.95
Naylor, Pauline, 1941.132;

    1948.96; 1950.71; 1952.72
Needham, Wilbur, 1935.49-50;
    1937.81
Neuman, Irene F., 1952.73
"New A.J. Cronin Opus, A,"
    1948.133
"New Books," (C.A.), 1935.1;
    (Anon.), 1950.14; (K. Brégy),
    1945.8; (M. Corcoran),
    1948.62; (P. Kirsch), 1933.23;
    (J. McSorley), 1941.127; (M.
    Reely), 1932.13
"New Books, The," (A. Bond),
    1950.45; (F. Robbins), 1931.18
"New Books Appraised: Fiction,"
    (R. Henderson), 1964.10; (M.
    Lacey), 1969.7; (L. Miller),
    1953.36; (E. Nichols), 1944.64;
    (C. Roth), 1948.117
"New Books Appraised: Too Late
    for Last Issue," 1950.94
"New Books Arrive at City Library,"
    1944.19
"New Books at Brunswick Library,"
    1941.24
"New Books at the Town Library:
    Book Reviews," 1948.58
"New Books: Fiction," 1941.136;
    1944.71; 1948.110
"New Books for Fall Reading,"
    1948.24
"New Books: The Public Library
    Presents," 1935.8
"New Cronin Book Relates Doctor's
    Bitter Struggles," 1948.24
"New Cronin Is a Smoothie,"
    1950.15
"New Cronin Novel," (Anon.),
    1944.20; (K. Dunlap), 1950.52;
    (W. Kirby), 1948.84; (J.
    Voiles), 1948.127
"New Cronin Novel Delightful Story
    of Orphan Youth," 1944.80
"New Cronin Novel Great Bit of
    Work," 1941.25
"New Cronin Novel Is Touching
    Story," 1950.44
"New Cronin Novel Shows Tragic
    Family," 1950.68
"New Fiction," 1933.7
"New Novel by Author of Hatter's

Castle Is Work of High
Quality," 1935.42
"New Novel by Cronin," 1935.31
"New Novels," (Anon.), 1931.45;
1933.8; 1935.9-10; (H.
Brighouse), 1937.47; (G.
Bullett), 1932.8; (H.
Harwood), 1931.12; 1932.10;
(Proteus), 1931.17; (P.
Quennell), 1933.30; 1935.55
"New Novels: Grand Canary,"
1933.1
"New Novels: Three Loves,"
1932.5
"New Offerings in America:
Cronin Scores New Success in
Latest Novel," 1948.103
"News," 1937.30; 1939.2; 1941.26
"News of New Books," 1937.108
"Newspaper Battlefield for
Cronin," 1958.8
Newton, Arthur Link, 1937.82
Nichols, Elizabeth P., 1944.64
Nichols, Lewis, 1940.13
"1941's Best Books," 1942.3
"1930s Sound Film," 1978.2
"Noble and Exciting: A.J.
Cronin's Novel Something to
Delight the Fastidious
Reader," 1941.116
"Noble Priest's Life Struggle in
Cronin Novel: Superficial
Study Avoids Deep Conflict,
Shuns Controversial," 1941.27
"No Hope for the Sinner Is A.J.
Cronin's View," 1950.87
"No Joy Forever," 1956.18
"Nonfiction," 1951.3; 1952.17-18
Normandin, Fern, 1958.19
North, Sterling, 1944.65;
1948.97-99; 1950.72-74;
1953.38; 1956.20
Northern Light, The, 1958.1-15,
17-28; 1959.1; 1960.1
"Note," 1937.31
"Note for Vacationist: Read
Grand Canary," 1933.24
"Notes about New Books and
Libraries," 1953.35
"Notes and Comment," 1941.119
"Notes on Fiction," 1932.6

"Noteworthy New Fiction," 1941.28
"Not Only the Doctors Will Read
The Citadel," 1937.66
Nourse, John, 1937.83
"Novel by a Doctor about a Doctor,
A," 1937.58
"Novelist A.J. Cronin Dies at 84
in Switzerland," 1981.3
"Novel Moves with Speed of Comic
Strip," 1948.50
"Novel of Class Struggle, A,"
1935.59
"Novel of Last Year Attacks
Medical System," 1938.15
"Novel of Suspense," 1953.40
"Novel of the Week," 1953.33
"Novel Revolves Around Life of
Priest in China, Scotland,"
1941.129
"Novels," 1948.89
"Novels for Summer Reading,"
1948.26
"Novels Revived," 1950.16

O., M.J., 1958.20
O., O., 1948.100; 1950.75;
1952.74; 1953.39
O., P., 1947.2
"Obituary: Dr. A.J. Cronin,"
1981.4-5
O'Dell, Scott, 1948.101
"Of Books and Men," 1948.27
"Of Books 'N' Things," 1937.53
"Of Sponge-Cake and Buttermilk,"
1948.115
"Oft-Wounded Knight: A.J. Cronin
Creates More Masterly Misery,"
1948.109
"Old-Fashioned Success Story of
A.J. Cronin, Doctor-Novelist,
The," 1952.79
O'Leary, Mary C., 1952.75
O'Leary, Theodore M., 1950.76
O'N., H., 1937.84
O'Neill, Frank, 1952.76
"One Man's Fight Against Failure,"
1948.73
"On Slum Clearance: How to Blow
Up a Sewer--A Literary Idea,"
1937.32
"On the Shelf at Clarkston,"

1952.56
Orebaugh, Vernon, 1944.66
"Other Books," 1950.17
"Other New Novels," 1964.3
"Outstanding Novels," 1945.15
"Overextension by A.J. Cronin,"
    1950.2
"Over-Possessive Father-Love
    Cronin Novel Tragic Theme,"
    1950.77
Owens, Olga, 1941.133; 1944.67
"Owner-Editor Meets the Test,
    An," 1958.18

P., A.H., 1948.102
P., D.T., 1952.77; 1953.40;
    1958.21
P., F., 1948.103; 1961.9
P., M., 1940.14; 1944.68;
    1948.104
P., U., 1948.105
Paige, Mary, 1945.14
"Painter's Peregrinations, A,"
    1956.22
"Paperbacks: Fiction," 1971.1
"Paper Goes On," 1958.9
Paschall, Alma, 1950.77
Pascone, Tere, 1948.106
Paterson, Isabel, 1937.85
"Pattern of Murder," 1953.44
Patterson, William D., 1952.78
Paulding, Gouverneur, 1952.79
Paulus, John D., 1948.107
Pearson, Flaval, 1950.78
Pearson, R.N., 1952.80
Pekar, Joe, 1941.134
"Persecuted for His Art," 1956.8
Petersen, Scarborough, 1944.69
Phillips, Alice Swaright, 1935.51
Phillips, Marie Tello, 1935.52
"Physician Clicks Again," 1933.33
"Physician-Novelist," 1952.86
"Physician Sails the Sea, A,"
    1953.4
"Pilgrims, Not Strangers," 1959.2
Pippett, Aileen, 1961.10
Pippett, Roger, 1953.41; 1958.22
"Pit, The," 1935.64
"Plays for Stages and Students,"
    1940.10
Plomer, William, 1935.53

"Plot Is Old, Nicely Told,"
    1948.78
Pocketful of Rye, A, 1969.1-10;
    1970.1-2, 5; 1971.1
"Pocketful of Wry, A," 1964.12
Poore, Charles, 1958.23
Pope, J.S., 1935.54
"Popular Author Tells Own Story,"
    1952.54
"Popular Novel Reissued," 1950.18
Portersfield, Waldon, 1950.79
Pouder, G.H., 1969.9
Pray, Waldo, 1948.108
"Predestination?" 1933.9
"Pre-Issue Best Seller, A,"
    1941.134
Prescott, Orville, 1944.70;
    1945.15; 1950.80; 1953.42;
    1956.21
"Prescription," 1952.67
Presson, Mary Exley, 1948.109
"Previewing Books: Dr. Cronin
    Retells A Newsman's Saga,"
    1958.11
"Price of Reticence, The," 1953.31
Pride of Beauty, The, 1956.1.
    See also A Thing of Beauty and
    Crusader's Tomb
"Pride of Possessiveness, The,"
    1932.12
"Priest As Scapegoat in the Modern
    Catholic Novel, The," 1963.1
"Priest Is Main Character in New
    Cronin Novel," 1941.137
Prisoner, The, 1950.22, 91. See
    also The Spanish Gardener
"Prize Book Review," 1938.14
Proteus [pseud.], 1931.17
"Proud Man Who Found His Happiness
    in Humility, A," 1952.74
Proven, Grace, 1950.81; 1953.43
"Publishers Go Down Fighting As
    Los Angeles Comes of Age;
    Birds Grow Claws Like Badgers,"
    1948.101
"Purpose of Pity and Tenderness,
    A," 1944.81

Quennell, Peter, 1933.30; 1935.55

R., A.R., 1937.86

Radin, Dorothea P., 1941.135
"Radio/Books: Cronin's First
    Novel in Four Years Paints
    Unforgettable Picture of a
    Priest's Soul," 1941.65
Raven, Simon, 1958.24
"Read 'Em or Not," (Anon.),
    1937.33; (E. Dunton),
    1941.93
"Reader's Report, A," 1964.11
"Reading and Writing: A.J.
    Cronin Writes New Type of
    Novel," 1950.89
"Reading and Writing: A.J.
    Cronin's Memoirs Recall His
    Novels," 1952.85
"Reading and Writing: British
    Miners Reaching for the Sun,"
    1935.62
"Reading Glass: Current Reviews,
    The," 1944.67
"Recent Books: A Selection:
    Nonfiction," 1952.40
"Recent Fiction Chronicle,"
    1931.22
"Recollection of a Writer,"
    1981.7
Rector, Beulah, 1937.87
Redman, Ben Ray, 1956.22
Reed, Lois, 1952.81
Reely, Mary Katherine, 1932.13;
    1941.136; 1944.71; 1948.110
"Religion Presented Logically:
    A.J. Cronin Triumphs with
    Novel of a 'Mr. Chips' of the
    Church," 1941.68
"Research for Life," 1948.28
"Research Lab," 1948.29
"Reviewers on Library," 1948.30
"Reviews in Brief of Recent
    Worthwhile Books," 1941.143
Reynolds, Rossi, 1937.88
Rice, Joan, 1950.82
Rinker, Maxine, 1945.16
Ripley, Thomas, 1935.56
Roache, Mary C., 1948.111
Robbins, Frances Lamont, 1931.18
Roberts, Mary-Carter, 1941.137
"Robinson's Lost Memory," 1938.4
Robinson, Ted, 1941.138; 1944.72
Rodriguez, J.S., 1950.83

Rogers, W.G., 1948.112-116
"Romantic and Colorful," 1933.17
Ross, Mary, 1933.31; 1935.57-58;
    1937.89-90; 1941.139; 1953.44
Roth, Claire W., 1948.117
Rothermel, J.F., 1950.84; 1952.82
Rothman, Nathan L., 1944.73
Royer, Dorothy Pence, 1950.85
Rudkin, Marion, 1958.25
Russell, Richard M., 1948.118

S., D.S., 1937.91
S., F.M., 1937.92
S., H.B., 1935.59
S., H.L., 1948.119
S., M., 1961.11
S., M.B., 1944.74
S., R.I., 1952.83
S., T., 1952.84
"Sadistic Father, Criminal Butler,
    Mad Psychiatrist," 1950.39
"Saint As a Best Seller, The,"
    1941.99
"St. George of the Surgery,"
    1937.38
Salveson, Christopher, 1964.14
Scaife, Roger L., 1937.93
"Scanning New Books," 1937.68
"Scathing Indictment, A," 1937.5
"Scenes from a Frustrated Boyhood,"
    1944.45
Schulberg, Lucille, 1950.86
"Scotch Arrowsmith," 1948.98
"Scotch Horatio Alger, A," 1964.7
"Scotch Physician Has a Run of
    Hard Luck," 1948.63
"Scotch Priest in Fight for
    Right," 1941.73
"Scotch Sour," 1948.126
"Scottish-Born Author A.J. Cronin
    Dies at Age 84," 1981.6
"Scottish Novelist Writes of His
    Life As a Doctor," 1952.46
Scott, James, 1950.87
Scott, Kenneth W., 1948.120;
    1950.88
"Screen: 'The Citadel' at the
    Empire, The," 1937.57
Scruggs, Theodora, 1935.60
"Search for Justice," 1953.26
"Season's Best Sellers," 1937.105

"Season's Run, A," 1935.25
Seaver, Edwin, 1948.121
Selby, John, 1933.32; 1937.94;
    1941.140-48; 1944.75-76
"Selfless Life of Research,"
    1948.45
"Senior High Group," 1946.3
Sensabaugh, Mary Holmes, 1948.122
"'Sequel' to The Green Years Is
    a Distressingly Poor Novel,"
    1948.75
"Serious Novel: Troubled Priest
    Serves As Hero of Cronin
    Book," 1941.59
"Serpent in Eden," 1950.93
Shannon, T.V., 1941.149
Shannon's Way, 1948.1-10, 12-26,
    28-42, 44-75, 77-97, 100-112,
    117-35; 1950.16, 18, 64, 84,
    88; 1952.39; 1956.2, 13
"Shannon's Way," (R.N.), 1948.94;
    (O.O.), 1948.100; (K. Scott),
    1948.120; (A.W.), 1948.128
"Shannon's Way by A.J. Cronin,"
    1950.88
"Shannon's Way Gripping Sequel
    to The Green Years," 1948.96
"Shannon's Way Is Alive,"
    1948.131
"Shannon's Way Leads," 1948.37
"Shannon's Way: The August
    Selection by Dr. A.J.
    Cronin," 1948.38
Sherman, Thomas B., 1948.123;
    1950.89; 1952.85
"Shopping List," 1941.144
Shrapnel, Norman, 1958.26
Shucard, Alan R., 1975.5
Simms, Fenna B., 1935.61
Sims, Marian, 1944.77
Sink, E. Carl, 1937.95
Sinks, Naomi Bender, 1950.90
Slaughter, Frank G., 1952.86
Smith, H. Allen, 1933.33
Smith, Harrison, 1953.45
Smith, Henry H., 1952.87
Smith, Nelle Edwards, 1937.96
"Smother Love of a Father,"
    1950.92
"Social Fiction," 1942.7
"Society Doctor," 1937.61

Solomon, Gladys, 1937.97
"Some Very Nice Middle-of-Road
    Scotch-Irish," 1944.54
Song of Sixpence, A, 1964.1-5, 7,
    9-14; 1968.1; 1969.4
Soskin, William, 1935.62
Spanish Gardener, The, 1950.1-2,
    4-15, 17, 19-35, 37-42, 44-71,
    73-87, 89-97; 1951.4-6;
    1956.13; 1981.8. See also
    The Prisoner
"Spanish Gardener: A New Novel
    by A.J. Cronin Tells of a
    Doting Father's Evil Effect
    on His Son, The," 1950.79
"Speaking of Books," 1941.121;
    1942.8
"Spongecake and Buttermilk: A
    New A.J. Cronin Homily,"
    1948.116
Spry, Dick, 1952.88
Stafford, Hazel Straight, 1937.98
Stafford, Russell Henry, 1941.150
"Stage and Screen, The," 1940.15
Starr, Jimmy, 1952.89
Stars Look Down, The, 1935.1-26,
    29, 32-37, 39-42, 44-66;
    1936.1-2; 1937.4, 31, 67, 81;
    1941.101, 103; 1942.1; 1944.10,
    34; 1948.46, 65, 127; 1956.21;
    1981.9
"Stars Look Down, The," 1935.54
"Stars Look Down Is Finely, If
    Not Greatly, Written,"
    1935.47
"Stars Look Down on Scene of
    Powerful Novel by Cronin, The,"
    1935.21
"Stars Look Down Powerful Novel of
    English North Country, The,"
    1935.32
"Sterling North Reviews the Books,"
    1950.74; 1953.38; 1956.20
"Stethoscope and Stylus," 1952.84
Stevens, George, 1937.99
Stevens, Marion, 1941.151
"Stirs Controversy," 1937.39
Stith, Lucia, 1948.124
Stoer, Marion West, 1950.91
"Story of Disillusion, A," 1937.6
"Story of Doctor's Progress,"

1948.124
"Story of Industrial England,
    A," 1935.29
"Story of Life As It Is," 1935.65
"Storyteller of Finesse," 1961.7
Strong, L.A.G., 1931.19; 1932.14
"Study of a Doctor's Success and
    Failure," 1937.41
"Suave Egoist and His Guilty
    Past, A," 1961.6
Sugrue, Thomas, 1950.92
Sullivan, Richard, 1953.46
Sullivan, Robert, 1944.78
"Summer Mixture: Saarinen May
    Be Caviar, but Cronin and
    Paul are Plain Fare, A,"
    1948.6
"Sure-Fire Cronin," 1948.39
"Survey of the Year's Best:
    English Coal Mine," 1935.50
Sweeney, Frank, 1937.100
"Swift-Moving Story," 1950.58
Sylvia, 1948.125

Taylor, Howard, 1944.79
Taylor, Pamela, 1952.90
Tebbel, John, 1981.10
Temple, Ruth Z., 1968.1
Templeton, Lucy Curtis, 1941.152
"Tense and Poignant Novel,"
    1950.48
Terry, C.W., 1948.126
Theall, D. Bernard, 1952.91
"Theme of Novel Is Regeneration
    by Love's Power," 1933.27
"They're Wondering What You'll
    Read," 1937.73
Thing of Beauty, A, 1956.1-22;
    1957.1. See also Crusader's
    Tomb and The Pride of Beauty
"This Week's Reprints," 1946.4
"This World of Books," 1937.46
Thomas, A.M., 1952.92
Thompson, B.J., 1952.93
Thompson, Ralph, 1937.101;
    1941.153
Thomson, William S., 1941.154
"Thoughts of a Novelist," 1952.34
Three Loves, 1932.2-14; 1933.9-
    10, 18, 20, 22, 34; 1935.64;
    1942.1; 1975.5

Tinkle, Lon, 1950.93
Tobias, Rowena W., 1941.155
"Today and For Ever," 1941.122
"Today's Book," (M. Morris),
    1935.48; (N. Smith), 1937.96
"Today's Book: Dr. Cronin's
    Scotch Arrowsmith," 1948.99
"Today's Books," 1950.70
"Today's New Book: Calvinism and
    Scant Fare," 1944.65
Todd, Madonna, 1935.63
To Live Again, 1953.11-12. See
    also Beyond This Place
Tooill, Kenneth D., 1937.102
"Too-Possessive Father," 1950.59
Torinus, John B., 1937.103
"To the Top in 90 Days," 1952.59
Townend, Marion, 1944.80
"Tragedy in a Garden," 1950.83
"Tragic Events from Man's Vanity
    in New Cronin Tale," 1950.55
Tucker, Martin, 1968.1
"Turning a New Leaf," 1944.39
"Turning Point, The," 1948.125
"Turning the Pages," 1941.94
"Twentieth Century (1914-1963):
    The Novel and the Short Story,
    The," 1964.6
"Twice-Told Tale," 1931.13
"Two-Room Houses of Miners' Row:
    An Honest Stirring Novel
    Written from the Depths of a
    Compelling Despair," 1935.58

Uden, Grant, 1933.34
Ulrich, Mabel S., M.D., 1937.104
"Undercover," 1950.34
"Under the Stars," 1935.51
"Unforgettable Realism," 1935.60
"'Unhand Me, Villain,'" 1933.18
"Universals of A.J. Cronin, The,"
    1941.91

V., M.J., 1942.7
Valentine, Dan, 1970.5
Van Doren, Dorothy, 1931.20;
    1935.64
"Vanity Destroys Three Lives,"
    1950.86
Vassalo, Carol, 1945.17
Vernon, Grenville, 1940.15

"Vicar Dedicates Life to
    Mankind," 1941.72
"View of English Medical Prac-
    tices, A," 1937.80
Vigil in the Night, 1939.3
"Vignettes," 1952.35
"Vital Novel, A," 1935.45
Voiles, Jane, 1944.81; 1948.127;
    1952.94; 1958.27

W., A.B., 1935.65
W., A.J., 1948.128
W., A.M., 1961.12
W., C.P., 1948.129
W., E.B., 1937.105
W., G., 1942.8
W., K., 1935.66
W., T.E., Jr., 1938.15
Wagner, Charles A., 1937.106;
    1941.156
Walbridge, Earle F., 1950.94;
    1952.95
Walker, Christin, 1941.157
Walker, Joan, 1953.47
Walker, Viola White, 1937.107
Walpole, Hugh, 1931.21
Walsh, Anne, 1948.130
Ward, A.C., 1975.6
Ware, Harlan, 1944.82; 1948.131;
    1952.96
Washer, Jane Dennie, 1969.10
"Ways of Fame, The," 1941.63
Wedman, Les, 1953.48
"Weekly Book Review," 1944.37
"Weeks Books: Unforgettable
    Portrait of Priest Given in
    The Keys of the Kingdom,"
    1941.128
Weeks, Edward, 1933.35
Weidman, Jerome, 1941.158
Weiner, Sam, 1948.132
Welbach, Thomas, 1933.36
"Well Worn Material Is Made
    Vital," 1944.78
Wendt, Lloyd, 1950.95
Werner, Hazen G., 1944.83
"What's Best Between Bookends:
    Cronin Masters a Difficult
    Theme," 1941.146
"What's Best Between Bookends:
    Your Christmas Book List,"
    1941.147
"When Fiction Invades the Convent,"
    1947.3
Whitford, R.C., 1948.133
Wilensky, Harry, 1937.108
Williamina, Sister M., S.S.J.,
    1947.3
Williams, Orlo, 1931.22
Williams, William Carlos, 1937.109
Willis, Marianna, 1951.6
Wilson, Emma A., 1938.16
Wilson, Kay, 1948.134; 1950.96
Wilson, William E., 1952.97
Winn, Elizabeth Smith, 1950.97
Winship, Elizabeth C., 1958.28
"With Pen and Scalpel," 1962.1
"With the New Books," 1944.60
Wood, James Playsted, 1952.98
Woods, Katherine, 1941.159
Works, Charles, 1952.99
"World-Famous Novelist Attacks
    the English Court, A,"
    1953.39
"World of Books, This," 1941.76
"World of Books: Author of
    Hatter's Castle Writes Another
    Novel of Substance and
    Strength," 1935.46
"Worth While Fiction of Recent
    Date," 1936.1
"Writers at Work," 1944.38
"Writes New Novel," 1941.148
"Writings on Readings," 1952.81
Wyatt, Euphemia Van Rensselaer,
    1940.16
Wyeth, Ola M., 1933.37

"Yet Another by Mr. Cronin,"
    1950.62
"Yoke of Father-Love, The,"
    1950.60
"Young Doctor Is Hero of New
    Cronin Novel," 1948.57
"Young Doctor's Career," 1937.69
"Young Doctor's Dilemma, A,"
    1937.7

Z., A.J., 1941.160
Z., R., 1944.84
Zwart, Elizabeth Clarkson,
    1948.135